OXFORD EARLY CHRISTIAN TEXTS

General Editor
HENRY CHADWICK

MELITO OF SARDIS

MELITO OF SARDIS

ON PASCHA

AND FRAGMENTS

TEXTS AND TRANSLATIONS

EDITED BY

STUART GEORGE HALL

OXFORD

AT THE CLARENDON PRESS

1979

Oxford University Press, Walton Street, Oxford OX2 6DP

OXFORD LONDON GLASGOW
NEW YORK TORONTO MELBOURNE WELLINGTON
KUALA LUMPUR SINGAPORE JAKARTA HONG KONG TOKYO
DELHI BOMBAY CALCUTTA MADRAS KARACHI
NAIROBI DAR ES SALAAM CAPE TOWN

ISBN 0 19 826811 4

*Printed in Great Britain
at the University Press, Oxford
by Eric Buckley
Printer to the University*

PREFACE

THIS book has been written in the hope that it will give a more secure foundation for the study of Melito than has been available hitherto. It is my wish and prayer that it will promote the understanding of a literature that has features of interest to Christian and Jew, theologian and classicist alike. It may also enable the Church to rediscover unappreciated treasures of its Passover inheritance.

My debts to scholars in Britain, Europe, and America, who have assisted me with advice and learned contributions, are too numerous to set out in detail. To one and all, my warmest thanks. But I cannot omit reference to successive professors and colleagues in the Department of Theology of the University of Nottingham who have sustained my work with constant support and interest; to Dr. Henry Chadwick who invited and encouraged me to edit the text; to Dr. Charles W. Hedrick and Dr. M. Van Esbroeck, each of whom made contributions without which the work would have been, if not impossible, then significantly impaired; and to Miss Molly Whittaker whose own work at Nottingham first led me to take up the study of Melito's text, and whose frequent help has continued even to the point of checking the proofs. Finally, my thanks to the staff of the Oxford University Press for valuable suggestions and corrections during the production of the book.

STUART G. HALL

Feast of St. Melito of Sardis
1 April 1978

CONTENTS

ABBREVIATIONS AND REFERENCES

THERE is no consolidated bibliographical list in this volume, but the reader should find the guidance he needs in appropriate parts of the book. The most important editions are mentioned in the Abbreviations paragraph below. The textual bases are set out fully in Part 8 of the Introduction. The history of the publication of *Peri Pascha* appears in Part 3 of the Introduction. Relevant secondary literature is cited *ad hoc* in the Introduction and notes. The following abbreviations appear:

Blank   J. Blank, *Meliton von Sardes Vom Passa, Die älteste christliche Osterpredigt* (Sophia 3; Freiburg im Breisgau, 1963)

Bonner   C. Bonner, *The homily on the passion by Melito bishop of Sardis and some fragments of the apocryphal Ezekiel* (Studies and documents 12; London and Philadelphia, 1940)

Fr(s).   Fragment(s)

GCS   *Die griechischen christlichen Schriftsteller der ersten drei Jahrhunderte*

HE   *Historia ecclesiastica*

HThR   *Harvard Theological Review*

IP   Ps.-Hippolytus *In sanctum Pascha*, edited by P. Nautin in *Homélies pascales*, i (Sources chrétiennes 27; Paris, 1950)

JBL   *Journal of Biblical Literature*

JTS   *Journal of Theological Studies* (N.S.—New series)

Nautin   P. Nautin, *Le Dossier d'Hippolyte et de Méliton* (Patristica 1; Paris, 1953)

Otto   I. C. T. Otto, *Corpus apologetarum christianorum*, ix (Jena, 1872)

PG   *Patrologiae cursus completus* accurante J.-P. Migne, *Series Graeca*

PL   *Patrologiae cursus completus* accurante J.-P. Migne, *Series Latina*

PP   Melito of Sardis *Peri Pascha*

RechSR   *Recherches de science religieuse*

RevSR   *Revue des sciences religieuses*

Richard   M. Richard, 'Témoins grecs des fragments xiii et xv de Méliton de Sardes', *Le Muséon*, 85 (1972), 309–36

Rucker I. Rucker, *Florilegium edessenum anonymum* (Sitzungsberichte der bayerischen Akademie der Wissenschaften phil.-hist. Abt. 1933, Heft 5)

SC *Sources chrétiennes*

Testuz M. Testuz, *Papyrus Bodmer xiii, Méliton de Sardes Homélie sur la pâque* (Geneva, 1960)

TU *Texte und Untersuchungen*

Van Esbroeck M. Van Esbroeck, 'Nouveaux fragments de Méliton de Sardes', *Analecta bollandiana*, 90 (1972), 63–99

VigChr *Vigiliae christianae*

References to *PP* are generally given by the numbers of the sections adopted by Bonner, Testuz, and Perler, and followed (with some small adjustments) in this edition. Numbers of lines (verses) in this edition are sometimes added in brackets for precision, and are used throughout the apparatus criticus and the index. In the New Fragments the same procedure is followed, using the sections established by Van Esbroeck. In the other fragments reference is made to lines or verses of the text in this edition.

Abbreviations in the apparatus and sigla in the text vary from text to text, and are indicated for each item in Part 8 of the Introduction.

INTRODUCTION

1. *The Life of Melito*

EARLY in his reign Victor, bishop of Rome from A.D. 189 to 199, was in dispute with the church of Ephesus. He objected to the practice of the Asiatic churches which observed the Pascha (Passover or Easter) at the time when the Jews kept Passover, i.e. on the 14th of their month Nisan; and he tried to impose the Roman practice of keeping the festival always on a Sunday, the day of resurrection.[1] Our oldest and most valuable reference to Melito comes from a letter in which the aged Polycrates, bishop of Ephesus, defends the local tradition:

We keep the day without tampering with it, neither adding nor subtracting. For in Asia also great luminaries lie sleeping, such as shall rise again on the day of the Lord's appearing, when he comes with glory from heaven to seek out all his saints: Philip, one of the twelve apostles, who sleeps at Hierapolis together with his two daughters who grew old in virginity; and his other daughter who lived in the Holy Spirit and rests at Ephesus; and furthermore John who leaned on the Lord's breast, who was a priest wearing the *petalon*, both martyr and teacher—he sleeps at Ephesus; and furthermore Polycarp at Smyrna, both bishop and martyr; and Thraseas, both bishop and martyr, from Eumenea, who sleeps at Smyrna; need I mention Sagaris, bishop and martyr, who lies at Laodicea? and furthermore the blessed Papirius, and Melito the eunuch whose whole career was in the Holy Spirit, who lies at Sardis awaiting the visitation from heaven when he shall rise from the dead? These all kept the fourteenth day of the Pascha in accordance with the Gospel, in no way deviating, but following the rule of faith.[2]

From this we may infer that Melito was more recently alive than the other deceased 'luminaries' of Asia; that he was an ascetic, since 'eunuch' at this period usually meant 'celibate';[3] that he was reputedly a prophet, like Philip's daughter;[4] that he was buried at Sardis; and that he was, like Polycrates, a Quartodeciman,

---

[1] Eusebius, *HE* 5. 23–5.   [2] *HE* 5. 24. 2–6.
[3] Following Matt. 19: 11–12.
[4] Polycrates appears to identify the Philip of Acts 21 : 8–9 with the disciple of Jesus.

i.e. he kept Pascha on 14th Nisan. His prophetic reputation is confirmed from Tertullian as Jerome reports him.[1] To the information that he was buried in Sardis Eusebius adds that he was bishop there.[2] Unfortunately we cannot be sure that this is not the historian's inference from Polycrates' words; all we can say is that it may well be true.[3] But it is odd that Polycrates omitted to state this important qualification for authority.

Eusebius is responsible for much of our remaining information about Melito. Most important are the list of his books[4] and two informative extracts. His quotation from Melito's apologetic pamphlet shows that it was composed during the reign of Marcus Aurelius, to whom it was clearly addressed,[5] thus fixing the date between 161 and 180. This can be further narrowed. Since it is addressed to a single emperor, it is probably later than the death of his adoptive brother and co-Augustus, Verus, in 169, and earlier than the elevation of his son Commodus to the same office in 177. Eusebius also quotes from Melito's collection of *Extracts* from the Old Testament.[6] Here Melito tells of his visit to the biblical lands in the East, a claim which is substantiated by the 'Hebrew' type of Old Testament canon which he claims to have learnt there, and perhaps also from some curious references in *Peri Pascha*.[7]

Other information from ancient sources is meagre. Clement of Alexandria knew his book on the Pascha, and mentioned it in his own on the same topic.[8] Early in the third century an anonymous writer cites Melito's books as 'proclaiming Christ God and Man'.[9] Origen,[10] followed by Gennadius,[11] attributes to Melito the view that God is corporeal. Gennadius also knows a sect of *Melitani* with chiliastic views,[12] who might derive from Melito. Otherwise,

---

[1] 'Huius elegans et declamatorium ingenium Tertullianus in septem libris quos scripsit adversus ecclesiam pro Montano cavillatur, dicens eum a plerisque nostrorum prophetam putari' (*De viris illustribus* 24 = *PL* 23. 678).

[2] *HE* 4. 26. 1.

[3] P. Nautin, *Lettres et écrivains chrétiens des II*[e] *et III*[e] *siècles* (Paris, 1961) 71–4, denies it; but see Perler 7–9.

[4] *HE* 4. 26. 2. See next section.

[5] *HE* 4. 26. 10 names his grandfather Hadrian. See Fr. 1.

[6] *HE* 4. 26. 13 f. = Fr. 3.   [7] See *PP* 93–4 and notes.

[8] *HE* 4. 26. 4; 6. 13. 9. See also below, pp. xix–xxi.

[9] *HE* 5. 28. 5, Fr. 8a.   [10] *Selecta in Genesim* (*PG* 12. 93A).

[11] *De ecclesiasticis dogmatibus* 4 (*PL* 58. 982).

[12] Ibid., 55 (*PL* 58. 994c).

we are limited to what can be inferred about Melito's thought from the surviving fragments of his writings and from the *Peri Pascha*. To these we now turn.

2. *The Writings of Melito*

Eusebius gives a list of the works of Melito.[1] Unfortunately this is unintelligible in places because of textual corruption; and the other versions of the list in the Syriac of Eusebius, in Rufinus' Latin version, and in Jerome's *De viris illustribus* 24, are all secondary attempts to clear up the difficulties. Furthermore, one cannot be sure that Eusebius had even handled the books he names, let alone read them. He could quite well have copied someone else's catalogue of books already lost,[2] and he seems to have derived from an earlier writer his knowledge of at least one of those which he quotes.[3] This makes almost worthless theological deductions based on the titles,[4] which would be of doubtful value even if the titles were more certainly known. At most we may say that they reflect some second-century theological interests. The list consists of:

1. *The two books On the Pascha.*[5] Eusebius' information on this work[6] is difficult to reconcile with the rediscovered *Peri Pascha*. The problems are discussed below.[7]

2. *That On conduct and prophets.*[8] Whether this concerned ethics and the Old Testament, or discipline and Montanism, or something else, we can only guess.

3. *The discourse On the Church.*[9]

4. *The discourse On the Lord's Day.*[10] The small surviving fragment (Fr. 16b) gives no indication of the purpose of the book.

5. *That On faith of man.*[11] The title is obscure, which probably led one scribe to write *On the nature of man* instead. But perhaps the

---

[1] *HE* 4. 26. 2. For comments, see Perler 11–14; G. Bardy in *Eusèbe de Césarée Histoire ecclésiastique i–iv* (SC 31, Paris, 1952) 208–9.

[2] W. Bauer, *Orthodoxy and heresy in earliest Christianity* (London, 1972) 152–5 (= *Rechtglaübigkeit und Ketzerei im ältesten Christentum* (Tübingen, 1934) 155–7).

[3] Fr. 4 from *On the Pascha*; see below.

[4] Blank 14–19 makes too much of them.

[5] τὰ περὶ τοῦ πάσχα δύο.

[6] *HE* 4. 26. 3–4, 6. 13. 9.

[7] pp. xix–xxi.

[8] τὸ περὶ πολιτείας καὶ προφητῶν.

[9] ὁ περὶ ἐκκλησίας . . . λόγος.

[10] ὁ περὶ κυριακῆς λόγος.

[11] ὁ περὶ πίστεως (φύσεως) ἀνθρώπου.

common reading means *On faith in a man*. It would then be a defence of Christian belief in Christ.

6. *That On creation*.[1]

7. *That On obedience of faith of (the)senses*.[2] This is usually taken (for no very good reason) to mean *On the subjection of the senses to faith*. Jerome and Rufinus separate the title into two books, *On (the obedience of) faith* and *On the senses*.

8. *That On soul and body*.[3] Represented by Fr. 13 and New Frs. I–III, and by the homily of similar title variously attributed to Alexander of Alexandria and to Athanasius. Some Greek letters follow the title which, if intelligible at all, indicate that the list has been crudely altered by additions. Some witnesses omit these letters, others so read as to imply . . . *or mind*. Modern editors suggest readings implying . . . *or unity*, . . . *or union*. See also no. 11 below.

9. *That On baptism and on truth and on faith and origin of Christ*.[4] Manuscript variations indicate what is in any case obvious, that this could be several titles and not just one. There is frail foundation for Perler's view that the book spoke of the birth of Christ in the soul at baptism,[5] or for Grapin's that the title originally spoke of the *creation and origin of Christ* (following a manuscript variant).[6] Fr. 8b is attributed to Melito's *On baptism*, and that may reasonably be supposed to be this work, or one of these works.

10. *His Word of prophecy* (or *A discourse of his on prophecy*).[7] Melito's work might have concerned the Old Testament, or some form of Christian prophecy. We do not know. Or it could even have been a prophecy of his own, i.e. like parts of *Peri Pascha* a discourse in which God or Christ speaks in the first person.

11. *That On soul and body*.[8] Perhaps identical with no. 8 above. It is not clear whether confusion in the manuscripts is the cause or the result of the repetition.

---

[1] ὁ περὶ πλάσεως.   [2] ὁ περὶ ὑπακοῆς πίστεως αἰσθητηρίων.

[3] ὁ περὶ ψυχῆς καὶ σώματος ηνενοισ (= ἦν· ἐν οἷς? : ἢ νοός some mss. : ἢ ἑνός Schwartz: ἢ ἑνώσεως Bardy).

[4] ὁ περὶ λουτροῦ καὶ (add. ὁ) περὶ (om.?) ἀληθείας καὶ περὶ πίστεως (κτίσεως?) καὶ γενέσεως Χριστοῦ.   [5] Perler 12 n. 1.

[6] See Bardy's *Eusèbe de Césarée Histoire ecclésiastique i–iv* (SC 31, Paris, 1952) 208 n. 7.   [7] λόγος αὐτοῦ προφητείας.   [8] ὁ (om.?) περὶ ψυχῆς καὶ σώματος.

12. *That On hospitality.*[1] This was an important subject in the early Church.[2]

13. *The key.*[3] Probably concerned with biblical exegesis, as was the spurious work of this title compiled in the Middle Ages and put out as Melito's.[4]

14. *The (books) On the Devil and the Apocalypse of John.*[5] Apparently one work in more than one book, but possibly two works. Origen preserves a tiny fragment which may be from this book (Fr. 5).

15. *The (discourse) On God embodied.*[6] Some early Christians held that God is a corporeal being, sharing the view of the Stoics that spirit is a very refined kind of matter. Tertullian, who knew of Melito, held this belief, and Origen attributes to Melito the view that man is bodily made in the image of God.[7] This title may therefore mean *On the corporeality of God.*[8] On the other hand Frs. 13 and 14 distinctly call Christ *incorporeal* before his incarnation, and this title could perfectly well refer to Christ as embodying God in his flesh.[9] We can only speculate as to the contents.

16. *Finally, the petition To Antoninus.*[10] Three paragraphs are preserved by Eusebius (= Fr. 1) and another in the *Chronicon Pascale* (= Fr. 2). The addressee of this apologetic work is clearly Marcus Aurelius, whose full name was Marcus Aurelius Antoninus Verus.[11] Eusebius is very confused about the names of the Antonine emperors, and may have invented the title *To*

---

[1] ὁ περὶ φιλοξενίας.

[2] See A. Harnack, *The mission and expansion of Christianity* II. iv (in the Harper reprint, New York, 1962, of the 1908 English edition, pp. 147–98; in *Die Mission und Ausbreitung des Christentums* i (Leipzig⁴, 1924) 170–220).

[3] ἡ κλείς.

[4] See J. B. Pitra, *Spicilegium solesmense* ii (Paris, 1855) XIII–XXXI and 1–549.

[5] τὰ περὶ τοῦ διαβόλου καὶ τῆς ἀποκαλύψεως Ἰωάννου.

[6] ὁ περὶ ἐνσωμάτου θεοῦ.

[7] See the excellent note of E. Evans, *Tertullian's treatise against Praxeas* (London, 1948) 234–6.

[8] So H. J. Lawlor and J. E. L. Oulton, *Eusebius bishop of Caesarea: The ecclesiastical history and The martyrs of Palestine* i (London, 1954) 132.

[9] So Bardy translates *Sur le Dieu incarné.*

[10] ἐπὶ πᾶσι καὶ τὸ πρὸς Ἀντωνῖνον βιβλίδιον.

[11] In *HE* 4. 13. 8 Eusebius names the addressee *Verus.*

Antoninus. A Syriac Apology to the same emperor,[1] while possibly ancient, is now universally regarded as inauthentic.[2]

17. *The Extracts.*[3] Despite his 'Finally' before the note of 16 above, Eusebius refers apparently to another work, and quotes its opening (Fr. 3).[4] But it is possible that this is a descriptive reference to an item earlier in the list (e.g. 13, *The key*); equally, it is possible he derives his information from a secondary source (such as Clement of Alexandria) and added it to the list. The fragment states that the work was in six books. C. Bonner revived the suggestion that Fr. 15 is the conclusion of the same work, arguing that *On faith* is another title for it (cf. 5, 7, and 9 in the list above).[5] Otto attributed to it Frs. 9–12. See also Fr. 5.

Besides these works in Eusebius' list others have been attributed to Melito. For convenience, we list them continuing the same enumeration:

18. *On Christ's incarnation.*[6] This appears to be the title of the allegedly anti-Marcionite work from which Anastasius cited Fr. 6. It consisted of at least three books. But Melito is certainly not the author of the fragment as it now exists, and Anastasius was probably mistaken in his attribution.

19. *The discourse On the passion.*[7] Both Fr. 7, preserved by Anastasius, and Fr. 16 have been supposed to belong to this work. Both now appear to be quotations from *Peri Pascha*.

20. *On the cross.* This title is given in the lemma to Fr. 14. The authenticity is not certain, and we can only guess whether the fragment is from a work given a different title in Eusebius' list.

21. *On the faith.* This is the title of the work from which Fr. 15 is said to be taken. *Faith* appears in three titles attributed to Melito (nos. 5, 7, and 9 above), and the fragment could also be the end of *the Extracts* (see no. 17).

---

[1] Text in: W. Cureton, *Spicilegium syriacum* (London, 1855) 41–51; J. B. Pitra, *Spicilegium solesmense* ii (Paris, 1855) xxxvii–liii; I. C. T. Otto, *Corpus apologetarum christianorum* ix (Jena, 1872) 423–32 and 501–11.

[2] J. L. Jacobi, *Deutsche Zeitschrift für christliche Wissenschaft und christliche Leben* vii (1856) 105–8, and all subsequent studies. See especially Otto 379–86.

[3] (ἐν) ταῖς . . . ἐκλογαῖς.

[4] *HE* 4. 26. 12–14.

[5] Bonner 48–50, citing Roerdam in Otto 456. So M. Richard, *Le Muséon* 85 (1972) 321.

[6] περὶ σαρκώσεως Χριστοῦ.   [7] (ἐκ) τοῦ λόγου εἰς πάθος.

22. A number of very late works exist in manuscripts under the name of Melito, such as those described by Otto 390–1. These may be safely ignored.

3. *The Discovery, Identification, and Date of* Peri Pascha

In 1932 F. G. Kenyon[1] described what appeared to be a fifth-century papyrus codex, which contained chapters from the *Book of Enoch* and an unknown homily or homilies. Some leaves of the codex were in the Chester Beatty collection, others in the library of the University of Michigan. By 1936 C. Bonner[2] had identified the homiletic material as a work of Melito. On the strength of the designation given by Anastasius Sinaiticus to a tiny fragment (Fr. 7), Bonner took the homily to be a work called *On the passion*, and so he entitled it in his *editio princeps*.[3] The codex itself contains only the name Melito, as did the long Syriac extracts previously known as Fr. 16. Bonner was able to identify and use further fragments in Greek,[4] Coptic,[5] and Syriac.[6] More important discoveries were soon made. W. H. Willis[7] announced in 1958 the discovery of a Coptic papyrus, in his opinion probably from the third century,[8] containing the second half of the homily; this is unfortunately still not published, but a photocopy of all but a few fragments of the *Peri Pascha* material has been available to the author of this edition, and is referred to from § 49 onwards. In 1960

[1] 'The Chester Beatty biblical papyri', *Gnomon* 8 (1932) 46–9.
[2] 'The homily on the passion by Melito bishop of Sardis', *Mélanges F. Cumont* (Annuaire de l'Institut de philologie et d'histoire orientale et slave 4; Brussels, 1936) 107–19; 'The new homily of Melito and its place in Christian literature', *Actes du Ve Congrès International de Papyrologie, Oxford 1937* (Brussels, 1938) 94–7.
[3] *The homily on the passion by Melito bishop of Sardis and some fragments of the apocryphal Ezekiel* (Studies and documents 12; London and Philadelphia, 1940).
[4] P. Oxy. 1600, in B. P. Grenfell and A. S. Hunt, *The Oxyrhynchus papyri* 13 (London, 1919) 19 ff. See C. Bonner in *Actes* p. 94, and recension in S. G. Hall, *JTS* N.S. 19 (1968) 504–8.
[5] W. E. Crum and H. I. Bell, *Coptica* iii (Copenhagen, 1922) 47–9. See C. Bonner, 'A Coptic fragment of Melito's Homily on the Passion', *HThR* 32 (1939) 141–2.
[6] J. B. Pitra, *Analecta sacra* iv (Paris, 1883) 199 and 433; Otto 421–3 and 499–501.
[7] See *Proceedings of the IXth International Congress of Papyrology, Oslo 1958* (Oslo, 1961) 381–92.
[8] Art. cit. 389. But experts to whom I have shown my photocopy, including Professor T. Orlandi, suggest the sixth, or at earliest the fifth, century.

H. Chadwick[1] published a critical text of a Latin epitome, full enough in parts to be textually significant, preserved under the names of Leo and Augustine. But the most important find was a Greek copy, complete except for the first page, in a Bodmer papyrus codex. This was edited by M. Testuz.[2] Not only did this enable numerous gaps to be filled where the Chester Beatty–Michigan codex was damaged, but it provided a title: 'Melito's On Pascha'.[3] This suggested that we were now in possession of a paschal discourse, a sermon for the Passover (or Easter) celebration of the Quartodecimans. It also raised the problem of its relation to the 'two books On the Pascha' mentioned by Eusebius, of which more must soon be said. But first we should mention further textual discoveries. M. Richard identified and J. N. Birdsall published[4] a Georgian version of *PP* 1–45, circulating as a separate homily under the name of 'Meletius the bishop', and M. Van Esbroeck has identified, edited and published[5] a Georgian version of the remainder of the homily, again circulating separately, under the pseudonym of John Chrysostom. The Georgian provides useful supplementary evidence where the text is doubtful. All this material except the Mississippi Coptic and the Georgian of §§ 46–105 was available to O. Perler[6] when he composed his edition of the Greek with French translation, introduction, and notes in 1966. The work was thus available to the learned public in a reasonably complete form. The present edition aims to take account of the complete Coptic and Georgian evidence, and of the substantial criticisms which Perler's text received.[7] But Perler remains a useful working edition, and his introduction and notes are valuable.

The Greek papyri and the Mississippi Coptic carry the name of Melito, which also appears with fragments of the work in Greek

[1] 'A Latin epitome of Melito's Homily on the Passion', *JTS* n.s. 11 (1960) 76–82.

[2] *Papyrus Bodmer XIII, Méliton de Sardes Homélie sur la Pâque* (Geneva, 1960).

[3] μελίτωνος περι πασχα at the beginning and end of the text. The same appears at the end of the Mississippi Coptic version.

[4] J. N. Birdsall, 'Melito of Sardis Περὶ τοῦ πάσχα in a Georgian version', *Le Muséon* 80 (1967) 121–38.

[5] M. Van Esbroeck, 'Le traité sur la pâque de Méliton de Sardes en géorgien', *Le Muséon* 84 (1971) 373–94; id. 'Les œuvres de Méliton de Sardes en géorgien', *Bedi Kartlisa* 31 (1973) 48–63.

[6] *Méliton de Sardes Sur la pâque et fragments* (SC 123, Paris, 1966).

[7] See S. G. Hall, 'The Melito papyri', *JTS* n.s. 19 (1968) 476–508.

(Fr. 7) and Syriac. Although *PP* contains nothing internally which decisively links it to the second century or to Asia Minor, there are no elements in it which clearly suggest a later date or another background, and a great many which make sense if we assume that Melito was the author. Some of these features are brought out in the notes to Peri Pascha in this edition; but more detailed literary comparisons can often be found in Perler's notes. Some specific points deserve mention, however. First, the extravagant rhetorical forms which appear so often in *PP* are very like those characteristic of the orators of the 'Second Sophistic' who flourished in second-century Asia.[1] Secondly, the style and content tend to agree with those of most of the fragments of Melito. Thirdly, the use of the Bible, with its frequent quotations from the Old Testament as Scripture, while the New Testament is alluded to but never quoted, agrees with early practice rather than later. Fourthly, the argument is often illuminated by the assumption that controversy with Marcionites is in mind. Fifthly, the author appears to use the *Gospel of Peter*, which would be more likely before 200 than after. Sixthly, there is apparently some debt to Jewish paschal traditions,[1] which is agreeable with an early date and Quartodeciman background. The early date is probable, and the authorship might have gone unchallenged but for the complications arising from Eusebius' notices, to which we now turn.

The first problem arises from the fact that Eusebius speaks of 'The two books On the Pascha'. This could refer to separate works, but more naturally suggests a single work in two parts.[2] But the work entitled *On Pascha* is in the Greek codices apparently single and complete. Secondly, Eusebius quotes as the beginning of *On the Pascha* a passage which forms no part of the rediscovered homily.[3] Thirdly, we are told that Clement of Alexandria mentions Melito in his own book on the Pascha, which he wrote 'ostensibly because of Melito's'.[4] If we take this with the alleged quotation just referred to, which speaks of a dispute at Laodicea, and with Melito's reputation as a faithful Quartodeciman, it leads naturally to the supposition that Melito's *On the Pascha* known to

[1] See § 5 below.
[2] Apart from the wording Τὰ περὶ τοῦ πάσχα δύο, Eusebius refers to it in 4. 26. 3 as if it were a single work. See Perler 16; also V. Pseftogas, Μελίτωνος Σάρδεων "Τὰ περὶ τοῦ πάσχα δύο" (*Analecta Vlatadon* 8; Thessaloniki, 1971) 24–9.
[3] *HE* 4. 26. 3 = Fr. 4.   [4] 4. 26. 4, 6. 13. 9.

Eusebius was a controversial defence of a Quartodeciman paschal practice.[1] The rediscovered *Peri Pascha* is not such a work. Scholars remain very divided on the answer to these questions. A few argue from them that *PP* is not by Melito.[2] Others argue that the homily is simply another work of Melito, quite distinct from that mentioned by Eusebius.[3] More complicated theories include that of O. Perler,[4] who proposed that the homily is the first part of what Eusebius knew, the second part being a Quartodeciman liturgy of which a fragment is preserved in Papyrus Bodmer XII. S. G. Hall[5] proposed dividing the homily into two parts in accordance with Jewish evidence and the Georgian version. A. Hansen[6] arrived independently at the same position. V. Pseftogas[7] has argued that the homily constitutes the second part of a double work, the first part being the sixth paschal homily attributed to John Chrysostom but also preserved under the name of Hippolytus (*IP*). But if a connection with the books noted by Eusebius is to be preserved, the other difficulties must be dealt with, too. The second of these, the alleged quotation from *On the Pascha* (Fr. 4) may be explained as a chronological note added to the manuscript by an early scribe, or even by the author himself. Perler[8] adduces parallels for such a practice. The third difficulty, that Clement's references, and therefore Melito's book, were of a polemical character, is really based on supposition. The expression 'because of' need not imply that Clement was attacking Melito; and even if it does, the disagreement might have been

[1] So, e.g., O. Bardenhewer, *Geschichte der altkirchlichen Literatur* i[2] (Freiburg im Br., 1913) 457.

[2] P. Nautin, 'L'homélie de "Méliton" sur la passion', *Revue d'histoire ecclésiastique* 44 (1949) 429–38; id., *Le Dossier d'Hippolyte et de Méliton* (Patristica 1; Paris, 1953) 53–5; J. P. Audet, *Revue biblique* 75 (1968) 150–1.

[3] Blank 14–15; P. K. Christos, Κληρονομία 1 (1969) 65–6.

[4] O. Perler, *Ein Hymnus zur Ostervigil von Meliton? Papyrus Bodmer XII* (Paradosis 15; Freiburg Schw., 1960).

[5] S. G. Hall, 'Melito in the light of the Passover Haggadah', *JTS* n.s. 22 (1971) 29–46.

[6] A. Hansen, 'The *Sitz im Leben* of the paschal homily of Melito of Sardis with special reference to the paschal festival in early Christianity', Doctorate dissertation at Northwestern University, 1968 (unpublished), 67–9.

[7] V. Pseftogas, Μελίτωνος Σάρδεων "Τὰ περὶ τοῦ πάσχα δύο" (*Analecta Vlatadon* 8; Thessaloniki, 1971).

[8] Perler 19–20. But even before the discovery of *PP* the same had been suggested by W. Bauer, *Orthodoxy and heresy in earliest Christianity* (London, 1972) 152–3 = *Rechtgläubigkeit und Ketzerei* (Tübingen, 1934/1964) 155–6.

exegetical rather than liturgical;[1] some of Melito's statements
about the Old Testament might well interest or provoke Clement.
It is in any case worth reflecting that Eusebius may have got
all his information about Melito's *On the Pascha* from Clement.
Eusebius is unscrupulous in his use of secondary sources.[2] If we
have Eusebius reporting what he thought Melito must have
written, on the basis of statements and allusions in Clement, we
can hardly rely on the verbal details. Thus while the exact relation of the homily to the two books On the Pascha reported by
Eusebius remains uncertain, the difficulties are not substantial
enough to call in question the authenticity of the homily.

Attempts to date *PP* more precisely within the life-span of
Melito depend on the identity of the two works just discussed. In
Eusebius' chronological note, alleged to be part of *On the Pascha*,[3]
we read: 'Under Servillius Paulus proconsul of Asia, at the time
when Sagaris bore witness . . .' Servillius Paulus is not known to
historians. But though the Greek and Syriac texts of Eusebius
are unanimous, the Latin of Rufinus gives the name as Sergius
Paullus. This may be an accidental assimilation to the biblical
text of Acts 13: 7, where the name Sergius Paulus appears. But it
might still be correct, since one L. Sergius Paulus was consul for
the second time in 168, and apparently City Prefect the year
before. Allowing for time when other proconsuls are known, he
could have been proconsul in Asia in 166–7 (May–May) or before
162.[4] Though little more than guess-work, the later date is usually
preferred. Perler points out that if one is emending the text of
Eusebius the reading *Servillius Pudens* would require very little
change in the Greek. The proconsul would then be the Q.
Servilius Pudens who was consul in 166. He might have served in

---

[1] O. Casel, *Jahrbuch für Liturgiewissenschaft* 14 (1938) 8–9; B. Lohse, *Das Passafest der Quartadecimaner* (Gütersloh, 1953) 124; Perler 21–2; cf. W. Huber, *Passa und Ostern* (Berlin, 1969) 39–41.

[2] See B. Gustaffson, 'Eusebius' principles in handling his sources as found in his Church History books i–viii', *Studia Patristica* 4 (*TU* 78; Berlin, 1961) 429–41.   [3] *HE* 4. 26. 3 = Fr. 4.

[4] See alternative dates between 160 and 170 given by various authorities cited in H. J. Lawlor and J. E. L. Oulton, *Eusebius, The ecclesiastical history and The martyrs of Palestine* ii (London, 1954) 148; Perler 23–4; A. Hansen, 'The *Sitz im Leben* of the paschal homily of Melito of Sardis . . .', Doctorate disser-tation at Northwestern University 1968, 69–72. Hansen's grounds for linking *PP* with the effects of L. Verus' journey through Asia in 166 are tenuous (op. cit. 97–9, 117–19).

Asia after that year. The martyrdom of Sagaris unfortunately gives no further precision to the date; attempts to date it themselves depend upon this same chronological note. To sum up, then, we may say that the notice about *On the Pascha* points to a date between 160 and 170, but neither the identification of that work with *PP* nor the precise date can be fixed with assurance.

4. *Outline of* Peri Pascha

PP falls naturally into two divisions marked by the doxology in 45. I have called these 'Books'.[1] Each is in turn divided by the doxologies in 10 and 65.[2] The division at 10 is structurally quite clear. But the second Book might well be subdivided differently. Perler actually makes a break between 71 and 72 the principal division in the whole work, but this seems perverse. For alternative analyses see Blank 42 and Perler 42–4.

ANALYSIS

Book I: The paschal narrative and its interpretation.

1. *Prologue*: The mystery of the Pascha, 1–10.
2. *The paschal events anticipate the Gospel*, 11–45.
   a. The institution of the Pascha, 11–15.
   b. The slaying of the first-born of Egypt, 16–29.
   c. Why the blood of the lamb saved Israel, 30–3.
   d. The power of the Old Testament mystery explained from an artist's procedure, 34–8.
   e. The models fulfilled:
      i. The Law and the People, 39–43;
      ii. The paschal sacrifice, 44–5.

Book II: The meaning of the Pascha.

3. *What constitutes the Pascha?* 46–65.
   a. Introduction, 46–7.
   b. The suffering one:
      i. The creation and fall of man, 47–8;
      ii. Man's degradation under sin, 49–53;
      iii. Man divided by death, 54–6.

---

[1] See § 5 of Introduction.
[2] The fourfold division marked by doxologies is defended by P. K. Christos in *Κληρονομία* 1 (1969) 65–78.

5. Peri Pascha *as a Literary and Liturgical Document*

There is no question that *PP* is a work of Greek rhetoric. The use of verbal and stylistic tricks is fully discussed by C. Bonner,[1] who claims the homily as the earliest example of Christian art prose. He noted especially exclamation, question, anaphora, repetition, antithesis, oxymoron, and paronomasia. Nevertheless he attributed Melito's parallelisms and the hymnic Οὗτος (Οὗτός ἐστιν) and Ἐγώ (Ἐγώ εἰμι) formulae to biblical or oriental sources.[2] Others have emphasized further the debt to Greek rhetoric, A. Wifstrand[3] especially assembling parallels from the writings of the Asian school associated with the 'Second Sophistic'. His main witness is Maximus of Tyre (A.D. *c.* 125–85), but he quotes also Favorinus (A.D. *c.* 80–150), Ps.-Dio Chrysostom, Lucian (A.D. *c.* 120–?), Polemo (A.D. *c.* 88–145), and others. Melito may thus

---

[1] Bonner 20–7.
[2] Following E. Norden, *Agnostos theos* (Stuttgart⁴, 1956) 177–207.
[3] A. Wifstrand, 'The homily of Melito on the passion', *VigChr* 2 (1948) 201–23; see also T. Halton, 'Stylistic device in Melito *Peri Pascha*', in *Kyriakon, Festschrift J. Quasten* (Münster Westf., 1970) i. 249–55.

be seen introducing into Christian circles—perhaps clumsily and extravagantly—the rhetorical style to which his compatriots were greatly addicted.[1]

Melito may well have influenced the development of Christian liturgy. O. Perler[2] has suggested that the paschal *Praeconium* still in use in the Latin rite originates in the form of declamation known as *laus*, and that Melito is a very early example of such a declamation for the Pascha. E. J. Wellesz[3] claims that Melito represents the point at which the Greek and Syriac styles of religious recitation converged, at a date far earlier than Ephrem Syrus and Basil of Seleucia, to whose fifth-century writings it had previously been traced. He suggested that, although *PP* was not intended for singing like Romanos' *Kontakia* in the later period, it was probably intoned with the kind of cantillation customary in Scripture reading.

Whatever truth there may be in these theories, it is certainly to be hoped that *PP* will supply valuable information about the paschal observance of second-century Christianity. One great question has been the subject-matter or content of the Quartodeciman paschal festival. It was once widely held that the Quartodecimans, keeping Pascha on 14 Nisan, the day of the Jewish Passover (Pascha) festival, commemorated the death of Jesus, whereas those who with the Romans observed Pascha on a Sunday celebrated rather the resurrection.[4] Scholars now more readily recognize a similar content in both observances, the differences being more in the external nature than in the actual content of the commemoration.[5] But B. Lohse[6] has tried to show

---

[1] See A. Boulanger, *Aelius Aristide et la sophistique dans la province d'Asie Mineure au IIe siècle de notre ère* (Paris, 1923) esp. 1–57 and 133–5; G. W. Bowersock, *Greek sophists in the Roman empire* (Oxford, 1969) esp. 17–58.

[2] Perler 26–8.

[3] 'Melito's homily on the passion, an investigation into the sources of Byzantine hymnography', *JTS* 44 (1943) 41–52; also, *A history of Byzantine music and hymnography* (Oxford, 1949) 157–66.

[4] References in B. Lohse, *Das Passafest der Quartadecimaner* (Gütersloh, 1953) 31; most recently A. Baumstark, *Comparative liturgy* (London, 1958) 164–74.

[5] So principally F. E. Brightman, 'The Quartodeciman question', *JTS* 25 (1924) 254–70; O. Casel, 'Art und Sinn der ältesten christlichen Osterfeier', *Jahrbuch für Liturgiewissenschaft* 14 (1938) 1–78; R. Cantalamessa, *L'omelia 'In S. Pascha' dello Ps.-Ippolito di Roma* (Milan, 1967) 84–6; W. Huber, *Passa und Ostern* (Berlin, 1969) 12–31 and 148–56.

[6] B. Lohse, *Das Passafest der Quartadecimaner* (Gütersloh, 1953) 62–89; see J. Jeremias, in *Theological dictionary of the New Testament* 5, 901–4; F. L. Cross, *JTS* N.S. 11 (1960) 162–3.

that the Quartodecimans observed a Passover simultaneously with that of the Jews and partly similar in content, and he has been followed by eminent authorities. The special feature of Lohse's case is the argument that the Quartodeciman celebration was directed towards the hope of Christ's return. The faithful fasted in the evening for the Jews, read and expounded Scripture (Exodus 12—the point is based on Melito's evidence), and looked forward to the Lord's *parousia*, ending their Pascha with a celebration of love-feast and eucharist in the early morning. But apart from the reading and exposition, it is difficult to see that *PP* contains any evidence to support such a scheme. Though Lohse tries to find it,[1] *PP* scarcely contains any eschatological material of the kind suggested. In fact, Lohse's evidence comes largely from the *Epistola Apostolorum*, the Quartodeciman provenance of which is by no means certain. *PP* seems rather to suggest that commemoration of the whole saving work of Christ as the fulfilment of the ancient Pascha is the theme of the Quartodeciman observance. And it should be pointed out that *PP* was dispersed and used in parts of the world where Quartodeciman practice was not found, and was certainly copied and used long after the practice was generally condemned: the Greek and Coptic texts are from Egypt, and the Latin and Georgian show its wide use in both east and west at a late date.

Another vexed question is the part played by Gospel chronology in the Quartodeciman controversy. Early critical study asked whether the Quartodeciman practice was compatible with the passion chronology of St. John's Gospel, the authenticity of that work being a prime concern.[2] To this day some maintain that the Quartodecimans saw their observance as fulfilling Christ's command to repeat the Passover which he ate on the eve of his passion.[3] Others find the Quartodecimans led by Apollinaris of Hierapolis supporting the coincidence of Christ's death with that of the paschal lambs, and thus the johannine chronology.[4] In that

---

[1] Op. cit. 81.

[2] See B. Lohse, op. cit. 22–6.

[3] C. C. Richardson, 'The Quartodecimans and the Synoptic chronology', *HThR* 33 (1940) 177–90; B. Lohse, op. cit. 123–4.

[4] See the fragment of Apollinaris in Perler 244–7; Blank 26–41; W. H. Cadman, *Studia patristica* 5 (*TU* 80, Berlin, 1963) 8–16; R. Cantalamessa, op. cit. 79–80.

case Melito might have belonged to the Roman party, not the Quartodecimans.[1] *PP* entirely fails to resolve this problem. While one passage refers to Christ's death on 'the great feast', which some interpret as 15 Nisan in agreement with the Synoptic Gospels,[2] it is followed by another which appears to make his death simultaneous with the Passover meal, thus agreeing with St. John.[3] The origins of the Christian paschal observance in its various forms remain obscure, and the obscurity is not removed by the knowledge that the variety goes back into pre-Christian Judaism.[4] But we may be fairly sure that many early Christians did not observe the Pascha at all. Those with Gnostic and Marcionite leanings would repudiate such a ceremony as Judaizing, along with the whole Old Testament Law. The context of *PP* may well have included resistance to such forms of Christianity, and it is notable that Melito in the fragments as well as *PP* shows signs of preoccupation with the authority and interpretation of the Old Testament.

One thing which *PP* makes clear is that the reading of Exodus 12 was from an early date part of the Christian paschal observance. This has no exact parallel in Jewish practice, though there are traces of the reading and exposition of this chapter on pre-paschal sabbaths.[5] But it is attested by the Ps.-Hippolytus *In sanctum pascha* (*IP*) which cites and expounds a slightly different set of verses. This reading established itself in every traditional lectionary for the paschal vigil with the single exception of Rome, and it should not therefore be considered a Quartodeciman characteristic. At one time it was thought that *PP* implied a reading of Exodus in Hebrew, but this view must now be discarded.[6]

PP shows signs of direct debt to the Jewish Passover recitation called the Haggadah. It has been claimed that it simply is a

[1] W. Huber, op. cit. 39–40—an unlikely theory.

[2] *PP* 79 and notes thereto; Perler 21; W. Huber, *Passa und Ostern* (Berlin, 1969) 44.

[3] *PP* 80 and notes thereto; B. Gärtner, *John 6 and the Jewish Passover* (Lund, 1959) 32; Blank 78.

[4] See A. Jaubert, *La Date de la Cène* (Paris, 1957) = *The date of the Last Supper* (New York, 1965); J. Carmignac, 'Comment Jésus et ses contemporains pouvaint-ils célébrer la Pâque à une date non officielle?' *Revue de Qumran* 5 (1964) 57–79; J. van Goudoever, *Biblical calendars* (Leiden², 1961).

[5] See S. G. Hall, *JTS* N.S. 22 (1971) 34–6.

[6] On the reading see references in n. 2 to *PP* 1.

Christian Passover Haggadah.[1] But neither the shape nor the contents of *PP* 1–45 support this view, unless a very wide view is taken of the character of a Passover Haggadah. On the other hand, the second part of *PP* corresponds structurally to the requirements of the Mishnah in *Pesachim* 10. 4 that the father of the household 'begins with the disgrace and ends with the glory', and that he follows the pattern of Deuteronomy 26: 5–9. It also contains a number of specific points suggesting an origin in the Jewish Passover traditions: a close verbal correspondence between *PP* 68 and Mishnah *Pesachim* 10. 5; the use of the term ἀφικόμενος which could already be a Jewish paschal title of Messiah (*PP* 66; 86); and the exposition of the unleavened bread and bitter herbs (*PP* 93), which along with the Pascha (paschal lamb) itself is a required subject for the Jewish Haggadist.[2] The presence of such Jewish influences in *PP* is particularly interesting in the light of the power of the Jewish community in civic life at Sardis, where they possessed a magnificent basilica-synagogue at the heart of the city,[3] and it reflects a period when intercourse between Jews and Christians was still possible. But of course we cannot tell whether Melito inherited much of his thinking and formulation from earlier generations of Christians.

Finally, something must be said about the connection between Pascha and Christian initiation. The practice of baptism at the paschal festival was clearly established, though neither universal nor exclusive, by the beginning of the third century.[4] Attempts have been made to trace this practice to an early date, including New Testament documents themselves. F. L. Cross judged 1 Peter to be a paschal baptismal liturgy, and based his argument

[1] F. L. Cross, *JTS* N.S. 11 (1960) 162–3; *The early Christian fathers* (London, 1960) 104–9.

[2] This whole argument is fully documented in S. G. Hall, 'Melito in the light of the Passover Haggadah', *JTS* N.S. 22 (1971) 29–46. See also notes to text.

[3] See D. G. Mitten, 'A new look at ancient Sardis', *The biblical archaeologist* 29 (1966) 28–68; the records of the archaeological campaigns under the supervision of G. M. A. Hanfmann in *Bulletin of the American schools of oriental research* 170 (April 1963) 38–48; 174 (April 1964) 30–44; 187 (October 1967) 9–62; 199 (October 1970) 7–58; etc.; also A. T. Kraabel, 'Melito the bishop and the synagogue at Sardis: text and context', *Studies presented to G. M. A. Hanfmann*, ed. D. G. Mitten and others (Mainz, 1971) 77–83; R. L. Wilken, 'Melito and the sacrifice of Isaac', *Theological studies* 37 (1976) 53–69.

[4] Tertullian *De baptismo* 19 (Corpus Christianorum series Latina i. 293); Hippolytus, *Apostolic tradition* 20 (ed. G. Dix, London, 1937, 30–2).

partly on the use of the 'paschal pun' (deriving *pascha* from *paschein* 'to suffer') which occurs in *PP* 46 and might be implied in 1 Peter. J. Blank[1] and O. Perler[2] both find that the insinuation of baptismal terminology into *PP* 13–15, 30, and 67, and the appeal to the nations to receive light and cleansing in 103, are enough to demonstrate that *PP* was followed by a baptism. G. Racle[3] adds reference to passages where Christ speaks as Father, Light, Grace, etc. (*PP* 9; 73; 79; 89–90). Perler even claimed[4] that the liturgical fragment in Papyrus Bodmer XII reflects a paschal baptism and *agape* associated with *PP*. But R. Cantalamessa[5] is right to express caution. He finds that both *PP* and *IP* contain baptismal material, but notes the absence of indications that a rite was actually administered in connection with the homily. The practice of paschal baptism in the second century must therefore remain unproven, however theologically appropriate or intrinsically likely it may be thought; and if it is used in interpreting *PP*, it must be regarded as supposition, not certainty.

6. *The Fragments*

The fragments generally follow the numbering of Perler 218–47, which is the same as that of Otto and Goodspeed where they agree.[6] I have followed Perler in giving Otto's Fr. 8 as 8a and Goodspeed's Fr. 8 as 8b. The last of Otto's fragments, Fr. 16 is in fact a catena from *PP* and therefore not reproduced. Instead, I have included a recently discovered item as Fr. 16b, and a possible Melito fragment from Bodmer Papyrus 12 as Fr. 17. Beyond that, the elements of an entire homily recently edited from the Georgian are included separately as New Fragments, since they seemed to deserve separate treatment. The textual basis of all the fragments here printed is set out on pp. xlviii–l.

[1] Blank 56–7, 74–5, 92–5.

[2] Perler 144–5, 172–3, 204–7.

[3] 'A propos du Christ-Père dans l'Homélie pascale de Méliton de Sardes', *RechSR* 50 (1962) 400–8.

[4] O. Perler, *Ein Hymnus zur Ostervigil von Meliton?* (Paradosis 15; Freiburg Schw., 1960) esp. 37–67.

[5] *L'omelia* 282–333. G. F. Hawthorne, 'Christian baptism and the contribution of Melito of Sardis reconsidered', *Studies in honour of A. P. Wikgren*, ed. D. Aune (Novum Testamentum supplements 33; Leiden, 1972) 241–51, exaggerates the anti-sacramental case.

[6] Otto 374–501; E. J. Goodspeed, *Die ältesten Apologeten* (Göttingen, 1914) 307–13.

Besides individual studies and versions, collected editions and translations have appeared. Note particularly for the Greek fragments M. J. Routh, *Reliquiae sacrae* i (Oxford², 1846) 111–53; E. J. Goodspeed, *Die ältesten Apologeten* (Göttingen, 1914) 307–13. For the Syriac, W. Cureton, *Spicilegium syriacum* (London, 1855) 31–2 and 52–6; J. B. Pitra, *Spicilegium Solesmense* ii (Paris, 1855) lvi–lviii; I. Rucker, *Florilegium Edessenum anonymum* (Sitzungsberichte der bayerischen Akademie der Wissenschaften, phil.-hist. Abt. 1933, Heft 5 (Munich, 1933) 12–16, 55–60, and 67–73; P. Nautin, *Le Dossier d'Hippolyte et de Méliton* (Patristica 1; Paris, 1953) 43–73 (cf. 83–4). Both Greek and Syriac fragments appear with Latin version in Otto 374–486 and 497–511, and with French version in Perler 218–47. Weighty studies of the material available were produced by A. Harnack in *Die Überlieferung der griechischen Apologeten des zweiten Jahrhundert* (*TU* I. i, Leipzig, 1882) 241–71, and in *Geschichte der altchristlichen Literatur bis Eusebius* i (Leipzig, 1893) 246–55. R. M. Grant has published some fragments in English in his *Second Century Christianity* (London, 1946) 73–4, and in his survey in *Biblical and patristic studies in memory of R. P. Casey* (edd. J. N. Birdsall and R. W. Thompson; Freiburg im Br./New York, 1963) 179–218.

Fragment 1 consists of three passages preserved in Eusebius *HE* 4. 26. 5–11 from Melito's petition addressed to Marcus Aurelius between about 170 and 177. The style is more classical and formal than that of *PP*, but the differences are sufficiently accounted for by the difference between a written apologetic argument and a liturgical homily intended to be declaimed or even intoned. The arguments are very similar to those in the first few chapters of Athenagoras' *Plea* to the same emperor, written towards the end of the same decade: appeal is made to the humanity and philosophy of the emperor, the punishment of Christians is acknowledged proper if based on justice, the emperor is implored to become acquainted with Christians before condemnation is allowed, and the laying of information and the taking of property and life are deplored. Details of his argument have been traced also to Justin.[1] But Melito pioneers two important points familiar in later Christian apologetic: the coincidence of the rise of the Empire under Augustus with the origin of Christianity, and the

---

[1] R. Weijenbourg, 'Méliton de Sardes lecteur de la première Apologie et du Dialogue de Saint Justin', *Antonianum* 49 (1974) 362–6.

(false) notion that persecution was carried out originally and exclusively by notoriously bad emperors.

Fragment 2 is a sentence preserved in the seventh-century *Chronicon pascale*, apparently from the same book as Fr. 1. The introductory lemma and the content suggest that it is genuine.

Fragment 3, preserved in Eusebius *HE* 4. 26. 13–14, is important for its references to Melito's visit to Palestine, for the first use of the term *Old Covenant* or *Old Testament* to refer to the Bible, and for the earliest surviving Christian list of Old Testament books.

Fragment 4, from Eusebius *HE* 4. 26. 3–4, is very obscure. It is not clear whether it is part of *On the Pascha* or an attached note. See pp. xix–xxi above. The sentence following the quotation is included in the text because of its implications for Eusebius' own source.

Fragment 5 comes from Origen's *Selecta in Psalmos*, commenting on Psalm 3. It might derive from Melito's *On the devil and the Apocalypse of John* (Otto, Perler), but could equally well be from the *Extracts* or some other book.

Fragment 6 is preserved in a Christological book called *The Guide* by Anastasius Sinaiticus of the seventh–eighth century. Otto[1] and Harnack[2] both argued for its authenticity, followed by Bonner[3] and Blank.[4] It has been defended again by Cantalamessa[5] and Grant.[6] Nautin[7] substantially rejects it because of its late technical vocabulary, and Richard[8] dismisses it as a manifest forgery in the interests of diphysite Christology. I have argued against Anastasius' attribution to Melito on the following grounds:[9]

(i) Against Anastasius' assertion that the passage is anti-Marcionite must be set his statement that it replies to points based on scriptural texts which a Marcionite would not use; Christ's

[1] Otto 442–4.

[2] A. Harnack, *Die Überlieferung der griechischen Apologeten* (*TU* I. 1, Leipzig, 1882) 254–9.   [3] Bonner 28–9.   [4] Blank 52–3.

[5] R. Cantalamessa, *La cristologia di Tertulliano* (Paradosis 18, Freiburg Schw., 1962) 108–10; *RevSR* 37 (1963) 15–16 and 22–3.

[6] R. M. Grant in *Biblical and patristic studies in memory of R. P. Casey* (edd. J. N. Birdsall and R. W. Thompson, Freiburg im Br./New York, etc., 1963) 196.

[7] P. Nautin, *Le Dossier d'Hippolyte et de Méliton* (Patristica 1, Paris, 1953) 84, cf. 41.

[8] M. Richard, *Le Muséon* 85 (1972) 310.

[9] S. G. Hall, 'The Christology of Melito: a misrepresentation exposed', *Studia Patristica* 13 (*TU* 116, Berlin, 1975) 154–68.

hunger, thirst, sorrow, etc., are concerned, as the wider context shows, with incidents in Matthew, Mark, and John or Luke 3. Either Anastasius' testimony is worthless, or else it indicates controversy with other than Marcionite objectors.

(ii) The passage contains many expressions and concepts for which Melito's time and writings present no sufficient parallel: *real* and *non-imaginary* in Christological context[1] the distinction of *soul and body* in Christ's manhood; reference to Christ's *human nature like ours*;[2] the idea of *godhead hidden in flesh*, and even the word *godhead*;[3] *the same one being at once God and perfect Man*;[4] *his two essences*;[5] the three-year ministry of Jesus; *true God pre-eternally existing*.[6] Melito could not have been first with so many things in so short a passage.

(iii) At the same time the characteristic features of Melito's Christology are absent: pre-existence stated in terms of creation, law, and prophets; the personal identity of Creator and Incarnate; the close relation of Christ to the Father of quasi-modalist and theopaschite kind; functional and titular speech about Christ. In these, *PP* and the other fragments largely agree.

(iv) The same features which argue a date later than Melito also point to a fourth-century controversial background, probably in the area of Antiochene anti-Arianism. The thought and language find ready parallels in Athanasius, Eudoxius, Apollinaris, and Diodore.

Fragment 7 is a slight misquotation by Anastasius of two phrases from *PP* 96.

Fragment 8a is not a quotation from Melito, but from a third-century writer against those who denied the deity of Christ. His report of the general drift of Melito's Christology is verified from *PP* and the fragments.

Fragment 8b is an interesting piece of argumentative rhetoric. It dwells on the universality of water-washing or bathing as a source of brightness, strength, and fruitfulness, and especially the nightly refreshing of the sun in the ocean. The writer sees this as arguing that Christ the heavenly Sun is appropriately baptized in Jordan. The baptism of the heavenly Christ was in various ways rejected by Marcionites, Gnostics, and Adoptionists in the

---

[1] ἀληθής, ἀφάνταστος.   [2] τῆς καθ' ἡμᾶς ἀνθρωπίνης φύσεως.
[3] θεότης.   [4] θεὸς γὰρ ὢν ὁμοῦ τε καὶ ἄνθρωπος τέλειος ὁ αὐτός.
[5] τὰς δύο αὐτοῦ οὐσίας.   [6] θεὸς ἀληθὴς προαιώνιος ὑπάρχων.

b

second century, and some such opponents must be envisaged. There are certainly enough points of contact with *PP* and the other fragments to make authenticity plausible: the use of high-flown rhetorical forms generally; elaborate analogies from nature and art as in *PP* 35–9; interest in heavenly bodies, including use of terminology resembling that in *PP* 82–3; emphasis on the heavenly Christ as King and Captain, as in *PP* 105 and Fr. 15; emphasis on the personal identity of the heavenly Christ with the subject of Jesus' human experiences, as in *PP* 93, Frs. 13–15, and New Fr. II; interest in the baptism of Christ, which appears (though not conspicuously) in Fr. 15. 35 and New Fr. II. 6. On the other hand, the style, language, and content have more in common with other texts. In particular, there are substantial affinities with *IP*: specific parallels of thought and language in *IP* 1–3, pointed out by Pseftogas;[1] the same heavy verbose style which distinguishes *IP* from *PP*; and particularly words and expressions of a kind unusual in Melito but characteristic of *IP*.[2] Further there are remarkable similarities to Theophilus *Ad Autolycum* 1. 12–13, of a kind not paralleled in Melito.[3] The fragment must be regarded as doubtfully authentic.[4]

Fragments 9, 10, and *11* are the authentic items in a group which also includes Fr. 12. The style in various ways resembles that of *PP* and the content is compatible with authenticity.[5] All three are concerned with the offering of Isaac in sacrifice (Genesis 22), and its Christian interpretation. Otto's suggestion that they derive from the *Extracts* is plausible but not demonstrable. Each fragment makes a different point. Fr. 9 refers to Christ's binding like the binding of Isaac, and to the fact that both Isaac and Christ carried wood to the place of slaughter. But it chiefly emphasizes the astonishing character of Abraham's deed (and by implication of God's sacrifice of his Son), and the silence of Isaac which resembles that of Christ. Fr. 10 draws the parallel between

---

[1] V. S. Pseftogas, Μελίτωνος Σάρδεων "Τὰ περὶ τοῦ πάσχα δύο" (*Analecta Vlatadon* 8; Thessaloniki, 1971) 190, 200–1, 236–8.

[2] μυστικός, *IP* 1. 2, 2. 1, etc.; μυστικῶς, *IP* 6. 1, 10. 1, etc.; noun formations in -μα, -ήριον.

[3] Some pointed out by R. M. Grant in *VigChr* 4 (1950) 33–6.

[4] So R. M. Grant in *Biblical and patristic studies in memory of Robert Pierce Casey*, ed. J. N. Birdsall and R. W. Thompson (Freiburg, etc., 1963) 200.

[5] See B. Lohse, *Die Passa-Homilie des Bischofs Meliton von Sardes* (Leiden, 1958) 5–6.

the sacrifice of the ram in substitution for Isaac and the sacrifice of Christ as a ransom for mankind. Fr. 11 draws from the idea of the ram entangled in the tree a type of Christ fastened to the cross in the same place.

These fragments together with Fr. 12 are preserved in a number of manuscripts of a catena (i.e. a compilation of patristic comments) on Genesis, some of which are in Paris and others in Rome. They also stand in Nicephorus Theotokes, Catena on the Octateuch (Leipzig, 1772) cols. 281–3, which was based on other manuscripts. There are important studies in D. Lerch, *Isaaks Opferung christlich gedeutet* (Tübingen, 1950) 27–43; F. Nikolasch, *Das Lamm als Christussymbol in den Schriften der Väter* (Vienna, 1963) 24–60; R. L. Wilken, 'Melito and the sacrifice of Isaac', *Theological Studies* 37 (1976) 53–69.

Fragment 12 is controversial. It comes from the same catenae as Frs. 9–11. The ideas in it are not at first sight incompatible with Melito's use of the Isaac story in *PP* and the other fragments. But the writer claims knowledge of the Syriac and Hebrew (i.e. Aramaic) versions of the Bible, and uses such information twice in his explanation of the ram in the tree. The information is inaccurate, and might have been picked up by Melito in Palestine. Scholarly opinion has moved against authenticity, however. Against attribution to Melito must be reckoned:

(i) The catena manuscripts are not unanimous in giving it Melito's name: one gives no name, two others give that of Eusebius.

(ii) The opening sentence (with slightest variation) stands in Montfaucon's Roman edition of the LXX beside Genesis 22: 13 under the name of Eusebius of Emesa.

(iii) Reference to the Syriac text is extremely improbable as early as the second century. Origen in his scrupulous researches on the scriptural text never refers to it. It begins to be used by Antiochene writers of the fourth century such as Diodore of Tarsus—a context into which Eusebius of Emesa naturally fits. G. Mercati,[1] who makes this point, suggests that the false attribution arose from a confusion in a catena manuscript between τῷ αὐτῷ, *on the same (passage)*, and τοῦ αὐτοῦ, *of the same (author)*.

(iv) The fragment ends with reference to the two provisions for

---

[1] G. Mercati, *Biblica*, 26 (1945) 1–5.

forgiveness, suffering for Christ (i.e. martyrdom) and baptism. This is uniquely early if Melito wrote the passage.

(v) Several things distinguish the style from *PP* and Frs. 9–11: pedantic and prosaic method, the reverential adjective in *the holy cross*, and the precise reference to the end of the book of Ezekiel. It is best left to Eusebius of Emesa.[1]

Fragment 13 is here reproduced in its customary place, and, with certain exceptions, in its customary form. This is partly for convenience, representing the fragment as reproduced by Otto and Perler, and partly because this form is the only one in which the surviving documents attribute this or related material to Melito. In fact we probably have a Georgian version (or revision) of the greater part of the homily from which the words of Fr. 13 are drawn. This homily is discussed and reproduced below as New Frs. I–III; Fr. 13 is contained in New Fr. II. 4 and II. 11–14.

Fr. 13 was preserved in a Syriac florilegium of Christological texts, probably made from Greek material at Edessa in the fifth century.[2] It is selected to demonstrate that the limitations and sufferings of the divine Son of God belong personally to him and are undertaken solely for the purpose of man's salvation. This special emphasis is characteristic of the Christological debates of a later date, but is no reason to question Melito's authorship. In the content are a great many ideas, anthropological and theological, which are also present in *PP*, and the form and expression are quite similar.

The heading in the florilegium attributes the fragment to 'Melito bishop of Sardis, from his treatise *On soul and body*' (see nos. 8 and 11 in the works of Melito listed in part 2 of the Intro-

---

[1] Even this attribution meets difficulties, since Jerome writes (*Liber hebr. quaest. in Gen.*; *PL* 23. 1020A) 'Ridiculam rem in hoc loco Emisenus Eusebius est locutus: Sabecth, inquiens, dicitur hircus qui rectis cornibus et ad carpendas arboris frondes sublimis attollitur.' This does not agree with the interpretation ἄφεσις of Fr. 12, but rather with that found in the scholion to the Roman edition of the LXX, cited by Otto 452 from Woog, where Σαβέκ means *straight up* or *vertical* (ὄρθιος), and refers to the ram as a *goat climbing straight up a tree* (τράγος ὀρθὸς ἐπαναβεβηκὼς φυτῷ). However, Jerome maybe misunderstood Eusebius, for the selfsame scholion reconciles this with the interpretation *forgiveness* (ἄφεσις); in both, it says, *Sabek* means *lifted up* (ἐπηρμένος, cf. Jerome's *sublimis attollitur*), presumably meaning that in the one case *sins*, in the other the *ram*, are *lifted up*. This may in fact be Eusebius' view.

[2] I. Rucker, *Florilegium Edessenum anonymum* (Sitzungsberichte der bayerischen Akademie der Wissenschaften, phil.-hist. Abt. 1933) gives the fullest account of the principal manuscript, Brit. Lib. Syr. 729, addit. 12156.

duction above). This attribution has been questioned because the contents of the fragment reappear in a variety of forms, under the names of various more famous fathers, and, while progress has been made, the true relations between these are not finally resolved.

i. A 'Sermon of S. Alexander bishop of Alexandria, On soul and body and the passion of the Lord' contains the first part of Fr. 13. It is known in two Syriac manuscripts, Vat. Syr. 368 and Brit. Lib. addit. 17192 fo. 278a.[1]

ii. A fragment partially overlapping with the sermon of 'Alexander' (i), but fuller in wording, and fuller also than Fr. 13, of which it includes both parts. It follows the 'Alexander' homily in Vat. Syr. 368, and usually goes by the name given it by its first editor, the *Additamentum*.[2] In the florilegium from which Fr. 13 comes, it appears in Syriac under the name 'Of Alexander archbishop of Alexandria, extract from his treatise on the incarnation'.[3] The same fragment, in whole or part, is repeated in a florilegium of Timothy Ailuros, preserved in Syriac and Armenian, and in the *Fides patrum* of the Copt Paul ibn Raga, preserved only in Arabic and Ethiopic.[4]

iii. A Coptic version of the same homily as (i) above, but fuller and including all the *Additamentum* material.[5] It is headed 'Discourse which the holy patriarch abba Athanasius, archbishop of Rakote (Alexandria), pronounced on soul and body'.

iv. Ps.-Epiphanius *De resurrectione* 7–8[6] contains a substantial part of Fr. 13 in Greek. Other parts of the same work contain some sentences apparently culled from *PP*, and substantial parts of the *Additamentum* and 'Athanasius' homily (ii and iii above).

v. The Georgian homily from which New Frs. I–III come[7] contains not only Fr. 13, but all the *Additamentum* material, as

---

[1] A. Mai, *Bibliotheca nova patrum* (Rome, 1844) 529–39 = *PG* 18. 583–604; E. A. Wallis Budge, *Coptic homilies in the dialect of upper Egypt* (London, 1910) 407–24.

[2] A. Mai, op. cit. 539–40 = *PG* 18. 604–8.

[3] I. Rucker, *Florilegium Edessenum anonymum* 74–8 (fragment numbered 77); also in J. B. Pitra, *Analecta sacra* iv. 197–8 and 432.

[4] Details in P. Nautin, *Le Dossier d'Hippolyte et de Méliton* (Paris, 1953) 57–60, who has a convenient Latin version of the text.

[5] E. A. Wallis Budge, *Coptic homilies in the dialect of upper Egypt* (London, 1910) 115–32, 258–75.

[6] Text in P. Nautin, *Le Dossier d'Hippolyte et de Méliton* (Paris, 1953) 155–9.

[7] See below.

indicated in the notes to New Fragments. It is attributed to Athanasius, but circulated also under the name of Alexander.

vi. The Greek text of Fr. 13 is largely preserved in a homily on the Ascension preserved under the name of John Chrysostom.[1] In addition, this Greek text includes some expressions from the *Additamentum* and other material listed above.

In interpreting the Syriac evidence G. Krüger[2] argued that the *Additamentum*, represented also by Fr. 13, was part of a Melito homily *On soul and body* which was used as a source by Alexander, who wrote the shorter homily (i above). The discovery of the Coptic homily (iii above) suggested rather that both *Additamentum* and shorter homily (ii and i) were secondary to it. P. Nautin[3] argued that all the Syriac and Coptic material (including Fr. 13) goes back to a homily falsely ascribed to Alexander, itself based on Ps.-Epiphanius, and that the name Melito is wrongly introduced in the florilegium. But Nautin did not fully account for the affinities which exist between the various forms of the 'Alexander' homily and *PP*, which he was obliged to regard as inauthentic. W. Schneemelcher[4] argued that the attributions are secondary to either Melito or Alexander, and that Alexander (or whoever composed the 'Alexander' homily) used *PP* as a source. Scrupulously comparing the texts, O. Perler[5] came to the same conclusion. Further, both scholars proposed that a work by Melito, perhaps called *On soul and body*, was also a source for 'Alexander'. This conclusion appears to be confirmed by the discovery of the Georgian homily (v), which, despite later accretions, mistranslations, and attribution to Athanasius (or Alexander), probably represents a homily of the period and style of *PP*, and could well be the base from which the 'Alexander' complex derived the *Additamentum* material. Curiously, this implies that Krüger was right: the *Additamentum* is part of a Melito homily on which 'Alexander' is based—it is in fact the common ground between the two sets of material. If this is correct, Fr. 13 is an

---

[1] See M. Richard, *Le Muséon* 85 (1972) 309–17, for complete discussion and collated text.

[2] 'Meliton von Sardes oder Alexander von Alexandrien?' *Zeitschrift für wissenschaftliche Theologie* (1888) 434–48.

[3] *Le Dossier* 56–64, 151–2.

[4] 'Der Sermo "De anima et corpore" ein Werk Alexanders von Alexandrien?' *Festschrift G. Dehn* (Neukirchen, 1957) 119–43.

[5] 'Recherches sur le Peri Pascha de Meliton', *RechSR* 51 (1963) 407–21.

abbreviated version of the *Additamentum*, perhaps independently
derived from the Melito homily, pseudonymously preserved in
Georgian, *On soul and body*.

Fragment 14 is known only from the same Syriac florilegium
which is the prime witness for Fr. 13.[1] It consists of a series of
antitheses contrasting Christ's bodily humiliation with his un-
changing divine glory, a series which might have derived from
almost any period of ancient theology, including Melito's. It has
usually been accepted as authentic.[2] P. Nautin has, however,
rightly pointed out features which betray later theological
interests and terminology.[3] It cannot therefore be regarded as
authentic in its entirety.

Fragment 15 is a long series of statements about Christ, beginning
with his divine origin and following his career through creation,
Old Testament prophecy, incarnation, ministry, death, resurrection, and exaltation. Its style, and sometimes its wording,
resemble those of *PP* and the New Fragments. Because the introduction refers to these Christological truths being gathered 'from
the law and the prophets', it has been repeatedly suggested that
it forms the conclusion of Melito's *Extracts*.[4] The fragment is
attributed to Melito only in the one Syriac florilegium to which
we owe Frs. 13 and 14. Another form of the same text circulated
under the name of Irenaeus. This is most fully attested in the
Armenian manuscripts of the florilegium of Timothy Ailuros, but
in various abbreviated forms it appears also in Syriac versions of
the same florilegium, in the *Fides patrum* of the Copt Paul ibn Raga
(preserved in Arabic and Ethiopic only), and in the Syriac of
Severus' *Defence of Philalethes*. This material was edited by H.
Jordan,[5] who argued that the 'Melito' form was secondary to the
'Irenaeus' form, and that Irenaeus was the true author. P.
Nautin,[6] however, pointed out features which indicate the

---

[1] See esp. I. Rucker, op. cit. 14–16.

[2] e.g. by Otto, Harnack, and Krüger in studies already cited, and most
recently by R. Cantalamessa, 'Méliton de Sardes, une christologie antignostique
du iime siècle', *RevSR* 37 (1963) 1–26, who draws out similarity to *PP* and other
fragments.

[3] *Le Dossier* 73; see notes to text for details.

[4] T. S. Roerdam, cited with approval by Otto 456; Bonner 49 and Richard
321 concur. See item 17 in the list of Melito's works above.

[5] *Armenische Irenaeus-fragmente mit deutsche Übersetzung nach W. Lüdtke* (*TU* 36.
2, Leipzig, 1913) 56–99; conveniently summarized in Nautin 64–5; see also
Rucker 55–60 and Richard 321–2.   [6] Nautin 64–72.

priority of 'Melito'; but he regarded both forms as pseudonymous, arguing that the fragment was based on a passage of Hippolytus, with influence from *PP*. This also appears to be onesided, however, and it is probable that the two forms derive independently from a lost original form.[1] Discoveries such as the parallel passages in *PP* and the New Fragments, and more recently of a prayer in Greek attributed to John Chrysostom, which clearly incorporates a Greek text resembling the 'Irenaeus' form, have led M. Richard to attempt a Greek reconstruction with full apparatus criticus.[2] The same scholar has also discovered a Greek florilegium fragment from Athos Vatopedi 236 fo. 30ᵛ which gives the opening sentence in the 'Irenaeus' form.[3] We cannot be certain that Melito wrote the fragment, and it is possible that its resemblances to *PP* are due to imitation. But the claim that so much of Christ's career may be verified from the Old Testament ('the law and the prophets') is striking, and together with the parallel passages and similarities to *PP* suggests authenticity.

Fragment 16b. Older editors following Otto's numbering count as Fr. 16 the extracts from *PP*. It is pointless to reproduce these, and I have substituted the little scrap ascribed to *On the Lord's day* discovered by M. Richard.[4] It is very similar to passages in *PP* and Fr. 15. If genuine, it was apparently the source for some lines of Hesychius of Jerusalem, edited by M. Aubineau in *Homélies pascales* (SC 187; Paris, 1972) i. 5. 17–20 (p. 66).

Fragment 17 is associated with Melito only by the fact that it follows *PP* in the same Bodmer Papyrus Codex, in which it figures as Papyrus Bodmer XII. It is included here because Perler has argued that it is a liturgical fragment deriving from the Quartodeciman liturgy which followed *PP*, and perhaps itself composed by Melito.[5] There is little doubt that Perler is right to see it as a liturgical dialogue associated with initiation, but the remainder of his case remains speculative. If it is not a relic of an independent ceremony, like that of the 'bridechamber' practised by some

---

[1] V. Pseftogas, Τὸ ἀπόσπασμα ἐκ τοῦ "Περὶ πίστεως" τοῦ Μελίτωνος, ἀντιγνωστικὴ χριστολογικὴ ὁμολογία, *Kleronomia* 1 (1969) 247–73.   [2] Richard 324–7.

[3] M. Richard, 'Le florilège du cod. Vatopédi 236 sur le corruptible et l'incorruptible', *Le Muséon* 86 (1973) 249–73.

[4] Cod. Ochrid. Musée nat. 86 p. 145 and published first in *Symbolae Osloenses* xxxviii, p. 79 and again in Richard 324.

[5] See O. Perler, *Ein Hymnus zur Ostervigil von Meliton?* (Freiburg Schw., 1960) for full documentation.

gnostics, it is probably baptismal. But it should be recalled that *PP* contains no reference to imminent initiation ceremonies, nor does it use the bridal imagery (though the latter does appear near the end of Fr. 15).

New Fragments. We owe to M. Van Esbroeck the discovery and publication of three fragments from a Georgian homiliary of the tenth century which may well represent a lost homily of Melito.[1] The substantial New Fr. II contains much material in common with the *On soul and body* nexus which is discussed in the introduction to Fr. 13 above. There are strong codicological and stylistic reasons for regarding New Fr. I as the beginning of the same homily. New Fr. III is much more difficult to place with security, but may well be the end of the same homily.

The homiliary associates this homily with 14 September, which commemorated the Elevation of the Cross by the emperor Heraclius in A.D. 629 after he had recovered the cross, and the city of Jerusalem, from the Persians. One is therefore not surprised to find some references to the cross and to the building of Jerusalem or of churches, which were associated with the same events. If the homily is in fact much more ancient, some of these are probably secondary additions; some certainly seem superfluous. The other possibility, that the whole work is in fact a late construction designed for this festival, is ruled out by Van Esbroeck on the ground that in general it is surprisingly lacking in theologoumena of later date. Comparison with the cognate texts of the Alexander *De anima* nexus makes this clear. Where expressions of Christological precision occur as in II. 18, they manifestly disrupt the sequence of the text. We clearly have here material of importance for Melito studies. Elaboration of detail is beyond the scope of the present work, and notes to the text are generally confined to indicating parallels in the Melito corpus and the *De anima* nexus.

The present editor cannot read Georgian. He is deeply indebted to Dr. Van Esbroeck for permission to publish a translation direct from his Latin version, and for some corrections to the published text which are indicated in the notes. It has been possible to cite Greek material for substantial parts of New Fr. II, the sources for which are also stated in the notes.

---

[1] M. van Esbroeck, 'Nouveaux fragments de Méliton de Sardes', *Analecta Bollandiana* 90 (1972) 63–99, on which all the following observations are based.

7. *Theology*

We shall consider Melito's theology under four heads: (i) Doctrinal norms, especially Scripture; (ii) doctrine of man; (iii) doctrines of God and Christ; (iv) eschatology.

(i) *Doctrinal norms.* Melito has a clearly defined Old Testament canon and interpretative principles, a New Testament resembling ours but ill defined, and possibly a credal confession or hymn. It is clear from Fr. 3 that Melito listed the Old Testament books in Palestine and made extensive extracts from them. He quotes directly from Genesis, Exodus, Deuteronomy, Psalms, Isaiah, and Jeremiah.[1] He alludes more or less clearly to some other books. Most notably he appears to use the Wisdom of Solomon,[2] which is not in his canonical list; but the affinities may be due to a common tradition of exposition of the Exodus narrative. His text usually agrees with the LXX or one or other of its principal manuscripts, though the manuscripts of *PP* have themselves suffered corruption under the influence of biblical texts.[3] Early Christian variants attested in other patristic writings occur.[4] It is widely assumed, but not altogether certain, that these affinities are due to the use of a common collection of *testimonia*.[5] Melito's discussion of Old Testament interpretation is striking.[6] The words and deeds of the Gospel are anticipated by the *comparisons* ($\pi\alpha\rho\alpha\betao\lambda\alpha\iota$) and *models* ($\tau\upsilon\pio\iota$) of the Old Testament.[7] These include prophetic statements and the foreshadowings of Christ's passion in the sufferings of patriarchs, prophets, and people.[8] Melito compares these anticipations with the artist's preliminary sketch or the architect's model, which is necessary to exhibit *the shape of what is to be*, but thereafter is displaced by the real artefact.[9] Thus Israel gives way to the Church, the law to the Gospel, the earthly Jerusalem to the heavenly, the paschal lamb to Christ.[10] This passage appears to have been known to Tertullian, Origen,

---

[1] *PP* 47, 61–4, 72, 93.
[2] See *PP* 18–34 and notes.
[3] See *PP* 47 = Genesis 2: 16–17.
[4] See notes on the Deuteronomy text in *PP* 61 and the Isaiah texts in *PP* 64 and 72.
[5] J.-P. Audet, 'L'hypothèse des Testimonia', *Revue biblique* 70 (1963) 381–405.
[6] See J. Daniélou, 'Figure et événement chez Méliton de Sardes', in *Neotestamentica et patristica* (Supplements to Novum Testamentum 6; Leiden, 1962) 282–92; Blank 59–65; Perler 29–32.
[7] *PP* 35.
[8] *PP* 57–65; New Fr. II. 2–3.
[9] *PP* 36–8.
[10] *PP* 39–45.

and other writers.[1] Melito stands firm by Old Testament historicity, unlike the Alexandrian allegorists such as Origen, so that the Old Testament events and personalities exhibit Christ: he was himself 'in Abel murdered, in Isaac bound, in Jacob made an exile, etc.'.[2] He even holds that it was the mysterious presence of Christ in the original paschal lamb which turned aside the destroying angel.[3] It is emphasized that the one who becomes incarnate in Jesus is the same who thus worked in the Old Testament, both suffering and saving.[4] In addition, he was the source of creation and the providence behind all the saving history of the Old Testament.[5] Thus everything in the Old Testament is embraced in Jesus Christ.[6] At this point theology emerges from hermeneutic: Christ is the God and Father of all things old and new, and we reach the 'naïve modalism' discussed later. There is little doubt that Melito's concern with Old Testament is due to controversy with Marcionite and gnostic groups about the origin and authority of the ancient Scriptures. He would wish to affirm their authority and at the same time exculpate himself from any insinuation of Judaizing. Hence he insists that the models and parables are abrogated except in so far as they embody and prophesy the dispensation in Christ. Associated with the affirmation of the Old Testament would be the keeping of the Pascha as an annual festival, dear to Quartodecimans but probably widely rejected in radical Pauline vein by gnostic and Marcionite Christians. The same is true of the doctrine of creation, which figures repeatedly in *PP* 46–105. It is not surprising to learn that Melito's technical discussion of the authority of the old Scriptures has clear points of contact with the language of the Valentinian writer Ptolemaeus.[7]

Turning to the New Testament, it is clear that Melito knew the Gospels of Matthew and John and the Revelation of John, and there are indications of knowledge of Luke-Acts and some epistles.[8] There is nothing to support the view that he knew a

---

[1] Bonner 68–72 cites Tertullian, *Ad nat.* 1. 12; Origen, *Homily on Leviticus* 10. 1; Proclus in *PG* 65. 797; Ps.-Chrysostom in *PG* 59. 723 and 732–3.

[2] *PP* 69, cf. 59.   [3] *PP* 31–3.

[4] *PP* 66–71.   [5] *PP* 82–6.   [6] *PP* 5–11.

[7] B. Lohse, 'Meliton von Sardes und der Brief des Ptolemäus an Flora': in *Der Ruf Jesu und die Antwort der Gemeinde, Festschrift J. Jeremias* (Göttingen, 1970) 179–88.

[8] Bonner 39–41, with further evidence on Rev. from *PP* 105.

definite canon such as the Muratorian, much less that he composed it.[1] In fact he seems to have used the *Gospel of Peter* for episodes like the trial before Herod.[2] There are less clear affinities with texts such as the *Acts of Peter* and the *Acts of John*.[3] It should be noted that while Melito plainly knows some New Testament texts, they are neither quoted nor referred to as Scripture. This is coherent with his second-century date.

There are indications which convince some scholars that Melito knew and used a fixed 'rule of faith', baptismal creed, or Christological confession.[4] But it is doubtful if the evidence points to more than a collection of customary phrases or topics in which the faith could be summarized at the speaker's discretion.

(ii) *Doctrine of man*. Melito's anthropology is striking. He is a dichotomist: man consists of a body fashioned from earth and a soul (*psyche*) given by God, fitted beautifully together.[5] Man was created to enjoy Paradise, but chose freely to sin, and was cast into this world 'like a convict into prison'. This reflects the notion that Paradise is a physical location separated from earth by impassable seas or mountains.[6] Once in prison, man is subject to the tyranny of Sin and his colleague Death, both highly personified figures.[7] Thus Adam leaves to his descendants an unpleasant heritage, but although St. Paul's connection of death with sin is followed, there is no suggestion that sinfulness is itself communicated to Adam's progeny as in later Augustinian teaching. Melito is in line with the Antiochene Christian tradition which is Aristotelian and dichotomist, and his thought is very like that of his contemporary, Theophilus of Antioch.[8] The similarity of the anthropology to that in Alexander *De anima* and related texts has often been noted, and attention should be drawn to the interesting

---

[1] Against V. Bartlet, 'Melito the author of the Muratorian Canon', *Expositor* 7th series 3 (1906) 210–24.

[2] See notes on *PP* 93–8, and O. Perler, 'L'Évangile de Pierre et Méliton de Sardes', *Revue biblique* 61 (1964) 584–90.

[3] S. G. Hall, 'Melito's paschal homily and the *Acts of John*', *JTS* N.S. 17 (1966) 95–8; R. Cantalamessa, 'Il Christo "Padre" negli scritti del II–III sec.', *Rivista di storia e letteratura religiosa* 3 (1967) 1–27.

[4] C. H. Thomas, *Melito von Sardes* (Osnabruck, 1893) 109–13; Blank 93–7; Perler 208; V. Pseftogas, loc. cit. See especially *PP* 104 and Fr. 15.

[5] *PP* 47 and 55, with notes.   [6] *PP* 47–8.

[7] *PP* 47–56.

[8] See further A. Grillmeier, ' "Das Erbe der Sohne Adams" in der Homilia de Passione Melitos', *Scholastik* 20–4 (1949) 481–502.

phrase which refers to man as 'the Spirit's image' or 'the Father's image'.[1] The anthropology emphasizes the bodily or psycho-somatic character of human existence, and Melito draws from it the necessity for the bodily existence and passion of the Lord.[1]

(iii) *Doctrine of God and Christ.* Bonner characterized Melito's teaching by Harnack's phrase 'naïve modalism'; i.e. Christ is equated with God with no serious consideration of the implications. Bonner refers especially to the use of the title *Father* in speaking of Christ, and the epigram 'God is murdered'.[2] Attempts are made to modify this estimate, by interpreting *Father* as a reference to Christ's regenerating action, or emphasizing expressions which imply Christ's distinct personal pre-existence.[3] Others defend Melito from the imputation of formal heresy.[4] Nevertheless, Melito does attribute to Christ all the acts of God without exception; he rarely uses expressions which clearly imply a personal distinction of the Son from the Father; where the term *Logos* is used of Christ there is no suggestion of the Middle Platonist ideas which led Justin to think in terms of a *second God;*[5] and Melito addresses his doxologies to Christ rather than distinctly to the Father.[6] If not exactly a modalist, Melito shares the Christocentric monotheism of the *Acts of John*; Christ alone is God.[7] On the doctrine of incarnation, similarly, Melito's orthodoxy has been exaggerated. This has been largely due to reliance upon the authenticity of Fr. 6, with its clear statement of the two natures ($ο\dot{υ}σίαι$) and the human soul of Christ. This has excessively influenced interpretations of *PP*.[8] The Christology of *PP*, broadly supported by the fragments and New Fragments, is in fact fairly clear and coherent. The divine Lord identifies himself with

[1] *PP* 56.

[2] Bonner 27–8; *PP* 9 and 96.

[3] So G. Racle, 'A propos du Christ-Père dans L'Homélie pascale de Méliton de Sardes', *RechSR* 50 (1962) 400–8; id. *Studia Patristica* 9 (*TU* 94, Berlin, 1966) 264–5; R. Cantalamessa, *RevSR* 37 (1963) 4–10.

[4] A. Grillmeier, *Scholastik* 20–4 (1949) 484–5 n. 8; Blank 54.

[5] *PP* 9, 47; Fr. 2. V. Grossi, *Antonianum* 16 (1976) 257–69, disagrees.

[6] *PP* 10, 45, 65, 105; Fr. 15; New Fr. II. 23.

[7] Cf. *Acta Johannis* 77, 82, 103–4, etc.

[8] e.g. Bonner 28–9; R. Cantalamessa, *RevSR* 37 (1963) 22–4; id. *La cristologia di Tertulliano* (Paradosis 18; Freiburg Schw., 1962) 108–11; Perler 140. Cf. also G. Kretschmar, 'Christliches Passa im 2. Jahrhundert und die Ausbildung der christlichen Theologie', *RechSR* 60 (1972) 287–323.

suffering mankind, putting on like a garment the flesh which is the subject of man's defeat by sinful passion and death. In the flesh he dies, but his dying merely releases the divine Spirit, which destroys death and raises him to life again, and with him humanity (ὁ ἄνθρωπος).[1] Ideas of sacrificial or substitutionary death are presupposed rather than expressed, either in a series of rhetorical contrasts (PP 100–2; New Fr. II. 14) or in typological interpretations such as the paschal lamb (PP 67–8) or the offering of Isaac (Frs. 9–11). In so far as a notion of two natures is present (the term of course is not), they are Spirit and Body, the Lord and the Man he became. The one who created was himself enfleshed in a virgin, and in the body he suffered and rose. There is some advance in Christological terminology (e.g. the verb σαρκόω), and generally an emphasis on those features which gnostic heresy denied, such as the unity of Jesus Christ and the corporeal reality of his passion.[2] It is not surprising that allusions to Valentinian texts have been detected in PP.[3] In one particular there is a striking silence characteristic of the second century: where his account of Christ's death and the release of the Spirit invite some treatment of the theme of the descent into hell, so well favoured with myth and theology in later centuries, Melito is silent;[4] and the same silence distinguishes New Fr. II. 15–16 from the later texts based upon it.

(iv) *Eschatology. PP* gives little support, as we have said, for the view that it was associated with a vigil of waiting for the return of Christ. It has even been said that such expectation is entirely absent, or that there is deliberate de-eschatologizing.[5] But that is misleading. The homily concentrates on Christ as the exalted Lord whose work as paschal Lamb is complete, but his sovereignty extends to *the end*, to *eternity;* he is *Omega* as well as *Alpha*.[6] He is thus the judge of all.[7] Melito leaves room for the future

[1] See esp. *PP* 66–72 and nn.

[2] See R. Cantalamessa, 'Méliton de Sardes, une christologie antignostique du IIe siècle', *RevSR* 37 (1963) 1–26; S. G. Hall, 'The Christology of Melito', *Studia patristica* 13 (*TU* 116; Berlin, 1975) 154–68.

[3] T. Halton, 'Valentinian echoes in Melito *Peri Pascha*?' *JTS* N.S. 20 (1969) 535–8; G. Kretschmar, *RechSR* 60 (1972) 312–22.

[4] So A. Grillmeier, 'Der Gottessohn im Totenreich', *Zeitschrift für katholische Theologie* 71 (1949) 1–53 and 184–203, esp. 8–12.

[5] Blank 96; G. Racle, *Studia patristica* 9 (*TU* 94, Berlin, 1966) 269.

[6] *PP* 105.

[7] *PP* 104.

outworking of the victory which has already in principle raised up man and exalted him to heaven.[1] Christ is Lord of all history, past, present, and future, rather as depicted in the Revelation of St. John, and the future promises of *PP* 103 probably refer to a definite time of *parousia*.[2] But Melito never makes clear how the salvation won by Christ is actually appropriated by the individual, or how the past victory is related to the future consummation. No doubt the sacraments play a part. But in his surviving writings Melito is too occupied with the sufferings and glory of the triumphant Lord to deal with such matters.

8. *The text*

(i) *Peri Pascha*. The text is based on the following:

A   Chester Beatty and Michigan papyrus. Facsimile in F. Kenyon, *The Chester Beatty biblical papyri* 8 (London, 1941). Transcript in C. Bonner, *The homily on the passion by Melito bishop of Sardis and some fragments of the apocryphal Ezekiel* (Studies and documents 12; London and Philadelphia, 1941). Contains §§ 1–104 with gaps due to broken edges. Fourth century.

B   Papyrus Bodmer XIII. Transcript in M. Testuz, *Papyrus Bodmer XIII, Méliton de Sardes Homélie sur la Pâque* (Geneva, 1960). Contains §§ 6–105 in good condition. Third or early fourth century.

O   Oxyrhynchus papyrus 1600. Edited by B. P. Grenfell and A. S. Hunt, *The Oxyrhynchus papyri* xiii (London, 1919). New transcription in S. G. Hall, *JTS* N.S. 19 (1968) 504–8. Contains §§ 57–63, much mutilated. Fifth century.

C   Coptic version in one of two papyri indicated below.

C¹ Brit. Lib. Or. MS. 9035, published by W. E. Crum and H. I. Bell in *Coptica* iii (Copenhagen, 1922) 47–9. Contains §§ 12–16 in good condition. Probably fourth century.

C² Mississippi Coptic Codex I (the Crosby Codex). To be published by W. H. Willis; see his article 'The new collections of papyri at the University of Mississippi', *Proceedings of the Sixth International Congress of Papyrology, Oslo 1958* (Oslo, 1961) 381–92. Cited in his own Latin by the present editor from photographic copy of original. Contains §§ 48–105 with some damaged edges. Probably sixth century.

G   The Georgian version. Other indicators (G¹, G²; Gᵃ, Gᵗ) are given only when further precision is required. The readings are clear and the version almost complete, but translation and transmission have so corrupted the text that it is often impossible to cite relevant testimony.

---

[1] *PP* 71, 102.
[2] R. Vignolo, 'Storia della salvezza nel Peri Pascha di Melitoni di Sardi', *La scuola cattolica* 99 (1971) 3–26.

G¹   Text and English translation published by J. N. Birdsall, 'Melito of Sardis $\Pi\epsilon\rho\grave{\iota}$ $\tauο\hat{υ}$ $\pi\acute{α}σχα$ in a Georgian version', *Le Muséon* 80 (1967) 121–38. Contains §§ 1–45.

G²   Text and Latin translation published by M. Van Esbroeck, 'Le traité sur la Pâque de Méliton de Sardes en géorgien', *Le Muséon* 84 (1971), 373–94, with further material collated in 'Les œuvres de Méliton de Sardes en géorgien', in *Bedi Kartlisa* 31 (1973) 48–63. Contains §§ 46–105.

Gᵃ   In §§ 1–45, Iviron MS. 11 fos. 98–100, cited from J. N. Birdsall (see G¹). Tenth century.

     In §§ 46–105, Iviron MS. 11 fos. 89–94, cited from M. Van Esbroeck, 'Le traité' (see G²).

Gᵗ   In §§ 1–45, Tbilisi MS. S–1246, cited from J. N. Birdsall (see G¹). Seventeenth century.

     In §§ 46–105, Tbilisi MS. A–1109, cited from M. Van Esbroeck, 'Les œuvres de Méliton' (see G²). Ninth century.

L   Latin epitome preserved among spuria of St. Augustine and St. Leo. Critical edition by H. Chadwick in *JTS* n.s. 11 (1960) 76–82. Contains §§ 1–5 and (with many omissions) 64–104.

Lᵛ, L¹, Lᵐ, Lᵇ   Authorities cited by Chadwick (art. cit. 76–7) as V, L, M, B.

S¹   Syriac fragments in Brit. Lib. Syr. Add. 12156. Cited in Latin from I. C. T. Otto, *Corpus apologetarum* ix (Jena, 1872) 421–3 (Syriac text 499–501), with reference also to improved Latin version in P. Nautin, *Le Dossier d'Hippolyte et de Méliton* (Patristica 1; Paris, 1953) 46–9. Contains parts of §§ 70–104.

S²   Syriac fragment in Brit. Lib. Syr. Add. 12154. Cited in Latin from J. B. Pitra, *Analecta sacra* iv (Paris, 1883) 433 (Syriac text 199–200). Contains §§ 94–8.

In the text, apparatus, and notes the following abbreviations and signs appear:

add.	addit, -unt
Bonner	Reading of C. Bonner, *The homily on the passion* (see A above).
cf.	confer
Chadwick	Readings of L published in *JTS* N.S. 11 (1960) 76–82, or proposals on Greek readings communicated personally by H. Chadwick.
edd.	editores
Hall	Readings proposed by S. G. Hall in *JTS* N.S. 19 (1968) 476–508.
inc.	incipit, -iunt
inv.	invertit, -unt
LXX	Septuaginta

om.	omittit, -unt
par.	and parallel passages
Perler	Reading or note of O. Perler, *Méliton de Sardes Sur la Pâque et fragments* (SC 123, Paris, 1966).
pon.	ponit, -unt
praem.	praemittit, -unt
Testuz	Reading proposed by M. Testuz, *Papyrus Bodmer XIII* (see B above).
trsp.	transponit, -unt
txt.	textus, -um
v.	vide
Vg	Vulgata
vid.	videtur, -entur
vs.	versus, -um
vss.	versûs
Whittaker	Unpublished reading proposed by M. Whittaker.
Wifstrand	Reading proposed by A. Wifstrand, 'The homily of Melito on the passion', *VigChr* 2 (1948) 201–23.

[ ]	Square brackets indicate words or letters which do not appear in Greek manuscripts but probably stood in them before damage to the codices.
⟨ ⟩	Diamond brackets indicate words or letters omitted by the Greek witnesses and restored by conjecture or from the versions.
( )	Brackets round the number of a section, e.g. (43), indicate the numbering in the editions of Bonner, Testuz, and Perler where this has not been followed in the present edition.
( )	Brackets round the symbol of a witness, e.g. (G), indicate that the reading is partially, probably, or inexactly supported by that witness.
( )	Brackets after the symbol of a witness, e.g. B(-εται), indicate a comment or clarification by the editor on the reading of the witness.
[[ ]]	Double square brackets reproduce the brackets used by the scribe of B to delete errors.
.	A full stop is used to indicate a whole word in the text by one or more or its earlier letters: in vs. 8 ἀΐδ. κ. πρόσκ. indicates ἀΐδιον καὶ πρόσκαιρον.
-	A hyphen after part of a word indicates that only the first part of the word is being cited, or only the first part is relevant.
-	A hyphen before the later part of a word indicates that

	only the later part is being cited, or only the later part is relevant.
—	A dash between two words indicates that all the intervening words are being cited.
. . .	Three dots with space at either end indicate an omission of indefinite length, whether by a witness or by the editor.
[. . . .]	Dots enclosed in brackets indicate an estimated number of letters wanting.
. .	Dots below letters in a citation indicate that the letters are not wholly legible in the manuscript. e.g. αι

(ii) *Fragments 1, 3, 4,* and *8a.* Text from Eusebius, *Historia ecclesiastica* in the edition of E. Schwartz, *Eusebius Werke* II. i, *Die Kirchengeschichte* (*GCS* IX. i, Leipzig, 1903). The same text is unaltered in the Kleine Ausgabe[2] (Berlin reprint 1952) and in G. Bardy (SC 31 and 41). A selection of Schwartz's apparatus criticus is included.

Fragment 1 = *HE* 4. 26. 4–11 (*GCS* IX. i 384. 1–386. 15; SC 31 209–11)
Fragment 3 = *HE* 4. 26. 12–14 (*GCS* IX. i 386. 16–388. 8; SC 31 211)
Fragment 4 = *HE* 4. 26. 3–4 (*GCS* IX. i 382. 8–14; SC 31 209)
Fragment 8a = *HE* 5. 28. 5 (*GCS* IX. i 500. 23–4; SC 41 75)

(iii) *Fragment 2.* Text from *Chronicon paschale* i, ed. L. Dindorf (Bonn, 1832) 483; identical text in *PG* 92. 632A.

(iv) *Fragment 5.* Text from Origen, *Selecta in Psalmos* ad Psalm. 3, *PG* 12. 1120A

(v) *Fragments 6* and *7.* Text from Anastasius Sinaiticus, *Hodegus.* The wording of *PG* 89 is preserved, but the punctuation altered.
Fragment 6 = *Hodegus* 13, *PG* 89. 228D–9B
Fragment 7 = *Hodegus* 12, *PG* 89. 197A

(vi) *Fragment 8b.* Eclectic text based on published editions and collations, with apparatus criticus.

V Cod. Vatic. 2022 fo. 238; text printed in J. B. Pitra, *Analecta sacra* ii (Paris, 1884) 3–5.
A Ambros. I. 9. Sup. (page numbered 125); collation in J. L. Mercati, 'Symbolae melitonianae', *Theologische Quartalschrift* 26 (1894) 597–600.

Perler 228–32 has an eclectic text based on Pitra and Mercati.

Better critical text in A. Harnack, *Marcion* (Leipzig, 1924/ Darmstadt, 1960) 422*–23*, which offers readings proposed by Wilamowitz here adopted or noted.

(vii) *Fragments 9–12.* The text follows I. C. T. Otto, *Corpus apologetarum* ix (Jena, 1872) 416–18, with exceptions noted. A select apparatus is based on Otto 446–53, where the manuscript tradition is fully described, with reference also to J. B. Pitra, *Spicilegium solesmense* ii (Paris, 1855) lxiii–lxiv; M. J. Routh, *Reliquiae sacrae* i (Oxford², 1846) 122–4 and 150–3.

(viii) *Fragment 13.* English text translated from I. C. T. Otto, *Corpus apologetarum* ix (Jena, 1872) 419 (Latin) and 497 (Syriac), with reference also to I. Rucker, *Florilegium Edessenum anonymum* (Sitzungsberichte der bayerischen Akademie der Wissenschaften, phil.-hist. Abt. 1933) 12–14 (Syriac with Greek retroversion); P. Nautin, *Le Dossier d'Hippolyte et de Méliton* (Patristica 1; Paris, 1953) 61 (improved Latin version).
The Greek is reconstructed by M. Richard, *Le Muséon* 85 (1972) 312–17.

(ix) *Fragment 14.* English text based on same sources as Fr. 13 above: Otto 419–20 (Latin) and 498 (Syriac), with reference to Rucker 14–15 (Syriac with Greek retroversion and Nautin 73 (improved Latin).

(x) *Fragment 15.* At the head of the translation is given the opening of the 'Irenaeus' text-form. In the English, the words enclosed in diamond brackets ⟨ ⟩ are translated from Nautin 67 (Latin text based on oriental sources).
Under the heading 'Melito' is given, with some variations, an English version based on Nautin 65–6. From verse 4 onwards, it gives material common to both the 'Melito' and 'Irenaeus' text-forms, with the following exceptions:

[ ]   Words in square brackets stand only in the 'Melito' text-form and are probably not original.

⟨ ⟩   Words in diamond brackets are absent in the 'Melito' text-form. At certain points referred to in footnotes the two forms diverge, and I have followed one or the other.

The Greek of lines ⟨1⟩–⟨9⟩ and 18 is a fragment from a florilegium described by M. Richard, 'Le florilège du cod. Vatopédi 236 sur le corruptible et l'incorruptible', *Le Muséon* 86 (1973)

249–73, where it appears on p. 265. From verse 19 onwards it is based on M. Richard's reconstruction in *Le Muséon* 85 (1972) 317–31. He uses chiefly a Greek prayer from Paris gr. 1115 fos. 206ʳ–7ᵛ, which is clearly based on the same material as the Melito fragment.

(xi) *Fragment 16b.* Text reproduced from M. Richard, *Le Muséon* 85 (1972) 324 = *Symbolae Osloenses* fasc. XXXVIII, p. 79.

(xii) *Fragment 17.* Text reproduced from O. Perler, *Ein Hymnus zur Ostervigil von Meliton?* (*Papyrus Bodmer XII*) (Paradosis 15; Freiburg Schw., 1960) 9 (photograph and transcript).

(xiii) *New Fragments I–III.* One manuscript exists, in Georgian, Tbilisi A–144 fos. 208ᵛ–12ᵛ. Georgian text with parallel Latin in M. Van Esbroeck, *Analecta Bollandiana* 90 (1972) 72–89. The English text is translated from Van Esbroeck's Latin, with his kind permission. In the notes, the following sigla appear:

L   Latin version in *Analecta Bollandiana* 90 (1972) 72–89.
vE   Corrections to L communicated privately by Van Esbroeck to the present editor.
[ ]   Square brackets indicate words or letters unreadable in the Georgian.
⟨ ⟩   Diamond brackets indicate words added to the text by the present editor.

The Greek parallels are derived partly from reconstructions of M. Richard in *Le Muséon* 85 (1972) 311–17, and partly from Ps.-Epiphanius, *De resurrectione*, edited by P. Nautin in *Le Dossier d'Hippolyte et de Méliton* (Patristica 1; Paris, 1953) 151–9. The Greek and English (=Georgian) do not always agree. Parallels with other texts are repeatedly indicated in footnotes.

ΜΕΛΙΤΩΝΟΣ ΠΕΡΙ ΠΑΣΧΑ

1 Ἡ μὲν γραφὴ τῆς ἑβραϊκῆς Ἐξόδου ἀνέγνωσται
καὶ τὰ ῥήματα τοῦ μυστηρίου διασεσάφηται,
πῶς τὸ πρόβατον θύεται
καὶ πῶς ὁ λαὸς σώζεται
⟨καὶ πῶς ὁ Φαραὼ διὰ τοῦ μυστηρίου μαστίζεται⟩.　　　　5

2 τοίνυν ξύνετε, ὦ ἀγαπητοί,
ὅπως ἐστὶν καινὸν καὶ παλαιόν,
ἀΐδιον καὶ πρόσκαιρον,
φθαρτὸν καὶ ἄφθαρτον,
θνητὸν καὶ ἀθάνατον τὸ τοῦ πάσχα μυστήριον·　　　　10

3 παλαιὸν μὲν κατὰ τὸν νόμον,
καινὸν δὲ [κατὰ τὸν] λόγον·
πρόσκαιρον κατὰ τὸν [τύπον],
ἀΐδιον διὰ τὴν χάριν·
φθαρτ[ὸν διὰ τὴν] τοῦ προβάτου σφαγήν,　　　　15
ἄφθαρτον [διὰ τὴν] τοῦ κυρίου ζωήν·
θνητὸν διὰ τὴν [εἰς γῆν] ταφήν,
ἀθάνατον δ[ιὰ τ]ὴν ἐκ [νεκρῶν] ἀνάστασιν.

4 παλαιὸς [μὲν ὁ νόμος,]
[καινὸς δὲ ὁ] λόγος·　　　　20
πρόσκαιρο[ς ὁ τύπος,]
[ἀΐδιος δὲ ἡ χάρις·]
[φ]θα[ρτὸν τὸ πρόβατον,]
[ἄφθαρτος ὁ κύριος·]

Titulum μελειτων in capite A: μελιτωνος περὶ πάσχα ad calcem BC²: *The word of Meletius the bishop about the efficacy of the Passover (lit. fulfilment)* G
1 inc. AG¹L　　　5 vs. supplevi ex *et quomodo Pharao per mysterium verberatus est* LG: om. A　　　7 ὅπως GL(*quemadmodum*): ουτως A　　　8 ἀΐδ. κ. πρόσκ. AG: inv. L　　　12 κατ[ὰ A(vidit Bonner, nunc deperdita): *because of* G: *secundum* L　　　13 κατὰ τὸν [τύπον] A: *because of the type* G: *per exemplar* L: διὰ τὸν τ. Perler　　　15 [διὰ]: *propter* LG　　　16 [διὰ]: *propter* LG　　　17 [εἰς γῆν] Hall: *in the earth* G: om. L　　　19-21 restitui (Perler et Testuz secutus) ex AL: om. G　　　22-9 in A paene deperdita e GL restituta　　　22 δὲ Testuz: *sed* L: om. Perler　　　23 φ]θα[ρτὸν–30 ἀλ]λ' deest A　　　24 ἄφθαρτος Perler cum GL: δὲ add. Testuz

MELITO ON PASCHA[1]

1 The scripture from the Hebrew Exodus has been read
  and the words of the mystery have been plainly stated,[2]
    how the sheep is sacrificed
    and how the people is saved
    and how Pharaoh is scourged through the mystery.   5
2 Understand, therefore, beloved,
    how it is new and old,
      eternal and temporary,
      perishable and imperishable,
      mortal and immortal, this mystery of the Pascha: 10
3   old as regards the law,
    but new as regards the word;
  temporary as regards the model,[3]
    eternal because of the grace;
  perishable because of the slaughter of the sheep,   15
    imperishable because of the life of the Lord;
  mortal because of the burial in earth,
    immortal because of the rising from the dead.
4   Old is the law,
    but new the word;   20
  temporary the model,
    but eternal the grace;
  perishable the sheep,
    imperishable the Lord;

---

[1] Pascha has no English equivalent. It is the Greek form of the Aramaic *pasḥā*. It can denote the Passover festival, the Passover meal, the Passover lamb, or the Christian feast (Holy Week and Easter) which continues and replaces Passover.

[2] G. Zuntz's theory (*HThR* 36 (1943) 299–315) that this line refers to a translation or preliminary exposition is to be rejected (S. G. Hall in *Kyriakon, Festschrift J. Quasten* (Münster Westf., 1970) 236–48).

[3] τύπος, 'type', is rendered *model* as consistently as possible.

[μὴ συντριβεὶς[a] ὡς ἀμνός,]   25
[ἀνασταθεὶς δὲ ὡς θεός.]
[εἰ καὶ γὰρ ὡς πρόβατον εἰς σφαγὴν ἤχθη,[b]]
[ἀλλ' οὐκ ἦν πρόβατον·]
[εἰ καὶ ὡς ἀμνὸς ἄφωνος,[c]]
[ἀλ]λ' οὐδὲ ἀμνὸς ἦν.   30
ὁ μὲν γὰρ τύπος [ἐγένετο,]
[ἡ δὲ] ἀλήθεια ηὑρίσκετο.
5 ἀντὶ γὰρ τοῦ [ἀμνοῦ υἱὸ]ς ἐγένετο
καὶ ἀντὶ τοῦ προβάτου ἄν[θρωπ]ος,
[ἐ]ν δὲ τῷ ἀνθρώπῳ Χριστὸς ὃς κεχώρηκεν [τὰ] πάντα.   35
6 ἡ γοῦν τοῦ προβάτου σφαγὴ
καὶ ἡ τοῦ αἵματος πομπὴ
καὶ ἡ τοῦ νόμου γραφὴ εἰς Χριστὸν Ἰησοῦν κεχώρηκεν,
δι' ὃν τὰ πάντα[d] ἐν τῷ πρεσβυτέρῳ νόμῳ ἐγένετο,
μᾶλλον δὲ ἐν τῷ νέῳ λόγῳ.   40
7 καὶ γὰρ ὁ νόμος λόγος ἐγένετο,
καὶ ὁ παλαιὸς καινός,
συνεξελθὼν ἐκ Σιὼν καὶ Ἰερουσαλήμ,[e]
καὶ ἡ ἐντολὴ χάρις,
καὶ ὁ τύπος ἀλήθεια,   45
καὶ ὁ ἀμνὸς υἱός,
καὶ τὸ πρόβατον ἄνθρωπος,
καὶ ὁ ἄνθρωπος θεός.
8 ὡς γὰρ υἱὸς τεχθείς,
καὶ ὡς ἀμνὸς ἀχθείς,   50
καὶ ὡς πρόβατον σφαγείς,

25 μὴ συντριβεὶς Testuz: *not eaten* G: *non comminutus* L[v1] (cf. Ioh. 19:36 Vg.): *nam comminutus* L[mb] unde σφαγεὶς Perler   26 δὲ Testuz: *sed* LG: om. Perler   27 εἰ καὶ γὰρ scripsi: *although* G: *etenim* L[1mb]: *licet enim* L[v]: καὶ γὰρ Perler: γὰρ post ὡς Testuz   29 εἰ καὶ Hall: *although* G: *et* L[1mb]: *licet* L[v]: καὶ Testuz   31 ὁ μὲν AG: *illa* (. . . *fiebant*) L: τὰ μὲν Testuz   32 ἡ] δὲ Bonner: *but the* G: *haec* (. . . *reperiuntur*) L: τὰ δὲ Testuz   33 υἱὸ]ς A (Bonner, Hall)G: *dominus* L(†*est deus*† L[b]) unde θεὸς Testuz   36–442 silet L   36 προβά]του inc. B   37 ἡ τοῦ αἵματος πομπὴ scripsi: ἡ τοῦ [. . .]ου πομπὴ A([ἀ]μνοῦ vidit Bonner): τυπος του πασχα πομπὴ B: *the shedding of the blood* G   38 χ̅]ν̅ ι̅ν̅ A: χ̅ν̅ B: *our Lord Jesus Christ* G   39 ἐγένετο A: εγειν- B(ἐγίν-)   41 ὁ AG: om. B   ἐγένετο A: γέγονεν B: *was manifested as* G   42 καὶ AG[t]: om. BG[a]   44 καὶ AB: om. G   45 καὶ AG: om. B   46 ὁ BG: om. A   48 ὁ AG: om. B   50 ἀχθείς A: ευρεθις B: vs. om. G

not broken as a lamb,   25
    but resurrected as God.
For although *as a sheep he was led to slaughter,*
    yet he was not a sheep;
although *as a lamb speechless,*
    yet neither was he a lamb.   30
For the model indeed existed,
    but then the reality appeared.[4]

5 For instead of the lamb there was a Son,
    and instead of the sheep a Man,
   and in the Man Christ who has comprised all things.   35

6 Hence the slaying of the sheep
    and the distribution of the blood
  · and the scripture from the law have reached as far as Christ,
on whose account were all things in the ancient law,
    or rather, in the recent word.   40

7 For indeed the law has become word,
    and the old new
      (*having gone out* together *from Zion and Jerusalem*),
    and the commandment grace,
    and the model reality,   45
    and the lamb a Son,
    and the sheep a Man,
    and the Man God.

8 For as a Son born,
    and as a lamb led,   50
    and as a sheep slain,

[a] Cf. John 19: 36; Exod. 12: 10 (LXX), 46.   [b] Isa. 53: 7.   [c] Isa. 53: 7.   [d] Heb. 2: 10.   [e] Isa. 2: 3; cf. Mic. 4: 2.

[4] This sentence reappears in Ps.-Hippolytus, *In sanctum pascha* 2. 2 (ed. P. Nautin p. 119. 17), and Ephraim, *Hymns for the feast of the Epiphany* iii. 17 (ed. A. E. Johnston, *Nicene and post-Nicene fathers* 13, p. 270).

καὶ ὡς ἄνθρωπος ταφείς,
ἀνέστη ἐκ νεκρῶν ὡς θεὸς φύσει θεὸς ὢν καὶ ἄνθρωπος.
9 ὅς ἐστιν τὰ πάντα·
  καθ' ὃ κρίνει νόμος,   55
  καθ' ὃ διδάσκει λόγος,
  καθ' ὃ σώζει χάρις,
  καθ' ὃ γεννᾷ πατήρ,
  καθ' ὃ γεννᾶται υἱός,
  καθ' ὃ πάσχει πρόβατον,   60
  καθ' ὃ θάπτεται ἄνθρωπος,
  καθ' ὃ ἀνίσταται θεός.
10 οὗτός ἐστιν Ἰησοῦς ὁ Χριστός,
  ᾧ ἡ δόξα εἰς τοὺς αἰῶνας τῶν αἰώνων. ἀμήν.

11 Τοῦτό ἐστιν τὸ τοῦ πάσχα μυστήριον   65
  καθὼς ἐν τῷ νόμῳ γέγραπται,
  ὡς μικρῷ πρόσθεν ἀνέγνωσται·
  διηγήσομαι δὲ τὰ ῥήματα τῆς γραφῆς,
  πῶς ὁ θεὸς ἐντέταλται Μωυσεῖ ἐν Αἰγύπτῳ,
  ὁπότε βούλεται τὸν μὲν Φαραὼ δῆσαι ὑπὸ μάστιγα,   70
  τὸν δὲ Ἰσραὴλ λῦσαι ἀπὸ μάστιγος διὰ χειρὸς Μωυσέως.
12 Ἰδοὺ γάρ, φησίν, λήμψῃ[f] ἄσπιλον ἀμνὸν καὶ ἄμωμον,[g]
  καὶ πρὸς ἑσπέραν σφάξεις αὐτὸν μετὰ τῶν υἱῶν Ἰσραήλ,[h]
  καὶ νύκτωρ ἔδεσθε αὐτὸ μετὰ σπουδῆς·[j]
  ὀστοῦν οὐ συντρίψεις αὐτοῦ.[k]   75
13 οὕτως, φησίν, ποιήσεις.[l]
  ἐν μιᾷ νυκτὶ ἔδεσθε αὐτὸ[m] κατὰ πατριὰς καὶ δήμους,[n]
  περιεζωσμένοι τὰς ὀσφύας ὑμῶν
  καὶ αἱ ῥάβδοι ἐν ταῖς χερσὶν ὑμῶν.[o]

53 ἄνθρωπος AG : ‾ανθς‾ ‾θς‾ B   54 ὅς AG : ὅ B   55 κρίνει νόμος AG : κρινομενος B   58 γεννᾷ BG : γενναται A   63 ἐστιν AG : εν B   ὁ A : om. B   64 ᾧ BGᵃ : οὗ AGᵗ   τῶν αἰώνων AG : om. B   65 τοῦτό ἐστιν τὸ AG : τουτουτο εστι B   69 ὁ A : om. B   ἐντέταλται A : ἐντέλλεται B   ἐν A : ἐν τῇ B   70 ὁπότε βουλετε B(-ται) : οπωταν βουληται A   71 ἀπὸ A(G) : ὑπὸ B   Μωυσέως inc. C¹   72 ἰδοὺ γάρ AC : ειδου B : om. G   καί om. B   73 ἑσπέραν A : εσπερας B   74 αὐτὸ AB(sc. τὸ πάσχα) : αὐτὸν Bonner   75 ὀστοῦν : praem. καὶ B cum Exod. 12 : 10, 46 : txt. ACG   συντρίψεις AG : -ετε BC cum Exod. 12 : 10, 46   77 καὶ BC : κατὰ A : and family by family G   78 ὑμῶν : ⟨καὶ τὰ ὑποδήματα ἐν τοῖς ποσὶν ὑμῶν⟩ fortasse addendum cum CG(Exod. 12 : 11) : txt. AB

　　and as a man buried,

　he rose from the dead as God, being by nature God and Man.

9　For he is all things:

　　　inasmuch as he judges, Law;　　　　　　　　　　　　55

　　　inasmuch as he teaches, Word;

　　　inasmuch as he saves, Grace;

　　　inasmuch as he begets, Father;

　　　inasmuch as he is begotten, Son;

　　　inasmuch as he suffers, Sheep;　　　　　　　　　　　60

　　　inasmuch as he is buried, Man;

　　　inasmuch as he is raised, God.

10　This is Jesus the Christ,

　　　to whom be glory for ever and ever. Amen.

11　This is the mystery of the Pascha　　　　　　　　　　65

　　　just as it is written in the law,

　　　as it has just now been read.

　　But I will relate the words of the scripture,

　　　how God has given command to Moses in Egypt,

　　　when he intends to bind Pharaoh under a scourge　　70

　　　and to free Israel from a scourge by Moses' hand.

12　'Look,' he says, 'you shall *take* a lamb, spotless and unblemished,

　　and towards evening you shall slay it with *the sons of Israel,*

　　and in the night *you shall eat it with haste,*

　　and you shall *break no bone of it.'*　　　　　　　　　75

13　'*Thus*', he says, 'you shall *do*:

　　in one *night you shall eat it by families* and tribes,

　　　belted at your loins

　　　and with your staves *in your hands.*

ᶠ Exod. 12: 3.　　　ᵍ Cf. 1 Pet. 1: 19; Exod. 12: 5.　　ʰ Exod. 12: 6.
ʲ Exod. 12: 11.　　ᵏ Exod. 12: 10 (LXX), 46.　　ˡ Cf. Exod. 12: 11, 28.
ᵐ Cf. Exod. 12: 8, 12.　　　ⁿ Cf. Exod. 12: 3.　　　ᵒ Cf. Exod. 12: 11.

ἔστιν γὰρ τοῦτο πάσχα κυρίου,ᵖ 80
μνημόσυνον αἰώνιον�q τοῖς υἱοῖς Ἰσραήλ.

14 λαβόντες δὲ τὸ τοῦ προβάτου αἷμα
χρίσατε τὰ πρόθυρα τῶν οἰκιῶν ὑμῶν,
τιθέντες ἐπὶ τοὺς σταθμοὺς τῆς εἰσόδου
τὸ σημεῖον τοῦ αἵματοςʳ εἰς δυσωπίαν τοῦ ἀγγέλου.ˢ 85
ἰδοὺ γάρ, πατάσσω Αἴγυπτονᵗ
καὶ ἐν μιᾷ νυκτὶ ἀτεκνωθήσεται ἀπὸ κτήνους ἕως ἀνθρώπου.ᵘ

15 τότε Μωυσῆς σφάξας τὸ πρόβατον
[καὶ] νύκτωρ διατελέσας τὸ μυστήριον μετὰ τῶν υἱῶν Ἰσραὴλᵛ
ἐσφράγισεν τὰς τῶν οἰκιῶν θύρας 90
εἰς φρουρὰν τοῦ λαοῦ καὶ εἰς δυσωπίαν τοῦ ἀγγέλου.

16 Ὁπότε δὲ τὸ πρόβατον σφάζεται
καὶ τὸ πάσχα βιβρώσκεται
καὶ τὸ μυστήριον τελεῖται
καὶ ὁ λαὸς εὐφραίνεται 95
καὶ ὁ Ἰσραὴλ σφραγίζεται,
τότε ἀφίκετο ὁ ἄγγελος πατάσσειν Αἴγυπτον,ʷ
τὴν ἀμύητον τοῦ μυστηρίου,
τὴν ἄμοιρον τοῦ πάσχα,
τὴν ἀσφράγιστον τοῦ αἵματος, 100
τὴν ἀφρούρητον τοῦ πνεύματος,
τὴν ἐχθράν,
τὴν ἄπιστον·
(17) ἐν μιᾷ νυκτὶ πατάξας ἠτέκνωσεν.ˣ
17 περιελθὼν γὰρ τὸν Ἰσραὴλ ὁ ἄγγελος 105
καὶ ἰδὼν ἐσφραγισμένον τῷ τοῦ προβάτου αἵματι,
ἦλθεν ἐπ' Αἴγυπτον,
καὶ τὸν σκληροτράχηλον Φαραὼ διὰ πένθους ἐδάμασεν,

80 τοῦτο AC(G) : om. B   81 αιωνειον post Ἰσραήλ pon. B : txt. A
83 τ[ῶν–87 ἀτεκνω]θήσ. deest A   85 τὸ σημιον τοῦ αἵματος B : om. C : and
you shall mark (them) G   86 γάρ B : om. C : for, he says G   πατάσσω B :
I will smite CG cum Exod. 12 : 12   89 [καὶ] (A)CG : om. B   92 ὁπότε
δὲ BC : οποδ[. . . A   95 post 96 pon. C : txt. ABG   96 σφραγίζεται A :
ἐσφράγισται B   97 ἀφίκετο AG : αφικετε B(-ται)   ὁ BCG : om. A
99 ἄμοιρον Bonner : αμμρον AB : post ἄ[- desinit Cⁱ   105 τὸν ισλ AG :
αυτον B   106 καὶ ειδων A : κερεαις B : and he found every door G   107 ἐπ'
A : εἰς B

For *this* is *the Pascha of the Lord,*   80
    an eternal reminder for the sons of Israel.
14 *But* take *the blood* of the sheep
    and smear the front doors of your *houses,*
  putting *on the posts* of the entrance
    the *sign* of the *blood* to win the angel's respect.   85
  For look! I am *striking Egypt,*
    and *in* one *night* she will be made childless, both *beast* and *man.'*
15 Then Moses, when he had slain the sheep,
    and at night performed the mystery with *the sons of Israel,*
  marked the doors of the houses   90
    to protect the people and to win the angel's respect.[5]

16 But while the sheep is being slain
    and the Pascha is being eaten
    and the mystery is being performed
    and the people is making merry   95
    and Israel is being marked,
  then came the angel to *strike Egypt,*
    the uninitiated in the mystery,
    the non-participating in the Pascha,
    the unmarked with the blood,   100
    the unguarded by the Spirit,
    the hostile,
    the faithless;
17) in one *night* he *struck* and made her childless,
17 For when the angel had gone round Israel,   105
    and had seen him marked with the blood of the sheep,
  he went against Egypt,
    and tamed stiff-necked Pharaoh with grief,

[p] Cf. Exod. 12: 11, 27.   [q] Josh. 4: 7; cf. Exod. 14: 17.   [r] Cf.
Exod. 12: 7, 13, 22.   [s] Cf. Exod. 12: 23.   [t] Cf. Exod. 12: 23, 27.
[u] Cf. Exod. 12: 12.   [v] Cf. Exod. 12: 28.   [w] Cf. Exod. 12: 29.
[x] Cf. Exod. 12: 29.

[5] Melito regards the Pascha as an initiatory rite with apotropaic effect, and
insinuates into 14–16 the language of Christian baptism and unction, especially
σφραγίζειν, χρίειν, πνεῦμα, ἀμύητος. Justin draws a close parallel between the
paschal blood and the saving faith of Christians in *Dialogue* 40. 1 and 111. 3.

ἐνδύσας αὐτὸν οὐ στολὴν φαιὰν
οὐδὲ πέπλον περιεσχισμένον,   110
ἀλλ᾿ ὅλην Αἴγυπτον περιεσχισμένην
πενθοῦσαν ἐπὶ τοῖς πρωτοτόκοις αὐτῆς.

18 ὅλη γὰρ Αἴγυπτος γενηθεῖσα ἐν πόνοις καὶ πληγαῖς,
ἐν δάκρυσιν καὶ κοπετοῖς,
ἀφίκετο πρὸς τὸν Φαραὼ ὅλη πενθήρης   115
οὐ μόνον τῷ σχήματι ἀλλὰ καὶ τῇ ψυχῇ,
περιεσχισμένη οὐ μόνον τὰς στολὰς τῆς περιβολῆς
ἀλλὰ καὶ τοὺς μασθοὺς τῆς τρυφῆς.

19 ἦν δὲ καινὸν θέαμα ἰδεῖν,
ἔνθα κοπτομένους ἔνθα κωκύοντας,   120
καὶ μέσον Φαραὼ πενθήρη
ἐπὶ σάκκῳ καὶ σπόδῳ καθήμενον,
περιβεβλημένον τὸ ψηλαφητὸν σκότος[y] ὡς ἱμάτιον πενθικόν,
περιεζωσμένον ὅλ[ην] Αἴγυπτον ὡς κιθῶνα πένθους.

20 ἦν γὰρ περικειμένη Αἴγυπτος τὸν Φαραὼ   125
ὡς περιβολὴ κωκυτοῦ.
τοιοῦτος ὑφάνθη κιθὼν τῷ τυραννικῷ σώματι·
τοιαύτην ἐνέδυσεν στολὴν τὸν σκληρὸν Φαραὼ
ὁ τῆς δικαιοσύνης ἄγγελος·
πένθος πικρὸν καὶ σκότος ψηλαφητόν,[y]   130
καὶ ἀτεκνίαν καινὴν ἐπὶ τῶν πρωτοτόκων αὐτῆς.

21 ἦν γὰρ ταχινὸς καὶ ἀκόρεστος ὁ τῶν πρωτοτόκων θάνατος,
(21) ἦν [δὲ] καινὸν τρόπαιον ἰδεῖν
ἐπὶ τῶν πιπτόντων νεκρῶν ἐν μιᾷ ῥοπῇ.[z]
καὶ ἐγένετο τοῦ θανάτου τροφὴ   135
ἡ τῶν κειμένων τροπή.

109 οὐ A: om. BG   φεαν B(φαιὰν): φαιαινην A   110 οὐδὲ A: οὐ BG
111 ἀλλ᾿—περιεσχ. A(G): om. B   113 καὶ A: καὶ ἐν B   113–56 G
multum confusa et vix utilis   115 τὸν A: om. B   116 σχήματι B:
σώματι A: flesh (pl.) G   119 ἦν AG: νῦ B(νῦν)   120 κοπτομένους B:
καὶ add. AG   121 μέσον A: ἐν μέσῳ B   123 περιβ. B: καὶ περιβ. A
124 ὅλ[ην] A(Bonner): om. B   ὡς A: ω B   125 ἦν—περικ. B: η.[. . .]
μενην A   τὸν B: τω A   128 τοιαύτην—τὸν Testuz: . . .]εν στολὴν τ[
A(deest usque ad 132 ἀκόρεστ]ος): τοιαυτη εν εθηκεν τὸν B: bitter mourning was
spread out over him like a garment G   131 καινὴν scripsi: καὶ ἦν B   133 ἦν
[δὲ καιν]ον A(Bonner, Hall)G: ἦν καὶ τον B   134 πιπτοντω BG: προτων
[. . .] A   135 ἐγένετο ἡ A: εγεινετο B(ἐγίν-)   136 κειμένων B:
κριμενων A

    clothing him not with a grey garment
        nor a torn robe,   110
    but with all Egypt torn,
        grieving for her firstborn.

18 For all Egypt was in pains and disasters,
        in tears and sounds of mourning,
    and came to Pharaoh all grief-stricken   115
        not only in appearance but also in soul,
    with not only the garments she wore all torn,
        but also her delicate breasts.

19 And it was a strange sight to see,
        people beating themselves here, and wailing there,   120
        and in between grief-stricken Pharaoh
            seated on sack-cloth and ashes,
    clothed with the *darkness that could be grasped* as a mourning
    wearing all Egypt like a tunic of mourning.   [cloak,

20 For Egypt was surrounding Pharaoh   125
        like a robe of wailing.
    Such was the tunic woven for the tyrant's body;
    with such a garment did the angel of justice
        clothe harsh Pharaoh:
    bitter grief and *darkness that could be grasped*   130
    and strange bereavement of her firstborn.

21 For swift and insatiable was the death of the firstborn,
21) and there was a strange trophy to be seen
        for those falling dead in one moment,
    and the defeat of the prostrate   135
        became the food of death.[6]

---

y Exod. 10: 21.   z Cf. Wisd. 18: 12.

---

[6] The crude Greek word-play (τρόπαιον, ῥοπῇ, τροφή, τροπή) cannot be reproduced in English, but is easily paralleled in Greek rhetorical prose; cf. A. Wifstrand, *VigChr* 2 (1948) 208.

22 καινὴν δὲ συμφορὰν ἐὰν ἀκούσητε θαυμάσετε·
    τάδε γὰρ περιέσχεν τοὺς Αἰγυπτίους,
       νὺξ μακρὰ[a]
       καὶ σκότος ψηλαφητὸν[b]   140
       καὶ θάνατος ψηλαφῶν
       καὶ ἄγγελος ἐκθλίβων[c]
       καὶ ᾄδης καταπίνων τοὺς πρωτοτόκους αὐτῶν.

23 τὸ δὲ καινότερον καὶ φοβερώτερον ἀκοῦσαι ἔχετε·
    ἐν τῷ ψηλαφητῷ σκότει ὁ ἀψηλάφητος θάνατος ἐκρύβετο,   145
    καὶ τὸ μὲν σκότος ἐψηλάφων οἱ δυστυχεῖς Αἰγύπτιοι,
    ὁ δὲ θάνατος ἐξεραυνῶν ἐψηλάφα τοὺς πρωτοτόκους τῶν
       τοῦ ἀγγέλου κελεύοντος.   [Αἰγυπτίων

24 εἴ τις οὖν ἐψηλάφα τὸ σκότος
       ὑπὸ τοῦ θανάτου ἐξήγετο.   150
    καί τις πρωτότοκος χειρὶ σκοτεινὸν σῶμα ἐναγκαλισάμενος
    τῇ ψυχῇ ἐκδειματωθεὶς οἰκτρὸν καὶ φοβερὸν ἀνεβόησεν·
       Τίνα κρατεῖ ἡ δεξιά μου;
       τίνα τρέμει ἡ ψυχή μου;
       τίς μοι σκοτεινὸς περικέχυται ὅλῳ τῷ σώματι;   155
       εἰ μὲν πατήρ, βοήθησον·
       εἰ δὲ μήτηρ, συμπάθησον·
       εἰ δὲ ἀδελφός, προσλάλησον·
       εἰ δὲ φίλος, συστάθητι·
       εἰ δὲ ἐχθρός, ἀπαλλάγηθι, ὅτι πρωτότοκος ἐγώ.   160

25 πρὸ δὲ τοῦ σιωπῆσαι τὸν πρωτότοκον
    ἡ μακρὰ σιωπὴ κατέσχεν αὐτὸν προσειποῦσα·
       Πρωτότοκος ἐμὸς εἶ·
       ἐγώ σοι πέπρωμαι ἡ τοῦ θανάτου σιωπή.

137 θαυμασεται Α(-ετε) : -ητε Β   144 καινότερον Α : κεν- Β   145 ἀψηλάφ-
Α : ψηλαφ- BG(gripping) forsitan recte   146 ἐψηλάφων post δυστυχεῖς pon.
Β : txt. Α   150 ὑπὸ Β : ὑπὲρ Α   θανάτου Α : ἀγγέλου Β   151 καί
Α(G) : εἴ Β   πρωτότοκος Α(G) : -τοτόκου σῶμα Β   152 τῇ Β : τῇ δὲ Α
ἐκδειματωθεὶς Bonner : εκδιμαθεις Α : εκαιματωθεις Β   153 μου BG : om. Α
155 σκοτινος Α : σκότος BG   περικέχυται AG : περικειτε Β(-ται)   157 συμ-
edd. : συν- ΑΒ   159 συστάθητι Hall : συν[.]ανθησον Α : ευσταθησον Β :
draw near to me G : συγκάθισον Bonner   160 ἀπαλλάγηθι edd. : -ητι ΑΒ
161–281 G valde confusa et vix utilis   161 σειωπησε Β(σιωπῆσαι) : σειω-
πησασ Α   162 ἡ Α : om. Β   προσειπουσα Α : -ειπῶ Β   163 [[ει]]εμος ει
Β(sic) : εἰ μ[ὲν ἐ]μός Α(Hall) : ειμει [νό]μος Α(Bonner)

22 When you hear, you will marvel at a strange disaster.
    For these enclosed the Egyptians:
        long night
        and *darkness that could be grasped*   140
        and death grasping[7]
        and *angel crushing*
        and Hades swallowing their firstborn.

23 But the strangest and most dreadful thing you have still to hear.
    In the darkness that could be grasped lurked death that could
                                        not be grasped, 145
        and the wretched Egyptians were grasping at the darkness,
        while death was seeking out and grasping the firstborn of the
            at the angel's bidding.   [Egyptians

24 If therefore one was grasping at the darkness,
        he was led to execution by death.   150
    And one firstborn, as he clasped dark body in his hand,
        terrified in soul let out a piteous and dreadful cry:
        'Whom does my hand hold?
        Whom does my soul dread?
        Who is this dark one enveloping my whole body?   155
        If it is father, help;
        if mother, comfort;
        if brother, speak;
        if friend, support;
        if enemy, go away, for I am a firstborn.'   160

25 But before the firstborn grew silent,
        the long silence of death caught him and addressed him:
        'You are my firstborn;
        I am your destiny, the silence of death.'

    [a] Cf. Wisd. 17: 2.   [b] Cf. Exod. 10: 21.   [c] Ps. 35 (34 LXX): 5.

---

    [7] T. Halton notes the similarity to Homer's account of the blind Cyclops
feeling for his prisoners (χερσὶ ψηλαφάων), a passage favoured by orators (*Kyriakon, Festschrift J. Quasten* (Münster Westf., 1970) 251 f.).

26 ἕτερος δέ τις πρωτότοκος νοήσας τὴν τῶν πρωτοτόκων ἅλωσιν   165
ἑαυτὸν ἀπαρνεῖτο ἵνα μὴ θάνῃ πικρῶς·
Οὔκ εἰμι πρωτότοκος,
τριτῷ γεγέννημαι καρπῷ.
ὁ δὲ ψευσθῆναι μὴ δυνάμενος τοῦ πρωτοτόκου προσήπτετο,
πρηνὴς δὲ ἔπιπτεν σιγῶν.   170
ὑπὸ δὲ μίαν ῥοπὴν[d] ὁ πρωτότοκος καρπὸς τῶν Αἰγυπτίων ἀπώλετο·
ὁ πρωτόσπορος,
ὁ πρωτότοκος,
ὁ ποθητός,
ὁ περίψυκτος ἠδαφίσθη χαμαί·   175
οὐχ ὁ τῶν ἀνθρώπων μόνον,
ἀλλὰ καὶ τῶν ἀλόγων ζώων.
27 μύκημα δὲ ἐν τοῖς πεδίοις τῆς γῆς ἠκούετο
ἀποδυρομένων κτηνῶν ἐπὶ τῶν τροφίμων αὐτῶν·
καὶ γὰρ δάμαλις ὑπόμοσχος   180
καὶ ἵππος ὑπόπωλος
καὶ τὰ λοιπὰ κτήνη λοχευόμενα καὶ σπαργῶντα
πικρὸν καὶ ἐλεεινὸν ἀπωδύροντο ἐπὶ τῶν πρωτοτόκων καρπῶν.
28 οἰμωγὴ δέ τις καὶ κοπετὸς ἐπὶ τῇ τῶν ἀνθρώπων ἀπωλείᾳ ἐγένετο,
ἐπὶ τῇ τῶν πρωτοτόκων νεκρῶν.   185
ὅλη γὰρ ἐπώζεσεν Αἴγυπτος ἐπὶ τῶν ἀτάφων σωμάτων.[e]
29 ἦν δὲ θεάσασθαι φοβερὸν θέαμα
τῶν Αἰγυπτίων μητέρας λυσικόμους,
πατέρας λυσίφρονας,
δεινὸν ἀνακωκύοντας τῇ αἰγυπτιακῇ φωνῇ·   190
Δυστυχεῖς ἠτεκνώμεθα ὑπὸ μίαν ῥοπὴν ἀπὸ τοῦ πρωτοτόκου
καρποῦ.
ἦσαν δὲ ἐπὶ μασθῶν κοπτόμενοι,
χερσὶν τύπτοντες κροτήματα ἐπὶ τῆς τῶν νεκρῶν ὀρχήσεως.

165 νοήσας AG: ποιήσας Β   169 τοῦ πρωτοτόκου προσηπτε᾽τον Β(-ετο
Testuz): τους -ους προσ[. . . A   171 ἀπώλετο Β: απολλυ[. . . A(ἀπώλ-
λυτο?), tunc deest usque ad 177 κτηνῶν   175 περίψυκτος Whittaker:
-ψηκτος Β   ἠδαφίσθη: εδ- Β   177 ἀλόγων ζώων Β: . . .]κτηνῶν A
179 τροφίμων Β: τροφων A   184 οἰμωγὴ δ[έ τις] A(Hall): ομοια᾽η δε τις Β
ἐγένετο A: εγειν- Β(ἐγίν-)   185 τῇ Β: om. A   186 σωμάτων Β:
νεκρῶν A(G)   189 πατέρας BG: καὶ π. A   192 μασθῶν Β: -τῶν A
193 ὀρχήσεως AB: αἱρέσεως Testuz

26 But another firstborn, perceiving the seizure of the firstborn, 165
    denied his identity so that he might not die bitterly:
  'I am not a firstborn,
  I was begotten at third conception.'
  But he who could not be deceived fastened on the firstborn;
    headlong he fell, and was silent. 170
  At one moment the firstborn offspring of the Egyptians perished;
    the first begotten,
    the first born,
    the longed for,
    the fondled one was dashed to the ground; 175
    not the firstborn of men only,
      but also of dumb beasts.
27 Lowing was heard in the plains of the land
    from beasts bemoaning their nurslings;
  for cow with sucking calf 180
    and mare with sucking foal
  and the other beasts bearing young and distended with milk
  were bitterly and piteously bemoaning their firstborn offspring.
28 There was a howling and noise of grief at the loss of the men,
    at the loss of the firstborn dead. 185
  For all Egypt stank with the unburied bodies.
29 It was a terrible spectacle to watch,
    Egyptian mothers with hair undone,
      fathers with minds undone,
  dreadfully wailing in the Egyptian language: 190
    'By evil fate we are in one moment bereft of our firstborn
  And they were beating on their breasts,   [offspring.'
    striking blows with their hands for the dancing of the dead.[8]

d Cf. Wisd. 18: 12.   e Cf. Wisd. 18: 12.

---

[8] Apparently the dying of the firstborn is seen as a grotesque ballet, for
which the breast-beating constitutes the orchestral accompaniment (or perhaps
applause).

30 Τοιαύτη συμφορὰ περιέσχεν Αἴγυπτον,
    ἄφνω δὲ ἠτέκνωσεν αὐτήν.   195
    ἦν δὲ Ἰσραὴλ φρουρούμενος ὑπὸ τῆς τοῦ προβάτου σφαγῆς,
    καί γε συνεφωτίζετο ὑπὸ τοῦ χυθέντος αἵματος,[f]
    καὶ τεῖχος ηὑρίσκετο τοῦ λαοῦ ὁ τοῦ προβάτου θάνατος.
31 ὦ μυστηρίου καινοῦ καὶ ἀνεκδιηγήτου·
    ἡ τοῦ προβάτου σφαγὴ ηὑρίσκετο τοῦ Ἰσραὴλ σωτηρία,   200
    καὶ ὁ τοῦ προβάτου θάνατος ζωὴ τοῦ λαοῦ ἐγένετο,
    καὶ τὸ αἷμα ἐδυσώπησεν τὸν ἄγγελον.
32 λέγε μοι, ὦ ἄγγελε, τί ἐδυσωπήθης;
    τὴν τοῦ προβάτου σφαγὴν ἢ τὴν τοῦ κυρίου ζωήν;
    τὸν τοῦ προβάτου θάνατον ἢ τὸν τοῦ κυρίου τύπον;   205
    τὸ τοῦ προβάτου αἷμα ἢ τὸ τοῦ κυρίου πνεῦμα;
33 δῆλος εἶ δυσωπηθεὶς
    ἰδὼν τὸ τοῦ κυρίου μυστήριον ἐν τῷ προβάτῳ γινόμενον,
    τὴν τοῦ κυρίου ζωὴν ἐν τῇ τοῦ προβάτου σφαγῇ,
    τὸν τοῦ κυρίου τύπον ἐν τῷ τοῦ προβάτου θανάτῳ,   210
    διὰ τοῦτο οὐκ ἐπάταξας τὸν Ἰσραὴλ
    ἀλλὰ μόνην Αἴγυπτον ἠτέκνωσας·

34 Τί τοῦτο τὸ καινὸν μυστήριον,
    Αἴγυπτον μὲν παταχθῆναι εἰς ἀπώλειαν,
    τὸν δὲ Ἰσραὴλ φυλαχθῆναι εἰς σωτηρίαν;   215
    ἀκούσατε τὴν δύναμιν τοῦ μυστηρίου.
35 οὐδέν ἐστιν, ἀγαπητοί, τὸ λεγόμενον καὶ γινόμενον
    δίχα παραβολῆς καὶ προκεντήματος·
    πάντα ὅσα ἐὰν γίνηται καὶ λέγηται παραβολῆς τυγχάνει,
    τὸ μὲν λεγόμενον παραβολῆς,
    τὸ δὲ γινόμενον προτυπώσεως·   220
    ἵνα ὡς ἂν τὸ γινόμενον διὰ τῆς προτυπώσεως δείκνυται,
    οὕτως καὶ τὸ λαλούμενον διὰ τῆς παραβολῆς φωτισθῇ.

199 ὦ Bonner: ο A(Bonner, iam non videtur): τοῦ B   καινοῦ καὶ A: om.
B: inexpressible new G   201 ἐγένετο A: εγειν- B(ἐγίν-)   207 δῆλος εἶ
δυσωπηθεὶς B: δηλωση ο εδυσοπηθης A(num quid inter δηλωση et ο defractum
sit non liquet): but it appears to thee that thou wast propitiated G   208 τῷ B:
τωτου A   217–18 txt. B: inter λεγόμε[νον et προκεντήμα]το[ς breviorem tex-
tum habuisse vid. A, tunc deest usque ad 222 δ]είκνυται   219 γίνηται Testuz:
γεινετε B: γίν. καὶ om. G fortasse recte   λεγητε B(-ται)   223 λαλούμενον
A: λεγόμενον B   φωτισθῇ B: εφοτισθη AG(v. Birdsall p. 137 ad loc.)

30 Such was the calamity that encompassed Egypt,
       and suddenly made her childless.   195
   But Israel was guarded by the slaughter of the sheep,
       and was even illuminated together by the shed blood,[9]
   and the death of the sheep became a wall for the people.
31 O strange and inexpressible mystery!
       The slaughter of the sheep was found to be Israel's salvation, 200
       and the death of the sheep became the people's life,
           and the blood won the angel's respect.
32 Tell me, angel, what did you respect?
       The slaughter of the sheep or the life of the Lord?
       The death of the sheep or the model of the Lord?   205
       The blood of the sheep or the Spirit of the Lord?
33 It is clear that your respect was won
       when you saw the mystery of the Lord occurring in the sheep,
           the life of the Lord in the slaughter of the lamb,
           the model of the Lord in the death of the sheep;   210
       that is why you did not strike Israel,
           but made only Egypt childless.

34 What is this strange mystery,
       that Egypt was struck for destruction,
       while Israel was protected for salvation?   215
   Hear what is the force of the mystery.
35 What is said and done is nothing, beloved,
       without a comparison and preliminary sketch.
   Whatever is said and done finds its comparison—
       what is said, a comparison,   220
       what is done, a prefiguration—
   in order that, just as what is done is demonstrated through the
                                                  prefiguration,
   so also what is spoken may be elucidated through the comparison.

   f Cf. Exod. 10: 23; Wisd. 17: 5.

   _____

   9 The guarding and illumination reflect the terminology of Christian baptism
and unction. Cf. §§ 14–16.

36 τοῦτο δὴ γίνεται ἐπὶ προκατασκευῆς·
   ἔργον οὐκ ἀνίσταται,   225
   διὰ δὲ τὸ μέλλον διὰ τῆς τυπικῆς εἰκόνος ὁρᾶσθαι·
   διὰ τοῦτο τοῦ μέλλοντος γίνεται προκέντημα
   ἢ ἐκ κηροῦ ἢ ἐκ πηλοῦ ἢ ἐκ ξύλου,
   ἵνα τὸ μέλλον ἀνίστασθαι
   ὑψηλότερον ἐν μεγέθει   230
   καὶ ἰσχυρότερον ἐν δυνάμει
   καὶ καλὸν ἐν σχήματι
   καὶ πλούσιον ἐν τῇ κατασκευῇ
   διὰ μικροῦ καὶ φθαρτοῦ προκεντήματος ὁραθῇ.

37 ὁπόταν δὲ ἀναστῇ πρὸς ὃ ὁ τύπος,   235
   τό ποτε τοῦ μέλλοντος τὴν εἰκόνα φέρον,
       τοῦτ' ὡς ἄχρηστον γινόμενον λύεται,
   παραχωρῆσαν τῷ φύσει ἀληθεῖ τὴν περὶ αὐτοῦ εἰκόνα.
   γίνεται δὲ τό ποτε τίμιον ἄτιμον
   τοῦ φύσει τιμίου φανερωθέντος.   240

38 ἑκάστῳ γὰρ ἴδιος καιρός·
   ἴδιος χρόνος τοῦ τύπου,
   ἴδιος χρόνος τῆς ὕλης,
   ἴδιος χρόνος τῆς ἀληθείας.
   ποιεῖς τὸν τύπον·   245
   τοῦτον ποθεῖς
   ὅτι τοῦ μέλλοντος ἐν αὐτῷ τὴν εἰκόνα βλέπεις.
   προκομίζεις τὴν ὕλην τῷ τύπῳ·

---

224 δὴ Β: δε Α   227 τοῦτο Α: om. Β   γίνεται Testuz: γεινεσθαι ΑΒ
προκέντημα Α: -τος Β   229 ἀνίστασθαι Β(G): ἐγείρεσθαι Α   230 ὑψηλότερον
Α: η supra lineam add. Β(ῇ?)   232 καλὸν Β: καλλον Α(-ιον)   233 κατασκευῇ
Β: κατασκευηη Α(-ῇ ῇ?)   234 μικροῦ Bonner: μακρου ΑΒ: small G   προκεντήματος Α: κεντήματος Β   235 αναστεη Α(-αιη): $\overset{και}{αναστη}$ Β(sic)   προς ω
Α(πρὸς ὃ): om. Β   236 τό ποτε Α: $^{το}τε$ Β(sic)   τὴν ἴκονα φερων Β:
φέρον Α   237 τοῦτ' ὡς Α: τουτο ουτως Β   γεινομενον Α: om. Β   λυετε
ΑΒ(-εται): they destroy it G   240 φανερωθ[[θ]]εντος Β(sic): φανεροντος Α
241 ἑκάστῳ Α: εκαστ$\overset{ω}{ου}$ Β(sic)   241-5 restitui: ἐκ. γὰρ ἴδιος καιρός, τοῦ
τύπου ἴδιος χρόνος, τῆς ὕλης ἴδιος χρόνος, τῆς ἀληθείας ποιεῖ⟨ς⟩ τὸν τύπον Α
(Bonner; post ἀληθείας add. ⟨ἴδιος χρόνος⟩ Wifstrand): ἐκ. γὰρ ἴδιος χρόνος τ̄
τύπον Β   242-56 om. G   247 ἐν Β: τῷ Α   248 προκομιζις Β:
προκοπτει Α

36 This is just what happens in the case of a preliminary structure:[10]
 it does not arise as a finished work,   225
 but because of what is going to be visible through its image acting
         as a model.

For this reason a preliminary sketch is made of the future thing
 out of wax or of clay or of wood,
in order that what will soon arise
 taller in height,   230
 and stronger in power,
 and beautiful in form,
 and rich in its construction,
may be seen through a small and perishable sketch.

37 But when that of which it is the model arises,   235
 that which once bore the image of the future thing
  is itself destroyed as growing useless
having yielded to what is truly real the image of it;
and what once was precious becomes worthless
 when what is truly precious has been revealed.   240

38 For to each belongs a proper season:
 a proper time for the model,
 a proper time for the material,
 a proper time for the reality.

You make the model;   245
 you want that
 because you see in it the image of the future thing.
You produce the material before the model;

---

[10] The analogy in §§ 36–8 may have influenced Clement of Alexandria, Fr. 33 (Stählin iii. 218) and Origen, *In Lev. Hom.* x. 1 (*PG* 12. 525–6). A similar idea in another connection appears in Tertullian, *Ad nationes* 1. 12 (CChr. *SL* i. 31). The sketch may be that for a painter, or an architect's model, but most likely a sculptor's preliminary sketch for a statue.

ταύτην ποθεῖς
διὰ τὸ μέλλον ἐν αὐτῇ ἀνίστασθαι.   250
ἀπαρτίζεις τὸ ἔργον·
    τοῦτο μόνον ποθεῖς,
    τοῦτο μόνον φιλεῖς,
ἐν αὐτῷ μόνῳ τὸν τύπον καὶ τὴν ὕλην καὶ τὴν ἀλήθειαν βλέπων.

39 Ὡς γοῦν ἐν τοῖς φθαρτοῖς παραδείγμασιν,   255
    οὕτως δὴ καὶ ἐν τοῖς ἀφθάρτοις·
ὡς ἐν τοῖς ἐπιγείοις,
    οὕτω δὴ καὶ ἐν τοῖς ἐπουρανίοις.
καὶ γὰρ ἡ τοῦ κυρίου σωτηρία καὶ ἀλήθεια ἐν τῷ λαῷ προετυπώθη,
    καὶ τὰ τοῦ εὐαγγελίου δόγματα ὑπὸ τοῦ νόμου προεκηρύχθη.   260
40 ἐγένετο οὖν ὁ λαὸς τύπος προκεντήματος
    καὶ ὁ νόμος γραφὴ παραβολῆς·
τὸ δὲ εὐαγγέλιον διήγημα νόμου καὶ πλήρωμα,
    ἡ δὲ ἐκκλησία ἀποδοχεῖον τῆς ἀληθείας.
41 ἦν οὖν ὁ τύπος τίμιος πρὸ τῆς ἀληθείας   265
    καὶ ἦν ἡ παραβολὴ θαυμαστὴ πρὸ τῆς ἑρμηνείας·
τοῦτ᾽ ἔστιν ὁ λαὸς ἦν τίμιος πρὸ τοῦ τὴν ἐκκλησίαν ἀνασταθῆναι,
    καὶ ὁ νόμος θαυμαστὸς πρὸ τοῦ τὸ εὐαγγέλιον φωτισθῆναι.
42 ὁπότε δὲ ἡ ἐκκλησία ἀνέστη
    καὶ τὸ εὐαγγέλιον προέστη,
ὁ τύπος ἐκενώθη παραδοὺς τῇ ἀληθείᾳ τὴν δύναμιν,   270
    καὶ ὁ νόμος ἐπληρώθη παραδοὺς τῷ εὐαγγελίῳ τὴν δύναμιν.
43 ὃν τρόπον ὁ τύπος κενοῦται τῷ φύσει ἀληθεῖ τὴν εἰκόνα παραδούς,
    καὶ ἡ παραβολὴ πληροῦται ὑπὸ τῆς ἑρμηνείας φωτισθεῖσα,
οὕτως δὴ καὶ ὁ νόμος ἐπληρώθη τοῦ εὐαγγελίου φωτισθέντος,   275
    καὶ ὁ λαὸς ἐκενώθη τῆς ἐκκλησίας ἀνασταθείσης·

249 ταύτην Wifstrand: τουτον A: τουτο B   250 αὐτῇ Wifstrand: αυτω AB
252 τοῦτο A: -ον B   252 ποθεῖς–253 μόνον om. A   253 τοῦτο Testuz:
-ον B   254 μόνῳ A: om. B   καὶ–ὕλην om. A   255 γοῦν A: οὖν B
256 δὴ B: om. A   258 οὕτω B: οὐ A   261 τύπος προκέτηματος B:
προκέντημα τῆς ἐκκλησίας AG   264 ἀπο[δο]χεῖον A: αποδοχον B   266 ἦν
A: om. B   267 τοῦτ᾽ A: τοῦτο B   ἀνα]σταθῆναι A: ἀναστῆναι B
271 ἐ[κενώθη–273 τρόπον] deest A   273 ὁ τύπος κενοῦται Bonner: ὁ τ.
καινουται A: καινουται ὁ τ. B   274 ἡ παραβολὴ πληροῦται scripsi: παρα-
β[ολαὶ πλη]ροῦνται A(?): ἡ παραβολὴ καινουται B(ἡ π. κεν- Testuz): this parable is
fulfilled G   φωτισθισα B: φωτ[ισ]θ[. . . A(-εῖσαι?)   276 ἀνασταθείσ[ης
A: ανασθισης B

you want that
    because of what is going to arise in it.   250
You complete the work;
    you want that alone,
    you love that alone,
because in it alone you see the pattern and the material and the
          reality.
      255

39 As then with the perishable examples,
    so also with the imperishable things;
as with the earthly things,
    so also with the heavenly.
For the very salvation and reality of the Lord were prefigured in
         the people,
and the decrees of the gospel were proclaimed in advance by the 260
         law.

40 The people then was a model by way of preliminary sketch,
    and the law was the writing of a parable;
the gospel is the recounting and fulfilment of the law,
    and the church is the repository of the reality.   265

41 The model then was precious before the reality,
    and the parable was marvellous before the interpretation;
that is, the people was precious before the church arose,
    and the law was marvellous before the gospel was elucidated.

42 But when the church arose   270
    and the gospel took precedence,
the model was made void, conceding its power to the reality,
    and the law was fulfilled, conceding its power to the gospel.

43 In the same way as the model is made void, conceding the image
         to the truly real,
    and the parable is fulfilled, being elucidated by the interpretation,
just so also the law was fulfilled when the gospel was elucidated, 275
    and the people was made void when the church arose;

καὶ ὁ τύπος ἐλύθη τοῦ κυρίου φανερωθέντος,
καὶ σήμερον γέγονεν τά ποτε τίμια ἄτιμα
τῶν φύσει τιμίων φανερωθέντων.

44 Ἦν γάρ ποτε τίμιος ἡ τοῦ προβάτου σφαγή,
   νῦν δὲ ἄτιμος διὰ τὴν τοῦ κυρίου ζωήν·   280
τίμιος ὁ τοῦ προβάτου θάνατος,
   νῦν δὲ ἄτιμος διὰ τὴν τοῦ κυρίου σωτηρίαν·
τίμιον τὸ τοῦ προβάτου αἷμα,
   νῦν δὲ ἄτιμον διὰ τὸ τοῦ κυρίου πνεῦμα·   285
τίμιος ἄφωνος ἀμνός,
   νῦν δὲ ἄτιμος διὰ τὸν ἄμωμον υἱόν·
τίμιος ὁ κάτω ναός,
   νῦν δὲ ἄτιμος διὰ τὸν ἄνω Χριστόν.

45 ἦν τίμιος ἡ κάτω Ἰερουσαλήμ,
   νῦν δὲ ἄτιμος διὰ τὴν ἄνω Ἰερουσαλήμ·ᵍ   290
ἦν τίμιος ἡ στενὴ κληρονομία,
   νῦν δὲ ἄτιμος διὰ τὴν πλατεῖαν χάριν.
οὐ γὰρ ἐφ' ἑνὶ τόπῳ οὐδὲ ἐν βραχεῖ σχοινίσματι
   ἡ τοῦ θεοῦ δόξα καθίδρυται,
ἀλλ' ἐπὶ πάντα τὰ πέρατα τῆς οἰκουμένης   295
   ἐκκέχυται ἡ χάρις αὐτοῦ,
καὶ ἐνταῦθα κατεσκήνωκεν ὁ παντοκράτωρ θεὸς
   διὰ Χριστοῦ Ἰησοῦ·
ᾧ ἡ δόξα εἰς τοὺς αἰῶνας. ἀμήν.   300

46 Τὸ μὲν οὖν διήγημα τοῦ τύπου καὶ τῆς ἀνταποδόσεως ἀκηκόατε·
ἀκούσατε καὶ τὴν κατασκευὴν τοῦ μυστηρίου·
   τί ἐστιν τὸ πάσχα;
   ἀπὸ γὰρ τοῦ συμβεβηκότος τὸ ὄνομα κέκληται·
   ἀπὸ τοῦ παθεῖν τὸ πάσχειν.   305
μάθετε οὖν τίς ὁ πάσχων,
   καὶ τίς ὁ τῷ πάσχοντι συμπαθῶν,

280 τίμιος post προβάτου pon. A: txt. B   286 ἄφωνος AB: ⟨ὁ⟩ ἄ. Bonner (G)   ἀμνός A: ἄμωμος B: blameless lamb G   290 ἦν A: om. B   292 ἦν B: om. A   στενὴ B: κενη A: little G   294 οὐ γὰρ ἐφ' A(G): ου εν B   σχοινίσματι B: σθηματι A: place G   298 κατεσκήνωκεν A: -σεν B   299 χ̅υ̅ ι̅υ̅ A: ι̅υ̅ χ̅ο̅υ̅ B: Jesus Christ his Son Gᵃ: Jesus Christ Son of God Gᵗ   post ἀμήν desinit Gᴵ   302 ἀκούσατε A: om. B   303 inc. G²   304 τὸ A: om. B   305 txt. B: ἐκ γὰρ τοῦ παθε[. . . . . .]χειν A: a passione passio G   306 μάθετε AG: μάθε B

and the model was abolished when the Lord was revealed,
  and today, things once precious have become worthless,
    since the really precious things have been revealed.

44 Once, the slaying of the sheep was precious,   280
    but it is worthless now because of the life of the Lord;
  the death of the sheep was precious,
    but it is worthless now because of the salvation of the Lord;
  the blood of the sheep was precious,
    but it is worthless now because of the Spirit of the Lord;   285
  a speechless lamb was precious,
    but it is worthless now because of the spotless Son;
  the temple below was precious,
    but it is worthless now because of the Christ above.[11]

45 The Jerusalem below was precious,   290
    but it is worthless now because of *the Jerusalem above*;
  the narrow inheritance was precious,
    but it is worthless now because of the widespread bounty.
  For it is not in one place nor in a little plot
    that the glory of God is established,   295
  but on all the ends of the inhabited earth
    his bounty overflows,
  and there the almighty God has made his dwelling
    through Christ Jesus;
    to whom be glory for ever. Amen.   300

46 You have now heard the account of the model and what corresponds
  listen also to the constitution of the mystery.   [to it;
  What is the Pascha?[12]
    It gets its name from its characteristic:
    from *suffer* (*pathein*) comes *suffering* (*páschein*).[13]   305
  Learn therefore who is the suffering one,
    and who shares the suffering of the suffering one,

  ^g Gal. 4: 26.

[11] References to the temple and Jerusalem allude to the celebration of the
paschal sacrifice, restricted in the Deuteronomic code to Jerusalem. They gain
particular point from the cessation of sacrifice when the temple was destroyed.
Here the temple is taken as a model of the risen Christ, whose body it represents
in John 2: 19–21; cf. also Eph. 2: 14–22.

[12] Melito's question corresponds to the one to which the Jewish Passover
Haggadah gives the answer: 'What do you mean by this service?' (Exod. 12: 26).

[13] Text and interpretation are uncertain. The false etymology of the Aramaic
pascha as if it came from the root of the Greek *páschein* is widespread in early
Christianity. See C. Mohrmann, *Études sur le latin des chrétiens* i (Rome, 1961)
205–22 (= *Ephemerides liturgicae* 66 (1952) 37–52); A. Botte, 'Pascha', *L'Orient
syrien* 8 (1963) 213–26. The translation of πάσχειν as 'to keep the pascha'
(Testuz, Perler) should be avoided.

(47) καὶ διὰ τί πάρεστιν ὁ κύριος ἐπὶ τῆς γῆς
    ἵνα τὸν πάσχοντα ἀμφιασάμενος
    ἁρπάσῃ εἰς τὰ ὑψηλὰ τῶν οὐρανῶν.[h]

31

47 Ὁ θεὸς ἐν ἀρχῇ ποιήσας τὸν οὐρανὸν καὶ τὴν γῆν[j]
    καὶ πάντα τὰ ἐν αὐτοῖς διὰ τοῦ λόγου,
    ἀνεπλάσατο ἀπὸ τῆς γῆς τὸν ἄνθρωπον
    καὶ ἰδίαν πνοὴν μετέδωκεν.[k]
    τοῦτον δὲ ἔθετο εἰς τὸν παράδεισον κατὰ ἀνατολὰς

31

    ἐν Ἐδεμ, ἐκεῖ τρυφᾶν,[l]
    τάδε αὐτῷ νομοθετήσας διὰ τῆς ἐντολῆς·
    Ἀπὸ παντὸς ξύλου βρώσει φάγετε,
    ἀπὸ δὲ τοῦ ξύλου τοῦ γινώσκειν ἀγαθὸν καὶ πονηρὸν
    οὐ φάγεσθε·

32

    ᾗ δ' ἂν ἡμέρᾳ φάγῃ
    θανάτῳ ἀποθανῇ.[m]

48 ὁ δὲ ἄνθρωπος φύσει δεκτικὸς ὢν ἀγαθοῦ καὶ πονηροῦ,
    ὡσεὶ βῶλος γῆς ἑκατέρωθεν σπερμάτων,
    ἐδέξατο τὸν ἐχθρὸν καὶ λίχνον σύμβουλον,[n]

32

    καὶ προσαψάμενος τοῦ ξύλου παρέβη τὴν ἐντολὴν
    καὶ παρήκουσεν τοῦ θεοῦ.[o]
    ἐξεβλήθη γοῦν εἰς τοῦτον τὸν κόσμον
    ὡς εἰς δεσμωτήριον καταδίκων.[p]

49 Τούτου δὲ πολυχόου καὶ πολυχρονίου γενομένου,

33

    διὰ τῆς τοῦ ξύλου γεύσεως ⟨διαλυθέντος⟩
    καὶ εἰς γῆν χωρήσαντος,

308 inc. C² legi posse, valde mutilus   τῆς γῆς B : τὴν γῆν A   309 ἀμφια-
σάμενος BG : [ε]ιασαμενος A(ιασ-)   311 ἐν–316 τρυφ]ᾶν deest A   311 ἐν–326
καὶ deest C²   314 ειδειαν πνοη B : spiritum viventem G : εἴδει ἀναπνοὴν Testuz
316 τρυφαν B : . . .]αν A : ad servitium suum et ad delectationem G : ἐτρύφησαν Testuz
318 ξύλου BG : τοῦ ἐν τῷ παραδισω add. A(Gen. 2 : 16)   φάγ]ετε AG : φάγῃ B(Gen.
2 : 16)   319 γεινωσκει[ν A(Bonner, at χεινῳσκ[nunc praebetur ; cf. Gen. 2 :
17) : γεινωσκοντος B : ad scientiam G   ἀγαθὸν A : καλὸν B(Gen. 2 : 17)   321 φάγῃ
Bonner : φευγη A : φαγεσθαι B(-εσθε, cf. -ητε vel -ησθε Gen. 2 : 17) : edetis G
322 ἀποθανῇ A : αποθανισθε B(-εισθε, Gen. 2 : 17) G   324 γῆς ἑκατέρωθεν B : τῶν
ἑκατέρων A   325 τὸν A : om. B   ἐχθρὸν Bonner G : εχρον A : αιχρον B   326 legi
potest C² usque ad finem, hic illic mutilus   328 γοῦν A : οὖν B   329 κατα-
δίκων Bonner : -κουν A : -κος B : -κοι vel -κων C ut vid.   330 πολυχόου Bonner :
-χροος A(Bonner, sed -χρους video) : -χοος B : in magnam tribulationem G(πολυπό-
νου?) : π. καὶ om. C ut vid.   πολυχρονου A(C) : -κρανου B forsitan recte   331 δια-
λυθέντος restitui ex ⲁϥⲃ̄]ⲱⲗ ⲉ̅ⲃⲟⲗ C : om. AB   332 καὶ ante 331 διὰ trsp. Bonner

7) and why the Lord is present on the earth
   to clothe himself with the suffering one
       and carry him off to the heights of heaven.   310

47 When *God in the beginning* had *made the heaven and the earth*
   and all the things in them by his word,[14]
   he fashioned from the earth man,
   and gave him a share of his own *breath.*
   This man he set *in the paradise eastward*   315
   in Eden, there to live in bliss,
   laying down this law for him by his command:
   '*Of every tree in the paradise by all means eat,*
   but of the tree of knowing good and evil
       you shall not eat;   320
   and on the day you eat
       you shall certainly die.'

48 But the man, being naturally receptive of good and evil,
   as a clod of earth is of seed from either side,
   accepted the hostile and greedy adviser,   325
       and by touching the tree he broke the command
           and disobeyed God.
   So he was cast out into this world
       as into a convicts' prison.[15]

49 This man having become very prolific and very long-lived,   330
       when through the tasting of the tree he was dissolved
           and sank into the earth,

h Cf. 2 Cor. 12: 2.   j Gen. 1: 1.   k Gen. 2: 7.   l Gen. 2: 8, 15.
m Gen. 2: 17.   n Cf. Gen. 3: 1–6.   o Cf. Gen. 3: 11, 17.   p Cf.
Gen. 3: 17–24.

---

14 *By his word* is best taken with what precedes, contrasting creation by mere
fiat with the privileged creation of man, as in Theophilus, *Ad Autolycum* 2. 18
(Grant 56–7). One might find here the personal divine Logos, associated with
what precedes (Perler) or with what follows (Testuz); but the text does not
require it.

15 The idea of earth as a prison corresponds to the Egyptian bondage of
Jewish Passover tradition (Deut. 26: 5–6). Bonner ad loc. suggests Platonic
influence, but Melito is more probably interpreting Rom. 5: 12–6: 14 (A.
Grillmeier, *Scholastik* 20–4 (1949) 489–94) on the consequences of Adam's sin.

κατελείφθη ὑπ' αὐτοῦ κληρονομία τοῖς τέκνοις αὐτοῦ·
κατέλιπεν γὰρ τοῖς τέκνοις κληρονομίαν
    οὐχ ἁγνείαν ἀλλὰ πορνείαν,   33[.]
    οὐκ ἀφθαρσίαν ἀλλὰ φθοράν,
    οὐ τιμὴν ἀλλὰ ἀτιμίαν,
    οὐκ ἐλευθερίαν ἀλλὰ δουλείαν,
    οὐ βασιλείαν ἀλλὰ τυραννίδα,
    οὐ ζωὴν ἀλλὰ θάνατον,   34^c
    οὐ σωτηρίαν ἀλλὰ ἀπώλειαν.
50 καινὴ δὲ καὶ φοβερὰ ἡ τῶν ἀνθρώπων ἐπὶ τῆς γῆς ἐγίνετο ἀπώλεια.
    τάδε γὰρ συνέβαινεν αὐτοῖς·
    ἀνηρπάζοντο ὑπὸ τῆς τυραννικῆς ἁμαρτίας,
    καὶ ἤγοντο εἰς τοὺς χώρους τῶν ἐπιθυμιῶν   345
    ἐν οἷς περιηντλοῦντο ὑπὸ τῶν ἀκορέστων ἡδονῶν,
    ὑπὸ μοιχείας,
    ὑπὸ πορνείας,
    ὑπὸ ἀσελγείας,
    ὑπὸ φιλαργυρίας,   350^l
    ὑπὸ φόνων,
    ὑπὸ αἱμάτων,
    ὑπὸ τυραννίδος πονηρᾶς,
    ὑπὸ τυραννίδος παρανόμου.
51 καὶ γὰρ πατὴρ ἐπὶ υἱὸν ξίφος ἐπηνέγκατο,   355
    καὶ υἱὸς πατρὶ χεῖρας προσήνεγκεν
    καὶ μασθοὺς τιθηνοὺς ἀσεβὴς ἐτύπτησεν·
    καὶ ἀδελφὸς ἀδελφὸν ἀπέκτεινεν,
    καὶ ξένος ξένον ἠδίκησεν,
    καὶ φίλος φίλον ἐφόνευσεν,   360
    καὶ ἄνθρωπος ἄνθρωπον ἀπέσφαξεν τυραννικῇ δεξιᾷ.
(52) πάντες οὖν οἱ μὲν ἀνθρωποκτόνοι,

333–4 txt. B: κατελιφθη ὑπ αὐτοῦ κληρονομια τοῖς τέκνοις αὐτοῦ κληρονομιαν
A: *reliquit filiis suis hereditatem* CG   335 ἁγνείαν AC: αγειαν B(ἁγίαν): *bonam*
G   341 vs. ABG: om. C   342 ἡ A: om. B   345 χώρους B: χρόνους
A(*a tempore in tempus* G): *aquas* C: κλόνους Bonner   349 ὑπὸ ἀσελγείας BC:
ὑπο ἐπιθυμειας add. A: utrumque om. G   353 πο[νη]ρᾶς A: πονηρίας B:
fornicationis (πορνεία) C: *omnem* G (πάσης?)   357 ἐτύπτησεν A: ἔτυπτεν B
358 ἀπέκτεινεν–360 φίλον BCG: om. A   362–5 om. C   362 vs. AB:
om. G

an inheritance was left by him to his children;
   for he left his children as inheritance
      not chastity but promiscuity,   335
      not imperishability but decay,
      not honour but dishonour,
      not freedom but slavery,
      not royalty but tyranny,
      not life but death,   340
      not salvation but destruction.

50 The destruction of men upon earth became strange and terrible.
   For these things befell them:
     they were seized by tyrannical sin,
     and were led to the lands of the lusts,   345
     where they were swamped by insatiable pleasures,
       by adultery,
       by promiscuity,
       by wantonness,
       by avarice,   350
       by murders,
       by bloodshed,
       by wicked tyranny,
       by lawless tyranny.

51 For father took up sword against son,   355
     and son laid hands on father,
     and impiously smote the breasts that nursed him;
     brother killed brother,
     guest and host wronged each other,
     friend murdered friend,   360
     and man slew man with tyrannous right hand.

52) So all men became upon the earth either manslayers

οἱ δὲ πατροκτόνοι,
οἱ δὲ τεκνο[κτόνοι],
οἱ δὲ ἀδελφοκτόνοι ἐπὶ τῆς γῆς ἐγενήθησαν.   365

52 τὸ δὲ καινότερον καὶ φοβερώτερον ἐπὶ [τῆς γῆς] ηὑρίσκετο·
μήτηρ τις ἥπτετο σαρκῶν ὧν ἐγέννησεν,
⟨καὶ⟩ προσήπτετο ὧν ἐξέθρεψεν μασθοῖς,
καὶ τὸν καρπὸν τῆς κοιλίας εἰς κοιλίαν κατώρυσσεν,
καὶ φοβερὸς τάφος ἐγίνετο ἡ δυστυχὴς μήτηρ,   370
ὃ ἐκύησεν καταπίνουσα τέκνον †ουκετι προσλαλουν†.

53 πολλὰ δὲ καὶ ἔτερα, ξένα καὶ φοβερώτερα καὶ ἀσελγέστερα,
ἐν τοῖς ἀνθρώποις ηὑρίσκετο·
πατὴρ ἐπὶ παιδὸς κοίτην,
καὶ υἱὸς ἐπὶ μητρός,   375
καὶ ἀδελφὸς ἐπὶ ἀδελφῆς,
καὶ ἄρρην ἐπὶ ἄρρενος,
καὶ ἕτερος ἐπὶ τὴν γυναῖκα τοῦ πλησίον ἐχρεμέτιζον.�q

54 Ἐπὶ δὲ τούτοις ἡ ἁμαρτία ηὐφραίνετο,
ἡ τοῦ θανάτου σύνεργος ὑπάρχουσα   380
προοδοιπορεῖ εἰς τὰς τῶν ἀνθρώπων ψυχάς,
καὶ ἑτοιμάζει αὐτῷ τροφὰς τὰ τῶν νεκρῶν σώματα.
εἰς πᾶσαν δὲ ψυχὴν ἐτίθει ἡ ἁμαρτία ἴχνος
καὶ εἰς οὓς ἂν ἔθηκεν τούτους ἔδει τελευτᾶν.

55 πᾶσα οὖν σὰρξ ὑπὸ ἁμαρτίαν ἔπιπτεν
καὶ πᾶν σῶμα ὑπὸ θάνατον,   385

363 vs. AG: om. B: et nonnulli matricidae add. Gᵃ   364 οἱ δὲ τεκνω[κτονοι
A(Bonner, at οἱ δὲ[. . . nunc vid.)Gᵗ: vs. om. BGᵃ   365 οἱ δὲ ἀδ. BGᵗ: om.
AGᵃ   366 καιν. κ. φοβ. ACGᵗ: φοβ. κ. καιν. B   επει [τῆς γῆς ACG: om. B
367 μήτηρ Perler = C: . . .]τηρ A(Bonner): η μ̅η̅ρ̅ B   367 σαρ[κῶν–371
                                                            τις
κ]αταπεινουσα deest A   368 προσηπτετο B(sic): om. C: et comederunt G,
unde καὶ προσήπτετο scripsi   371 κ]αταπεινουσα A: εκατεπιουσα B   ουκετι
προσλαλουν B: ουκετι[. . . A: om. CG: ἀλλ' ἔτι πρὸς τούτοις Testuz: οὐκέτι
προσλαλῶ Perler (melius –ελάλουν): forsitan οὐ καταφιλοῦσα restituendum
372 δὲ ACG: om. B   ξ. κ. φοβ. κ. ἀσ. B: ξ. κ. φοβ. A: et nova et execrabilia et
horrenda C: execrabile et horrendum G   374 κοίτην BC: om. AG   375 καὶ B:
om. A(CG, sed etiam in 376–8)   378 ἐχρεμέτιζον Bonner(Jer. 5:8): εχρεμετιζω
                                                                            σ
A: εχρηματι[[ζ]]εν B (sic): om. CG   381 προοδοιπορεῖ B: προοδυπορευει A:
προωδοπόρει Bonner, Testuz   382 ἑτοιμάζει emendavi cum CG: ητυμαζεν
A: ετοιμαζι B(-ειν): ἡτοίμαζεν edd.   383 ψυχ. ἐτίθ. B: inv. A   384 εἰς
οὓς BC(G): ἴσος A

or parricides
or infanticides
or fratricides.[16]   365

52 But the strangest and most terrible thing occurred on the earth:
a mother touched the flesh she had brought forth,
and tasted what she had suckled at the breasts;
and she buried in her belly the fruit of her belly,
and the wretched mother became a terrible grave,   370
gulping, not kissing, the child she had produced.[17]

53 Many other things, strange and quite terrible and quite out-
                                                          rageous,
took place among mankind:
father for child's bed,
and son for mother's,   375
and brother for sister's,
and male for male's,
and *one man for the next man's wife, they neighed like stallions.*[18]

54 At these things sin rejoiced,
who in the capacity of death's fellow worker   380
journeys ahead into the souls of men,
and prepares as food for him the bodies of the dead.
In every soul sin made a mark,
and those in whom he made it were bound to die.

55 So all flesh began to fall under sin,   385
and every body under death,

q Jer. 5: 8.

---

16 This passage is inspired both by biblical ideas (Gen. 4: 8; Judg. 9: 5;
John 13: 8; Lev. 18: 21; Wisd. 12: 5) and by Greek mythological figures such
as Orestes, Agamemnon, and Medea.
17 Cannibalism by mothers is referred to in Deut. 28: 56–7; 2 Kings 6: 26–9;
Josephus, *De bello Iudaico* vi. 3. 4, etc. Melito is perhaps conscious of repeated
allegations that Christians were child-eaters, cf. Theophilus, *Ad Autolycum* iii.
3–5 (Grant 102–4).
18 The theme of sexual malpractice is a favourite in Christian apologetic
(Tatian, *Oratio ad Graecos* 33–4; Athenagoras, *Supplicatio* 34; Tertullian, *Ad
nationes* 1. 16). The influence of Leviticus 18 is possible here.

καὶ πᾶσα ψυχὴ ἐκ τοῦ σαρκίνου οἴκου ἐξηλαύνετο.
     καὶ τὸ λημφθὲν ἐκ γῆς εἰς γῆν ἀνελύετο,
     καὶ τὸ δωρηθὲν ἐκ θεοῦ εἰς ᾅδην κατεκλείετο·
     καὶ λύσις ἐγίνετο τῆς καλῆς ἁρμογῆς,
     καὶ διεχωρίζετο τὸ καλὸν σῶμα.   39

56 ἦν γὰρ ὁ ἄνθρωπος ὑπὸ τοῦ θανάτου μεριζόμενος.
     καινὴ γὰρ συμφορὰ καὶ ἅλωσις περιεῖχεν αὐτόν,
     καὶ εἵλκετο αἰχμάλωτος ὑπὸ τὰς τοῦ θανάτου σκιάς,
     ἔκειτο δὲ ἔρημος ἡ τοῦ πατρὸς εἰκών.   39
     διὰ ταύτην οὖν τὴν αἰτίαν τὸ τοῦ πάσχα μυστήριον
     τετέλεσται ἐν τῷ τοῦ κυρίου σώματι.

57 Πρότερον δὲ ὁ κύριος προῳκονόμησεν τὰ ἑαυτοῦ πάθη
     ἐν πατριάρχαις καὶ ἐν προφήταις καὶ ἐν παντὶ τῷ λαῷ,
     διά τε νόμου καὶ προφητῶν ἐπισφραγισάμενος.
     τὸ γὰρ μέλλον καινῶς καὶ μεγάλως ἔσεσθαι,   40
     τοῦτο ἐκ μακροῦ προοικονομεῖται,
     ἵν᾽ ὁπόταν γένηται πίστεως τύχῃ
     ἐκ μακροῦ προοραθέν.

58 οὕτω δὴ καὶ τὸ τοῦ κυρίου μυστήριον   405
     ἐκ μακροῦ προτυπωθέν,
     διὰ δὲ τύπον ὁραθέν,
     σήμερον πίστεως τυγχάνει τετελεσμένον
     καίτοι ὡς καινὸν τοῖς ἀνθρώποις νομιζόμενον.
     ἔστιν γὰρ καινὸν καὶ παλαιὸν τὸ τοῦ κυρίου μυστήριον·   410
     παλαιὸν μὲν κατὰ τὸν νόμον,
     καινὸν δὲ κατὰ τὴν χάριν.

387 σαρκεινου Α : σαρκικοῦ ΒC(σαρκικον graece)   388 καὶ τὸ Β(C) : om. Α
ἀνελύετο Β : κατελευετο Α   389 εἰς Β : τὸν add. Α   κατεκλείετο Β : κατε-
κλειτο Α   390 καλῆς ACG : γὰρ add. Β   391 καὶ : nam C(γὰρ graece)
καλὸν ΒC : om. Α   392 vs.: hominis C   ὁ Α : om. Β   θανάτου AG : θυ Β(θεοῦ)
394 εἵλκετο Α : ελικετο Β : iacuit G(ἔκειτο) : καὶ εἵλκ. om. C   395 ἔκειτο ΒC :
εἵλκετο AG   ἡ ΑC : om. Β   πατρὸς ΒCG : π̅ν̅σ̅ Α(πνεύματος)   396 οὖν Β :
γοῦν Α   399 παντὶ τῷ λαῷ BGᵗ : τῷ om. Α : apostolis omnibus C   402 προοι-
κονομιται Β(-εῖται)C : -ειτα Α : . . .]αι inc. O   403 ἵν᾽–τύχῃ ΒOC(G) : πειστεως
ειν[α τύχῃ Α   404 προοραθέν Α(O) : προτυπωθὲν οραθη Β   405 μυστήριον
ΒC : πάθος AOG   407 διὰ δὲ (τε Α) τύπον ὁραθέν AOC(G) : ὁραθεν^δε Β(sic)
408 τε[τελεσμένον–413 ἀλ]λ᾽ deest Α   409 καίτοι Testuz : κετοι ΒC(sic) :
longiorem perdidisse lectionem vid. O   410 γ]ὰρ καινὸ[ν καὶ παλαιὸν
OCG : γὰρ παλαιὸν καὶ κενον Β   411 νόμον Ο : τύπον Β(G)

and every soul was driven out of its fleshly dwelling.
And what was taken from earth was to earth dissolved,
    and what was given from God was confined in Hades;[19]
and there was separation of what fitted beautifully,   390
    and the beautiful body was split apart.

6 For man was being divided by death;
    for a strange disaster and captivity were enclosing him,
    and he was dragged off a prisoner under the shadows of death,
    and desolate lay the Father's image.[20]   395
This, then, is the reason why the mystery of the Pascha
    has been fulfilled in the body of the Lord.

7 But first the Lord made prior arrangements for his own sufferings
    in patriarchs and in prophets and in the whole people,
    setting his seal to them through both law and prophets.   400
For the thing which is to be new and great in its realization
    is arranged for well in advance,
so that when it comes about it may be believed in,
    having been foreseen well in advance.[21]

8 Just so also the mystery of the Lord,   405
    having been prefigured well in advance
        and having been seen through a model,
    is today believed in now that it is fulfilled,
        though considered new by men.
For the mystery of the Lord is new and old: 410
    old according to the law,
        but new with reference to the grace.

---

[19] The thought in 55–6 is closely paralleled in Alexander of Alexandria, *De anima et corpore*, PG 18. 589–92 (O. Perler, *RechSR* 51 (1963) 408).

[20] This refers to man as the image of God, not (as usual in patristic texts) to the Son as image of the Father. If it is true that Melito believed God to be corporeal, the reference is to man as a psychosomatic unity, and the image would not be merely the soul or reason as (e.g.) in Tatian, *Oratio ad Graecos* 7; 12–13; 15. The variant reading 'the spirit's image' may itself be successfully interpreted in terms of 1 Cor. 15: 45–9 (E. Peterson, *Frühkirche, Judentum und Gnosis* (Freiburg im Br., 1959) 138–40). The expression occurs in Tertullian, *Adversus Marcionem* ii. 9 (A. Orbe, 'Imago Spiritus', *Gregorianum* 48 (1967) 792–5); it may also express Origenistic thought in which man is in the image of the Logos-Spirit (O. Perler, 'Méliton "Peri pascha" 56 et la tradition géorgienne', in *Forma futuri, Studi in onore del Cardinale Michele Pellegrino* (Turin, 1975), 334–60; Perler rightly views the BCG reading as more original).

[21] For the thought and wording of 57–8 cf. Justin, *I Apology* 33. 2.

ἀλλ' ἐὰν ἀποβλέψῃς εἰς τὸν τύπον,
τοῦτον ὄψῃ διὰ τῆς ἐκβάσεως.

59 τοιγαροῦν εἰ βούλει τὸ τοῦ κυρίου μυστήριον ἰδέσθαι,   41?
ἀπόβλεψον εἰς τὸν Ἄβελ τὸν ὁμοίως φονευόμενον,
εἰς τὸν Ἰσὰκ τὸν ὁμοίως συμποδιζόμενον,
εἰς τὸν Ἰωσὴφ τὸν ὁμοίως πιπρασκόμενον,
εἰς τὸν Μωυσέα τὸν ὁμοίως ἐκτιθέμενον,
εἰς τὸν Δαυεὶδ τὸν ὁμοίως διωκόμενον,   42(
εἰς τοὺς προφήτας τοὺς ὁμοίως διὰ Χριστὸν πάσχοντας.

60 ἀπόβλεψον δὲ καὶ εἰς τὸ ἐν γῇ Αἰγύπτῳ πρόβατον σφαζόμενον,
τὸ πάταξαν τὴν Αἴγυπτον
καὶ σῶσαν τὸν Ἰσραὴλ διὰ τοῦ αἵματος.

61 Ἔστιν δὲ διὰ προφητικῆς φωνῆς τὸ τοῦ κυρίου μυστήριον κηρυσ- 425
φησὶν γὰρ Μωυσῆς πρὸς τὸν λαόν·   [σόμενον.
Καὶ ὄψεσθε τὴν ζωὴν ὑμῶν κρεμαμένην
ἔμπροσθεν τῶν ὀφθαλμῶν ὑμῶν νυκτὸς καὶ ἡμέρας,
καὶ οὐ μὴ πιστεύσητε ἐπὶ τὴν ζωὴν ὑμῶν.ʳ

62 ὁ δὲ Δαυεὶδ εἶπεν·   430
Ἵνα τί ἐφρύαξαν ἔθνη
καὶ λαοὶ ἐμελέτησαν κενά;
παρέστησαν οἱ βασιλεῖς τῆς γῆς
καὶ οἱ ἄρχοντες συνήχθησαν ἐπὶ τὸ αὐτὸ
κατὰ τοῦ κυρίου καὶ κατὰ τοῦ χριστοῦ αὐτοῦ.ˢ   435

63 ὁ δὲ Ἰερεμίας·
Ἐγὼ ὡς ἀρνίον ἄκακον ἀγόμενον τοῦ θύεσθαι.
ἐλογίσαντο εἰς ἐμὲ κακὰ εἰπόντες·

413 τύπον ABOGᵗ: μυστηριον C(graece)   414 τοῦτον cum 413
iungunt BC: txt. G: non liquent AO   ὄψῃ (A)OCG: οτει τὸ ἀληθὲς B   ἐκβάσεως B(OCG): εμβασεως A   415 τοιγαροῦν B: τοίνυν AO
416 τὸν Ἄβελ AOCG: om. B   417 συμποδιζ- BO: ποδειζ- A: Jacob
qui similiter ei alienus factus est add. G, cf. 483   421 διὰ B(O): τὸν add. A
πάσχοντας A(O): παθόντας B   422 τὸ BCG: τὸν AO   γῇ AC: τῇ
B(G)   423 τὸ πάταξαν τὴν B(CG): τὸν πατάξαντα A: τὸν παταξαν[. . O
424 σῶσαν B(CG): σώσαντα AO   425 δὲ BC: καὶ add. A: deest O
427 ὑμῶν AOCG: om. B   429 μη B: om. AO   πιστεύσητε BO: -σεται
A(-σετε)   430 εἶπεν BCG: om. A(O)   435 τοῦ¹ AO: om. B
436 Ἰερεμίας AB(O): dixit add. C(dicit G)   438 ἐλογίσαντο[desinit O
εἰς A: ἐπ' B(Jer. 11: 19)

But if you look carefully at the model,
 you will perceive him through the final outcome.

9 Therefore if you wish to see the mystery of the Lord,   4¹5
 look at Abel who is similarly murdered,²²
  at Isaac who is similarly bound,²³
  at Joseph who is similarly sold,²⁴
  at Moses who is similarly exposed,²⁵
  at David who is similarly persecuted,²⁶   420
  at the prophets who similarly suffer for the sake of Christ.²⁷

50 Look also at the sheep which is slain in the land of Egypt,
 which struck Egypt
 and saved Israel by its blood.

51 But the mystery of the Lord is proclaimed by the prophetic voice. 425
 For Moses says to the people:
  'And you shall see your life hanging
  before your eyes night and day;
  *and you will not believe on your life.'*²⁸

52 And David said: 430
  'Why have nations snorted,
  and peoples contemplated vain things?
  The kings of the earth stood by
  and the rulers assembled together
  *against the Lord and against his Christ.'*²⁹   435

53 And Jeremiah:
  'I am like a harmless lambkin led to be sacrificed.
  They devised evil things for me, saying:

^r Deut. 28: 66.   ^s Ps. 2: 1–2; cf. Acts 4: 25–7.

---

²² See Gen. 4: 1–12; Matt. 23: 35; Heb. 11: 4; 1 Clement 4. 1–7; Irenaeus, *Adversus haereses* 4. 25. 2. For the whole section cf. 69; Fr. 15. 19–27; Ps.-Cyprian, *Adversus Judaeos* 24–5; O. Perler, 'Typologie der Leiden des Herrn in Melitons *Peri Pascha*', in *Kyriakon* (Münster Westf., 1970) 256–65.

²³ See Gen. 22: 1–18; Frs. 9–12; 15. 21. Cf. D. Lerch, *Isaaks Opferung christlich gedeutet* (Tübingen, 1950); G. Vermes, *Scripture and tradition in Judaism* (Leiden, 1961) 193–227.

²⁴ See Gen. 37: 28.   ²⁵ See Exod. 2: 3.

²⁶ See 1 Sam. 23–6; 1 Clement 4. 13.   ²⁷ Cf. Matt. 5: 12.

²⁸ Melito's use of this testimonium is the earliest known, and differs from LXX text. His variants reappear in Novatian, *De trinitate* 9; Athanasius, *De incarnatione* 35; Gregory of Nyssa, *Testimonia adversus Judaeos* (PG 46. 213C); etc. The LXX form appears in Irenaeus 4. 10. 2, etc.; Tertullian, *Adversus Judaeos* 11. 9; etc. See J. Daniélou, 'Das Leben, das am Holze hängt', in *Kirche und Überlieferung* (Freiburg im Br., 1960) 22–34.

²⁹ A popular proof-text, following Acts 4: 25–7; see Justin, *1 Apology* 40. 11; Irenaeus, *Adversus haereses* 3. 12. 5.

Δεῦτε ἐμβάλωμεν ξύλον εἰς τὸν ἄρτον αὐτοῦ
καὶ ἐκτρίψωμεν αὐτὸν ἐκ γῆς ζώντων·   44
καὶ τὸ ὄνομα αὐτοῦ οὐ μὴ μνησθῇ.[t]

64 ὁ δὲ Ἡσαίας·
    Ὡς πρόβατον εἰς σφαγὴν ἤχθη,
    καὶ ὡς ἀμνὸς ἄφωνος ἐναντίον τοῦ κείραντος αὐτὸν
        οὗτος οὐκ ἀνοίγει τὸ στόμα αὐτοῦ·   44
    τὴν δὲ γενεὰν αὐτοῦ τίς διηγήσεται;[u]

65 πολλὰ μὲν οὖν καὶ ἕτερα ὑπὸ πολλῶν προφητῶν ἐκηρύχθη
    εἰς τὸ τοῦ πάσχα μυστήριον,
    ὅ ἐστιν Χριστός·
    ᾧ ἡ δόξα εἰς τοὺς αἰῶνας. ἀμήν.   45

66 Οὗτος ἀφικόμενος ἐξ οὐρανῶν ἐπὶ τὴν γῆν διὰ τὸν πάσχοντα,
    αὐτὸν δὲ ἐκεῖνον ἐνδυσάμενος διὰ παρθένου μήτρας
    καὶ προελθὼν ἄνθρωπος,
    ἀπεδέξατο τὰ τοῦ πάσχοντος πάθη
        διὰ τοῦ παθεῖν δυναμένου σώματος,   455
    καὶ κατέλυσεν τὰ τῆς σαρκὸς πάθη·
    τῷ δὲ θανεῖν μὴ δυναμένῳ πνεύματι
    ἀπέκτεινεν τὸν ἀνθρωποκτόνον θάνατον.

67 αὐτὸς γὰρ ὡς ἀμνὸς ἀχθεὶς
    καὶ ὡς πρόβατον σφαγείς,   460
    ἐλυτρώσατο ἡμᾶς ἐκ τῆς τοῦ κόσμου λατρείας
    ὡς ἐκ γῆς Αἰγύπτου,

442–50 continet L   442 Ἡσαίας ABC: ait add. LG   443 εισφαγην
A(εἰς σφαγὴν Bonner cf. Fr. 9.): ἐπὶ σφαγῇ B(cf. Isa. 53 : 7)   ἤχθη ACGL(Isa.
53 : 7): ἤχθην B   445 ουτος AB: sic LCG: οὗτως Bonner(Isa. 53 : 7)
αὐτοῦ AB: i]n sua humilita[te] add. C: in humilitate (sua add. G) iudicium eius
sublatum est add. LG: forsitan ἐν τῇ ταπεινώσει αὐτοῦ per homoeoteleuton excidit
446 δὲ AGL[vlm]: om. B(C)L[b]   αὐτοῦ τίς BCGL: αυτος A   διηγήσεται A(Isa.
53 : 8): -σηται B: quia lata est e terra vita eius add. G   447 μὲν οὖν A: μὲν
B: και (ante πολλὰ) C graece: et G   ἕτερα ACGL: τέρατα B   451 ουτος
BCG: ουτως A   452 μήτρας BCG: μαρίας A   454 [τοῦ–457 δυναμένῳ] deest
A   455 vs. B(G): om. C   459–76 continet L   459 αὐτὸς BL: ουτως
A(οὗτος Bonner): hic C: hic ipse G

---

[30] i.e. make the bread unusable with sawdust. Christians refer it to the cross
being laid upon the body of Christ (symbolized by bread).
This text first appears as a messianic testimony in Justin, *Dialogue with*

"Come on, let us put wood on his bread,[30]
   and wipe him out from the land of the living;   440
   and his name shall not be remembered."'

64 And Isaiah:
   '*As a sheep he was led to slaughter,*
   and as a lamb speechless before him that sheared him
      this one opens not his mouth: 445
   but his generation who shall tell?'[31]

65 Many other things have been proclaimed by many prophets
      about the mystery of the Pascha,
   which is Christ.
   To him be glory for ever. Amen   450

66 It is he who, coming from heaven to the earth because of the
                          suffering one,[32]
   and clothing himself in that same one through a virgin's womb,
      and coming forth a man,
   accepted the passions of the suffering one
      through the body which was able to suffer,   455
   and dissolved the passions of the flesh;[33]
   and by the Spirit which could not die
      he killed death the killer of men.

67 For, himself led as a lamb
   and slain as a sheep,   460
   he ransomed us from the world's service
      as from the land of Egypt,

   ᵗ Jer. 11: 19.   ᵘ Isa. 53: 7–8.

Trypho 72, who shares some of Melito's divergences from LXX. See also Tertullian, *Adversus Judaeos* 10. 12; *Adversus Marcionem* 3. 19. 3; 4. 40. 3. In Cyprian, *Testimoniorum liber* 2. 15. 20 it is associated with Deut. 28: 66 and Isa. 53: 7–8 as here.

[31] A messianic text in Acts 8: 32–3; 1 Clement 16. 7–8; Justin, *Dialogue with Trypho* 72. 3; etc. Melito shares some divergences from LXX with Barnabas 5. 2 and *Acts of Philip* 78 (R. A. Kraft, *JBL* 80 (1961) 371–3).

[32] The hymnic οὗτος (E. Norden, *Agnostos theos* (Leipzig, 1913) 250–63; A. Wifstrand, *VigChr* 2 (1948) 214–15) marks the point which in the Jewish Haggadah emphasized God's personal presence and work at the first Passover (S. G. Hall, *JTS* N.S. 22 (1971) 38–9). ἀφικόμενος may allude to the Passover *aphikomen* (M. Werner, *Hebrew Union College Annual* 37 (1966) 205–6; cf. D. Daube, *He that cometh* (London, 1966) 6–14).

[33] These anthropological and Christological expressions have verbal affinities with Valentinian terms in Clement, *Excerpta ex Theodoto* 45. 2; 59. 1; 61. 7 (T. Halton, *JTS* N.S. 20 (1969) 535–8).

καὶ ἔλυσεν ἐκ τῆς τοῦ διαβόλου δουλείας
ὡς ἐκ χειρὸς Φαραώ,
καὶ ἐσφράγισεν ἡμῶν τὰς ψυχὰς τῷ ἰδίῳ πνεύματι   465
καὶ τὰ μέλη τοῦ σώματος τῷ ἰδίῳ αἵματι.

68 οὗτός ἐστιν ὁ τὸν θάνατον ἐνδύσας αἰσχύνην
καὶ τὸν διάβολον στήσας πενθήρη
ὡς Μωυσῆς τὸν Φαραώ.

οὗτός ἐστιν ὁ τὴν ἀνομίαν πατάξας   470
καὶ τὴν ἀδικίαν ἀτεκνώσας
ὡς Μωυσῆς Αἴγυπτον.

οὗτός ἐστιν ὁ ῥυσάμενος ἡμᾶς ἐκ δουλείας εἰς ἐλευθερίαν,
ἐκ σκότους εἰς φῶς,
ἐκ θανάτου εἰς ζωήν,   475
ἐκ τυραννίδος εἰς βασιλείαν αἰώνιον,
καὶ ποιήσας ἡμᾶς ἱεράτευμα καινὸν
καὶ λαὸν περιούσιον αἰώνιον.ᵛ

69 οὗτός ἐστιν τὸ πάσχα τῆς σωτηρίας ἡμῶν.

οὗτός ἐστιν ὁ ἐν πολλοῖς πολλὰ ὑπομείνας·   480
οὗτός ἐστιν ὁ ἐν τῷ Ἀβὲλ φονευθείς,
ἐν δὲ τῷ Ἰσὰκ δεθείς,
ἐν δὲ τῷ Ἰακὼβ ξενιτεύσας,
ἐν δὲ τῷ Ἰωσὴφ πραθείς,
ἐν δὲ τῷ Μωυσῇ ἐκτεθείς,   485
ἐν δὲ τῷ ἀμνῷ σφαγείς,
ἐν δὲ τῷ Δαυεὶδ διωχθείς,
ἐν δὲ τοῖς προφήταις ἀτιμασθείς.

70 οὗτός ἐστιν ὁ ἐν παρθένῳ σαρκωθείς,
ὁ ἐπὶ ξύλου κρεμασθείς,   490

465 τῷ–466 τῷ AC(G)L: om. B   466 σώματος AC: nostri add. L(G)
468 στήσας BL: δήσας A: fecit CG   470 οὗτος B(C)GL: ουτως A
473 ῥυσάμενος ACGL: ῥυόμενος B   ἐκ B: τῆς add. A   εἰς B: τὴν add. A
474 vs. ABGL: om. C   476 αἰώνιον A: -ειαν B   477–8 vss. ACG:
om. B   478 περιούσιον AGᵗ: et regnum add. C   αἰώνιον AC: ut gloriam
ad eum semper dicamus G(ᵃ)ᵗ   480–9 ἐστιν cont. L   480 οὗτος BL:
ουτως A   481–9 om. C   481 οὗτος BGL: ουτως A   482 τῷ
B: om. A   483 ἐν δὲ AL: ὁ ἐν B   485 δὲ AL: om. B   486 vs.
AL: om. B: post 487 pon. G   488 δὲ AL: om. B   489–512 cont.
Sᴵ   489 ἐστιν A(GL): om. B   490 ξύλου A: τοῦ ξ. B: in terra C:
ligno GSᴵ   κρεμασθείς BGSᴵ: μὴ συντριβείς A: suspendit eum C

and freed us from the devil's slavery
    as from the hand of Pharaoh;
and he marked our souls with his own Spirit   465
    and the members of our body with his own blood.

68 It is he that clothed death with shame
    and stood the devil in grief
      as Moses did Pharaoh.
It is he that struck down crime   470
    and made injustice childless
      as Moses did Egypt.
It is he that delivered us from slavery to liberty,
    from darkness to light,
    from death to life,   475
    from tyranny to eternal royalty,
    and made us a new *priesthood*
    and an eternal *people personal to him*.[34]

69 He is the Pascha of our salvation.
It is he who in many endured many things: 480
it is he that was in Abel murdered,[35]
    and in Isaac bound,
    and in Jacob exiled,[36]
    and in Joseph sold,
    and in Moses exposed,   485
    and in the lamb slain,
    and in David persecuted,
    and in the prophets dishonoured.

70 It is he that was enfleshed in a virgin,
    that was hanged on a tree,   490

v Exod. 19: 5–6; 23: 22 (LXX); cf. 1 Pet. 2: 9.

---

34 This passage closely resembles Mishnah *Pesahim* x. 5 and *Exodus Rabbah* 12. 2; see S. G. Hall, *JTS* n.s. 22 (1971) 29–32.
35 The section resembles § 59; Fr. 15. 19–28; New Fr. II. 3–4.
36 Alluding primarily to the sojourn with Laban (Genesis 29–30), and typologically to Christ's sojourn in Egypt (Matt. 2: 13–23) or his rejection at home (Luke 4: 23–9; John 1: 11).

ὁ εἰς γῆν ταφείς,
ὁ ἐκ νεκρῶν ἀνασταθείς,
ὁ εἰς τὰ ὑψηλὰ τῶν οὐρανῶν ἀναλημφθείς.

71　οὗτός ἐστιν ὁ ἀμνὸς ὁ φονευόμενος·
οὗτός ἐστιν ὁ ἀμνὸς ὁ ἄφωνος·
οὗτός ἐστιν ὁ τεχθεὶς ἐκ Μαρίας τῆς καλῆς ἀμνάδος·　　　　49.
οὗτός ἐστιν ὁ ἐξ ἀγέλης λημφθείς,ʷ
　　καὶ εἰς σφαγὴν συρείς,ˣ
　　καὶ ἑσπέρας τυθείς,ʸ
　　καὶ νύκτωρ ταφείς,ᶻ
ὁ ἐπὶ ξύλου μὴ συντριβείς,ᵃ　　　　　　　　　　　　　　　500
εἰς γῆν μὴ λυθείς,
ἐκ νεκρῶν ἀναστάς,
καὶ ἀναστήσας τὸν ἄνθρωπον ἐκ τῆς κάτω ταφῆς.

72　Οὗτος πεφόνευται·　　　　　　　　　　　　　　　　　505
καὶ ποῦ πεφόνευται; ἐν μέσῳ Ἰερουσαλήμ.
⟨ὑπὸ τίνων; ὑπὸ τοῦ Ἰσραήλ.⟩
διὰ τί; ὅτι τοὺς χωλοὺς αὐτῶν ἐθεράπευσεν
καὶ τοὺς λεπροὺς αὐτῶν ἐκαθάρισεν
　　καὶ τοὺς τυφλοὺς αὐτῶν ἐφωταγώγησεν　　　　　　510
καὶ τοὺς νεκροὺς αὐτῶν ἀνέστησεν,
　　διὰ τοῦτο ἀπέθανεν.
ποῦ γέγραπται ἐν νόμῳ καὶ ἐν προφήταις·
Ἀνταπέδωκάν μοι κακὰ ἀντὶ ἀγαθῶν
καὶ ἀτεκνίαν τῇ ψυχῇ μου,ᵇ　　　　　　　　　　　　515
λογισάμενοι ἐπ' ἐμὲ κακὰ εἰπόντες·ᶜ
Δήσωμεν τὸν δίκαιον
　　ὅτι δύσχρηστος ἡμῖν ἐστιν;ᵈ

491–3 cont. L　　　491 ταφις B(-εἰς)CGL: μὴ λ[υ]θεὶς ταφείς A: sepultus
est neque putruit S¹　　　492 ἀνασταθεί[ς A(G): ἀναστάς B(CLS¹)
493 ὁ–ἀναλημφ. BCGL: καὶ ἀναστήσας τὸν ἄνθρωπον ἐκ τ[ῆς] κάτω ταφῆς ε[ἰ]ς
τὰ ὕψη τῶν οὐρανῶν A(S¹)　　　494–5 φο[νευόμενος … ἄφων[ος AS¹: ἀφ.…
φον. B: qui occisus est nihil dixit C: ligatus agnellus incorruptus qui ipse immolatus est
G　　495 cont. L　　ὁ² B: om. A　　497–500 cont. L　　500 ταφ[είς–
507 Ἰσραήλ⟩] deest A　　503–11 cont. L　　507 vs. scripsi ex a quibus?
ab Israhel LCS¹: om. BG　　509 καὶ AGL: om. B(C etiam in 510–11)
510 αὐτῶν AG: om. BC(L etiam in 509, 511)　　ἐφωτ- A: ἀνεφωτ- B
512 ἀπέθανεν scripsi e mortuus est CS¹(G): ἔπαθεν B: deest A　　513 που B:
ubi CG: ποὺ Perler: deest A　　ἐν² B(C): om. AG

that was buried in the earth,
that was raised from the dead,
that was taken up to the heights of the heavens.

71 He is the lamb being slain;   495
   he is the lamb that is speechless;
   he is the one born from Mary the lovely ewe-lamb;
   he is the one *taken from the flock*,
       and dragged *to slaughter*,
       and sacrificed *at evening*,[37]
       and buried *at night*;[38]   500
   who on the tree was *not broken*,
   in the earth was not dissolved,[39]
   arose from the dead,
   and raised up man from the grave below.

72 It is he that has been murdered.   505
   And where has he been murdered? In the middle of Jerusalem.
   By whom? By Israel.[40]
   Why? Because he healed their lame
   and cleansed their lepers
       and brought light to their blind   510
       and raised their dead,
           that is why he died.
   Where is it written in law and prophets,
   '*They repaid me bad things for good*
   and childlessness for my soul,   515
   when they devised evil things against me and said,
   "*Let us bind the just one*,
       because he is a nuisance to us'''?[41]

   ʷ Cf. Exod. 12: 5; 1 Sam. 17: 34.   ˣ Cf. Isa. 53: 7; *Evangelium Petri* iii.
6.   ʸ Cf. Exod. 12: 6.   ᶻ Cf. Exod. 12: 8, 10.   ª Cf. Exod. 12: 10
(LXX), 46; John 19: 32–7.   ᵇ Ps. 35 (34 LXX): 12; cf. 38 (37 LXX):
21.   ᶜ Jer. 11: 19; cf. Isa. 3: 9.   ᵈ Isa. 3: 10.

---

[37] Agreeing with the implication of John 19: 14 that Christ was executed
after noon (contrast Mark 15: 25).

[38] Christ's burial was 'late' according to Mark 15: 42 par., but the assimilation to the eating of the Passover 'at night' is forced.

[39] Compare § 55 and Acts 2: 31; Christ 'saw no corruption'.

[40] Throughout §§ 72–99 Melito shares with *Evangelium Petri* the tendency to
attribute the crucifixion directly and exclusively to Israel.

[41] Justin, *Dialogue* 17. 2; 133. 2 has the same wording of Isa. 3: 10. Contrast
[*cont. on p. 41*]

40   *ΜΕΛΙΤΩΝΟΣ ΠΕΡΙ ΠΑΣΧΑ*

73   τί ἐποίησας, ὦ Ἰσραήλ, τὸ καινὸν ἀδίκημα;
     ἠτίμησας τὸν τιμήσαντά σε·   52
     ἠδόξησας τὸν δοξήσαντά σε·
     ἀπηρνήσω τὸν ὁμολογήσαντά σε·
     ἀπεκήρυξας τὸν κηρύξαντά σε·
     ἀπέκτεινας τὸν ζωοποιήσαντά σε.

74   τί ἐποίησας, ὦ Ἰσραήλ; ἢ οὐ γέγραπταί σοι·   52
     Οὐκ ἐκχεεῖς αἷμα ἀθῷον,ᵉ
       ἵνα μὴ θάνῃς κακῶς;
     Ἐγὼ μέν, φησὶν Ἰσραήλ, ἀπέκτεινα τὸν κύριον.
     διὰ τί; ὅτι ἔδει αὐτὸν ἀποθανεῖν.
     πεπλάνησαι, ὦ Ἰσραήλ, τοιαῦτα σοφιζόμενος   53
       ἐπὶ τῇ τοῦ κυρίου σφαγῇ.

75   ἔδει αὐτὸν παθεῖν,ᶠ ἀλλ' οὐχ ὑπὸ σοῦ·
     ἔδει αὐτὸν ἀτιμασθῆναι, ἀλλ' οὐχ ὑπὸ σοῦ·
     ἔδει αὐτὸν κριθῆναι, ἀλλ' οὐχ ὑπὸ σοῦ·
     ἔδει αὐτὸν κρεμασθῆναι, ἀλλ' οὐχ ὑπὸ σοῦ   53
       τῆς δὲ σῆς δεξιᾶς.

76   ταύτην, ὦ Ἰσραήλ, πρὸς τὸν θεὸν ὤφειλες βοῆσαι τὴν φωνήν·
     Ὦ Δέσποτα, εἰ καὶ ἔδει σου τὸν υἱὸν παθεῖνᵍ
       καὶ τοῦτό σου τὸ θέλημα,
     πασχέτω δή, ἀλλὰ ὑπ' ἐμοῦ μή·   54
     πασχέτω ὑπὸ ἀλλοφύλων,
     κρινέσθω ὑπὸ ἀκροβύστων,
     προσηλούσθω ὑπὸ τυραννικῆς δεξιᾶς,
     ὑπὸ δὲ ἐμοῦ μή.

519–30 cont. L   519 καινὸν ACGL: κακὸν B   522 ὁμολογ.–523
τὸν om. L   523 ἀπεκήρ- A: ἀνεκήρ- B   524 τὸν ζ. σε AB: om.
C: salvatorem tuum G   527 θάνῃς A: ἀποθάνῃς B   528 ισηλ απεκτινα
B(= txt.)C(GL): ω ισλ απεκτεινας A   529 ἀποθανεῖν ACGᵗ⁽ᵃ⁾: παθεῖν
BL   532–3 cont. L   532 παθεῖν ABL: mori CGᵃ   533 vs.
AGLᵛˡᵐ: om. BCLᵇ   534 vs. ACGᵃ: om. BGᵗL   535–55 cont. L
535 κρεμασθῆναι ABC: ligno add. G: crucis suspendi patibulo L   ὑπὸ–536 δεξιᾶς
A(G): ὑπὸ τῆς [[σης]] δεξιᾶς σου B: per tuam dexteram LC   537 ταύτην
BCL: -ης A   πρὸς BCL: προτων A   τὴν A: om. B   539 σου τὸ BCGL:
ἐστιν A   540 δή Bonner: δε A: om. B(C)G(L sed cf. 541)   ὑπ' ἐμοῦ
μή B: ὑπ ἐμοῦ A   (μη above)   540–3 sic interpunxit Bonner cum CG: post 541
πασχ., 542 κριν., 543 προσηλ. interpunxit B: non liquent AL   541 πασχέτω
AB(C)G: plane add. L(δή?)   542 ακροβυσθων ACGL: προσηλύτων B
544 vs. om. C

73 What strange crime, Israel, have you committed?

> You dishonoured him that honoured you; 520
>
> you disgraced him that glorified you;
>
> you denied him that acknowledged you;
>
> you disclaimed him that proclaimed you;
>
> you killed him that made you live.

74 What have you done, Israel? Or is it not written for you, 525

> '*You shall not shed innocent blood*,'
>
>> so that you may not die an evil death?
>
> 'I did', says Israel, 'kill the Lord.
>
> Why? Because he had to die.'
>
> You are mistaken, Israel, to use such subtle evasions 530
>
>> about the slaying of the Lord.[42]

75   He *had to suffer*, but not by you;

> he had to be dishonoured, but not by you;
>
> he had to be judged, but not by you;
>
> he had to be hung up, but not by you 535
>
>> and your right hand.

76 This is the cry, Israel, which you should have made to God:

> 'Sovereign, if indeed your Son *had to suffer*,
>
>> and this is your will,
>
> then let him suffer, but not by me; 540
>
> let him suffer by foreigners,
>
> let him be judged by uncircumcised men,
>
> let him be nailed up by a tyrannical right hand,
>
>> but not by me.'

ᵉ Cf. Jer. 7: 6; 22: 3.   ᶠ Cf. Acts 17: 3.   ᵍ Cf. Acts 17: 3.

Justin, *Dialogue* 136. 2; 137. 3; Hegesippus ap. Eusebius, *HE* 2. 33. 15; Clement, *Stromateis* 5. 108. 2 (R. A. Kraft, *JBL* 80 (1961) 371–3).

[42] The same argument is challenged by Justin, *Dialogue* 95. 2. 3; 141. 1.

77　σὺ δὲ ταύτην, ὦ Ἰσραήλ, πρὸς τὸν θεὸν οὐκ ἐβόησας τὴν φωνήν,　545
　　οὐδὲ ἀφωσίωσαι τῷ δεσπότῃ,
　　οὐδὲ ἐδυσωπήθης τὰ ἔργα αὐτοῦ.

78　οὐκ ἐδυσώπησέν σε χεὶρ ξηρὰ ἀποκατασταθεῖσα τῷ σώματι,[h]
　　οὐδὲ ὀφθαλμοὶ πηρῶν διὰ χειρὸς ἀνοιγόμενοι,[j]
　　οὐδὲ λελυμένα σώματα διὰ φωνῆς ἀναπηγνύμενα.[k]　550
　　οὐδὲ τὸ καινότερόν σε ἐδυσώπησεν σημεῖον,
　　νεκρὸς ἐκ μνημείου ἐγειρόμενος ἤδη τεσσάρων ἡμερῶν.[l]

79　σὺ μὲν οὖν ταῦτα παραπεμψάμενος
　　ἔσπευσας ἐπὶ τὴν τοῦ κυρίου σφαγήν.

　　ἡτοίμασας αὐτῷ ἥλους ὀξεῖς καὶ μάρτυρας ψευδεῖς[m]　555
(79)　καὶ βρόχους καὶ μάστιγας[n]
　　καὶ ὄξος καὶ χολὴν[o]
　　καὶ μάχαιραν καὶ θλῖψιν ὡς ἐπὶ φόνιον λῃστήν.[p]
　　ἐπηνέγκω γὰρ αὐτοῦ καὶ μάστιγας τῷ σώματι[q]
　　καὶ ἄκανθαν τῇ κεφαλῇ αὐτοῦ·[r]　560
　　καὶ τὰς καλὰς αὐτοῦ χεῖρας ἔδησας[s]
　　αἴ σε ἔπλασαν ἀπὸ γῆς·[t]
　　καὶ τὸ καλὸν αὐτοῦ ἐκεῖνο στόμα τὸ ψωμίσαν σε ζωὴν[u]
　　ἐψώμισας χολήν.[v]
　　καὶ ἀπέκτεινάς σου τὸν κύριον ἐν τῇ μεγάλῃ ἑορτῇ.　565

80　καὶ σὺ μὲν ἦσθα εὐφραινόμενος,
　　ἐκεῖνος δὲ λιμώττων·
　　σὺ ἔπινες οἶνον καὶ ἄρτον ἤσθιες,
　　ἐκεῖνος δὲ ὄξος καὶ χολήν·

545 ταύτην BCGL: ταυτα A　　τὴν A: om. B　　φωνήν BCGL: σου add. A
546 ἀφωσίωσαι Testuz cum C(G) ex αποσειωσαι B: αφερεισω[A: inferre . . .
manus proprias pepercisti L　　548 ἀποκατασταθεῖσα B: απο[.] . . . . . αλμενη
A: ἀποκαθεσταμένη Bonner　　549 χειρὸς ABGL: eius add. C　　550 φωνῆς
(A)B(C)G: eius add. L　　553 πα[ραπεμψ.–556 καὶ] μάστ. deest A
554 ἔσπευσας Whittaker cum CG^tL^bv: εσπερας B　　555 αὐτῷ Testuz cum
CGL: σαιαυτω B　　556 καὶ β.–557 ὄξος om. L　　556 βρόχους B(G):
turbas C　　557 καὶ²–575 cont. L　　558 θλῖψιν AL: καὶ add. B
559 ἐπηνέγκω Hall cum CL(G^a): επηνεγκως A: ἐπενεγκὼν B　　γὰρ AB:
δε C(graece): et G: etiam L　　αὐτοῦ ACL: αυτω B: super eum G^a
560 ἄκανθαν AB: coronam spinae C: coronam spineam posuisti LG(^a)^t　　561 αὐτοῦ
AB(CG): illas add. L　　562 αἴ σαι ἔπλασαν BCGL: . . .]σεν A: αἷς σε
ἔπλα]σεν Bonner　　565 καὶ ABCG: om. L　　566 καὶ ABGL: om. C
ἦσθα A: ἦς B　　568 σὺ AB(G)L: μὲν add. C(graece)　　569 δὲ BCGL:
om. A

77 But you, Israel, did not make this cry to God, 545
    nor have you cleared yourself before the Sovereign,
    nor did you respect his deeds.

78 A withered hand restored to the body did not win your respect,
    nor eyes of disabled ones opened by a hand,
    nor impotent bodies made sound by a word; 550
nor did the most unprecedented sign win your respect,
    a corpse roused from a tomb already four days old.

79 So then, you set these things aside,
    and rushed to the slaying of the Lord.
You prepared for him sharp nails[43] and false witnesses 555
79)   and ropes and scourges
    and vinegar and gall[44]
    and sword and forceful restraint as against a murderous robber.
For you brought both scourges for his body
    and thorn for his head; 560
and you bound his good hands,
    which formed you from earth;
and that good mouth of his which fed you with life
    you fed with gall.
And you killed your Lord at the great feast.[45] 565

80 And you were making merry,[46]
    while he was starving;
you had wine to drink and bread to eat,
    he had vinegar and gall;

[h] Matt. 12: 10; cf. 12: 9–14 par.   [j] Cf. Matt. 9: 27–30; 20: 29–34 par.; John 9: 1–7.   [k] Cf. Matt. 9: 1–8 par.; John 5: 2–9.   [l] Cf. John 11: 17–44.   [m] Cf. Matt. 26: 59–60 par.   [n] Cf. Matt. 27: 26 par.   [o] Matt. 27: 34, 48 par.; John 19: 29; cf. Ps. 69 (68 LXX): 21.   [p] Matt. 26: 55 par.   [q] Cf. Matt. 27: 26 par.   [r] Cf. Matt. 27: 29 par.   [s] Cf. Matt. 27: 2 par.; John 18: 12.   [t] Cf. Gen. 2: 7; Job 10: 8; Deut. 32: 6.   [u] Cf. John 6: 63.   [v] Cf. Matt. 27: 34; Ps. 69 (68 LXX): 21.

---

[43] *Evangelium Petri* vi. 21 also refers to the nails, cf. John 20: 25.

[44] Melito alludes to Ps. 69 more closely than does Matthew. The gall and vinegar are combined also in *Evangelium Petri* v. 16, cf. Barnabas 7. 3–5.

[45] Perler (pp. 181–3) and W. Huber (*Passa und Ostern* (Berlin, 1969) 43–4) take this to imply that Melito dated the crucifixion on 15 Nisan, i.e. the day after the Passover meal. This day is called ἡ μεγάλη ἡμέρα τῶν ἀζύμων by Apollinaris of Hierapolis ap. *Chronicon paschale* (PG 92. 80); cf. John 19. 31 and *Martyria Polycarpi* 21. But the influence of John and *Evangelium Petri* on Melito would make him likely to follow their dating on 14 Nisan, and the festivities described in the lines following appear to refer to the Passover meal itself. Note especially εὐφραινόμενος, used of the paschal meal in § 16, and see B. Gärtner, *John 6 and the Jewish Passover* (Lund, 1959) 32.

[46] With § 80 cf. Ps.-Cyprian, *Adversus Judaeos* 39–40 (Van Damme pp. 119–20).

σὺ ἦσθα φαιδρὸς τῷ προσώπῳ,   570
 ἐκεῖνος δὲ ἐσκυθρώπαζεν·
σὺ ἦσθα ἀγαλλιώμενος,
 ἐκεῖνος δὲ ἐθλίβετο·
σὺ ἔψαλλες,
 ἐκεῖνος δὲ ἐκρίνετο·   575
σὺ ἐκέλευες,
 ἐκεῖνος δὲ προσηλοῦτο·
σὺ ἐχόρευες,
 ἐκεῖνος δὲ ἐθάπτετο·
σὺ μὲν ἐπὶ στρωμνῆς μαλακῆς ἦσθα κατακείμενος,   580
 ἐκεῖνος δὲ ἐν τάφῳ καὶ σορῷ.

81 ῏Ω Ἰσραὴλ παράνομε, τί τοῦτο ἀπηργάσω τὸ καινὸν ἀδίκημα,
 καινοῖς ἐμβαλών σου τὸν κύριον πάθεσιν,
  τὸν δεσπότην σου,
  τὸν πλάσαντά σε,
  τὸν ποιήσαντά σε,   585
  τὸν τιμήσαντά σε,
  τὸν Ἰσραὴλ σε καλέσαντα;
82 σὺ δὲ Ἰσραὴλ οὐχ εὑρέθης·
 οὐ γὰρ εἶδες τὸν θεόν,
 οὐκ ἐνόησας τὸν κύριον·   590
οὐκ ᾔδεις, ὦ Ἰσραήλ,
 ὅτι οὗτός ἐστιν ὁ πρωτότοκος τοῦ θεοῦ,
 ὁ πρὸ ἑωσφόρου γεννηθείς,ʷ
 ὁ τὸ φῶς ἐπανθίσας,
 ὁ τὴν ἡμέραν λαμπρύνας,   595
 ὁ τὸ σκότος διακρίνας,ˣ

572 ἦσθα A: ἧς B   575 δὲ B(G)L: om. C   576–7 om. L
576–602 cont. Sᴵ   577 δὲ C(graece): *et* GSᴵ: om. AB   578–93 cont. L
579 δὲ BCLSᴵ: om. A   580 στρωμνῆς μαλακῆς A: -ὴν -ὴν B   ἦσθα A:
ἧς B   581–2 σορῷ ὦ B(CG)LSᴵ: σορω in σαρω mutatum A   582 παράνομε τί BCGLSᴵ: παρανομετοδη vel -μεᶦτοδη A   583 καινοῖς BCLSᴵ: καὶ A
πάθεσιν BCL(Sᴵ): παθειν A   584–6 txt. BSᴵ: 586 om. A(G): qui te auxit qui
te plasmavit (πλάσσειν) C: dominatorem tuum et factorem tuum L   588 σε
καλέσ. A: inv. B   590 θ̄ν̄ (= θεόν) ABCSᴵ: dominum GL   595 ἐπανθίσας scripsi: απαντησας A: απανθησας B: splendere fecit G(C?): oriri fecit Sᴵ
(C?): ἐπαναστήσας Bonner   597 διακρίνας BCG: dissipavit Sᴵ unde δι[ανεί]μας
Bonner: δ[ιακρί]νας in A legendum

your face was bright,   570
  his was downcast;
you were triumphant,
  he was afflicted;
you were making music,[47]
  he was being judged;   575
you were giving the beat,
  he was being nailed up;
you were dancing,
  he was being buried;
you were reclining on a soft couch,[48]   580
  he in grave and coffin.[49]

81 O lawless Israel, what is this unprecedented crime you committed,
  thrusting your Lord among unprecedented sufferings,
    your Sovereign,
    who formed you,   585
    who made you,
    who honoured you,
    who called you 'Israel'?
82 But you did not turn out to be 'Israel';
  you did not 'see God',[50]   590
  you did not recognize the Lord.
You did not know, Israel,
  that he is the firstborn of God,
    who was begotten *before the morning star*,
    who tinted the light,   595
    who lit up the day,
    who divided off the darkness,

[w] Ps. 110 (109 LXX): 3.   [x] Cf. Gen. 1: 4.

---

[47] For music and dancing at Passover see J. Jeremias, *Eucharistic Words of Jesus* (London, 1966) 55 n. 1; W. C. van Unnik, 'A note on the dance of Jesus in the "Acts of John"', *VigChr* 18 (1964) 1–5.

[48] Jews recline at the Passover meal to symbolize freedom (J. Jeremias, *Eucharistic Words of Jesus* 48–9).

[49] Christ's tomb is depicted as a coffin in the baptistery at Dura-Europos (before 256); see illustration in F. van der Meer and C. Mohrmann, *Atlas of the Early Christian World* 46.

[50] This etymology of *Israel* appears already in Philo, *De mutatione nominum* 81, and perhaps lies behind John 1: 45–51. It arises from confusion with the etymology of Peniel in Gen. 32: 31. Cf. also John 9: 35–41.

[51] For §§ 82–5 cf. Fr. 15; New Fr. II. 18–20. Bonner pp. 25–7 postulated a common liturgical source with *Constitutiones Apostolicae* 8. 12, but exaggerates the resemblances.

ὁ ⟨τὴν⟩ πρώτην βαλβῖδα πήξας,
ὁ κρεμάσας τὴν γῆν,ʸ
ὁ σβέσας ἄβυσσον,
ὁ ἐκτείνας τὸ στερέωμα,ᶻ 600
ὁ κοσμήσας τὸν κόσμον,
(83)　ὁ τοὺς ἐν οὐρανῷ ἁρμόσας ἀστέρας,
ὁ τοὺς φωστῆρας λαμπρύνας,ᵃ
ὁ τοὺς ἐν οὐρανῷ ποιήσας ἀγγέλους,ᵇ 605
ὁ τοὺς ἐκεῖ πήξας θρόνους,
ὁ τὸν ἐπὶ γῆς ἀναπλασάμενος ἄνθρωπον.ᶜ
83　οὗτος ἦν ὁ ἐκλεξάμενός σε καὶ καθοδηγήσας σε
ἀπὸ τοῦ Ἀδὰμ ἐπὶ τὸν Νῶε,
ἀπὸ τοῦ Νῶε ἐπὶ τὸν Ἀβραάμ,
ἀπὸ τοῦ Ἀβραὰμ ἐπὶ τὸν Ἰσὰκ 610
καὶ τὸν Ἰακὼβ καὶ τοὺς ιβ πατριάρχας.ᵈ
84　οὗτος ἦν ὁ καθοδηγήσας σε εἰς Αἴγυπτον,
καὶ διαφυλάξας σε κἀκεῖ διαθρεψάμενος.
οὗτος ἦν ὁ φωταγωγήσας σε ἐν στύλῳ 615
καὶ σκεπάσας σε ἐν νεφέλῃ,
ὁ τεμὼν Ἐρυθρὰν καὶ διαγαγών σε
καὶ τὸν ἐχθρόν σου ἀπολέσας.
85　οὗτός ἐστιν ὁ ἐξ οὐρανοῦ σε μανναδοτήσας,
ὁ ἐκ πέτρας σε ποτίσας, 620
ὁ ἐν Χωρήβ σοι νομοθετήσας,
ὁ ἐν γῇ σοι κληροδοτήσας,
ὁ ἐξαποστείλας σοι τοὺς προφήτας,ᵉ
ὁ ἐγείρας σου τοὺς βασιλεῖς.
86　οὗτός ἐστιν ὁ πρός σε ἀφικόμενος, 625
ὁ τοὺς πάσχοντάς σου θεραπεύσας
καὶ τοὺς νεκρούς σου ἀναστήσας.

---

598 τὴν suppl. Bonner: om. AB　　βαλβῖδα Bonner: βαρβιδαν A: βασιλίδα B: *fundamentum* CS¹: *firmamentum* G　　600 vs. om. C　　603 ἁρμόσας A: ορμασας B(ὁρμήσας Testuz): *fixit* C: *disposuit* G　　605 ποιήσας B: πεποιη-κὼ[ς A　　606 θ[ρόνους–610 τὸ]ν deest A　　607 ἀναπλασάμενος Perler = CG: -ον B　　615–39 om. Gᵃ　　615–16 cont. L　　617 τεμὼν B(CG): τέμνων A　　διαγαγών B(CG): [δι]άγων A　　618 ἀπολέσας A: ἀποσκεδάσας B: *destruxit* CG　　619 σαι B(σε)CG: om. A: σοι Testuz　　620–1 ACGᵗ: om. B　　622 vs. A: om. BCG　　624 ἐγείρας A: ἐξεγ- B　　625–7 cont. L

who fixed the first marker,
who hung the earth,
who controlled the deep,   600
who spread out the firmament,
who arrayed the world,
(83)   who fitted the stars in heaven,
who lit up the luminaries,
who *made the angels* in heaven,   605
who established the thrones there,
who formed man upon earth.

83 It was he who chose you and guided you[52]
from Adam to Noah,
from Noah to Abraham,   610
from Abraham to Isaac
and Jacob and the twelve patriarchs.

84 It was he who guided you into Egypt,
and watched over you and there sustained you.
It was he who lit your way with a pillar   615
and sheltered you with a cloud,
who cut the Red Sea and led you through
and destroyed your enemy.

85 It is he who gave you manna from heaven,
who gave you drink from a rock,   620
who legislated for you at Horeb,
who gave you inheritance in the land,
who sent out to you the prophets,
who raised up your kings.

86 It is he who came to you,   625
who healed your suffering ones,
and raised your dead.

y Cf. Job 26: 7.   z Cf. Gen. 1: 6–8; Ps. 104 (103 LXX): 2.   a Cf.
Gen. 1: 14–18.   b Cf. Ps. 104 (103 LXX): 4.   c Cf. Gen. 2: 7.
d Cf. Acts 7: 8.   e Cf. Matt. 23: 34; Luke 11: 49.

---

52 In §§ 83–5 many biblical features are recalled, but affinities to the biblical
text are inexact and may well be indirect. Besides the pentateuchal narratives,
verbal approximations appear in such passages as Pss. 78 (77 LXX): 13–16,
24, 55; 105 (104 LXX): 39–40; 136 (135 LXX): 13–16. Similarities to
Constitutiones Apostolicae 6. 3. 1 and 6. 20. 6 led Bonner to postulate a common
liturgical source; but the common ground is all biblical, except the verb μαννα-
δοτεῖν.

οὗτός ἐστιν εἰς ὃν ἐτόλμησας·
οὗτός ἐστιν εἰς ὃν ἠσέβησας·
οὗτός ἐστιν εἰς ὃν ἠδίκησας·
οὗτός ἐστιν ὃν ἀπέκτεινας·   630
οὗτός ἐστιν ὃν ἠργυρίσω
ἀπαιτήσας παρ' αὐτοῦ τὸ δίδραχμα ὑπὲρ τῆς κεφαλῆς αὐτοῦ.ᶠ

87 Ἀχάριστε Ἰσραήλ, δεῦρο καὶ κρίθητι πρὸς ἐμὲ
     περὶ τῆς ἀχαριστίας σου.   635
πόσου ἀνετιμήσω τὸ ὑπ' αὐτοῦ πλασθῆναι;
πόσου ἀνετιμήσω τὴν τῶν πατέρων σου ἀνεύρεσιν;
πόσου ἀνετιμήσω τὴν εἰς Αἴγυπτον κάθοδον
     καὶ τὴν ἐκεῖ διατροφὴν διὰ τοῦ καλοῦ Ἰωσήφ;
88 πόσου ἀνετιμήσω τὰς δέκα πληγάς;   640
πόσου ἀνετιμήσω τὸν νυκτερινὸν στῦλον
     καὶ τὴν ἡμερινὴν νεφέλην
     καὶ τὴν δι' Ἐρυθρᾶς διάβασιν;
πόσου ἀνετιμήσω τὴν ἐξ οὐρανοῦ μαννοδοσίαν
     καὶ ἐκ πέτρας ὑδροπαροχίαν   645
     καὶ ἐν Χωρὴβ νομοθεσίαν
     καὶ τὴν γῆς κληρονομίαν
     καὶ τὰς ἐκεῖ δωρεάς;
89 πόσου ἀνετιμήσω τοὺς πάσχοντας
     οὓς αὐτὸς παρὼν ἐθεράπευσεν;   650
τίμησαί μοι τὴν ξηρὰν χεῖρα
     ἣν ἀπεκατέστησεν τῷ σώματι·ᵍ
(90) τίμησαί μοι τοὺς ἐκ γενετῆς τυφλοὺς
     οὓς διὰ φωνῆς ἐφωταγώγησεν·ʰ
τίμησαί μοι τοὺς κειμένους νεκροὺς   655
     οὓς ἐκ μνημείου ἀνέστησεν ἤδη τεσσάρων ἡμερῶν.ʲ

628 vs. ACG: om. B   629 vs. BCG: om. A   630–2 cont. L
631–2 vss. ABL: inv. G: 632 om. C   631 οὗτός ἐστιν BG: om. A(C item
629, 630)L   632 ὃν ἠργυρίσω scripsi: εἰς ὃν ἠργ- A: ὃν ἀπηργ- B: quem
vendidisti L(argento add. G)   633 ἀπαιτήσας B: ἀπήτησας A   634 ιηλ
δεῦρο BC(G): δευροι ω ισλ A   636 πλασθῆναι ACG: καθοδηγηθῆναι B
637 σου BC: om. A: vs. om. G   642 ἡμερινὴν B: ἡμέριον A   645 καὶ
A: τὴν add. B   υδροπαροχειαν B: ὑδροδοσίαν A   647 τὴν γῆς scripsi: τὴν
χῆν A: τὴν εγ γης B: τὴν ἐκ γῆς Testuz   653 τοὺς εγ γενετῆς τυφλοὺς
BCGᵗ: τὸν ἐκ γε]ϝετῆς τυφλων A(Hall)Gᵃ   654 οὓς BCGᵗ: quem Gᵃ: vs.
om. A   656 μνημιου B: mortuis C: sepulcris G   ἀνέστησεν ȳ δὴ δ ἡμερῶν B:

It is he that you outraged;
it is he against whom you sinned;
it is he that you wronged;   630
it is he that you killed;
it is he from whom you extorted money,
   demanding from him his two-drachma poll-tax.

87 Ungrateful Israel, come and take issue with me
    about your ingratitude.   635
How much did you value being formed by him?
How much did you value the seeking out of your fathers?
How much did you value the descent into Egypt
   and your sustenance there through handsome Joseph?
88 How much did you value the ten plagues?   640
How much did you value the nightly pillar
   and the daily cloud
   and the crossing of the Red Sea?
How much did you value the giving of manna from heaven
   and the supply of water from a rock   645
   and the law-giving at Horeb
   and the inheritance of the land
    and the benefits there?
89 How much did you value the suffering ones
   whom by his own presence he healed?   650
Value for me the withered hand
   which he restored to the body;
90) value for me those *blind from birth*
   to whom he brought light with a word;
value for me those who lay dead   655
   whom he raised from the dead *already four days* old.

. . .]ανεστησεν ηδε τ[circa 20 litterae]γεγων ωτων A(. . . ε]γειρων αὐτόν? cf.
G): *post tres dies* C: *eduxit vel quarti diei mortuum quem resuscitavit* G

---

^f Cf. Matt. 17: 24–7.   ^g Cf. Mark 3: 1–5 par.   ^h Cf. John 9: 1–7.
^j Cf. John 11: 17–44.

90 ἀτίμητοι αἱ παρ' αὐτοῦ σοι δωρεαί·
    σὺ δὲ ἀτίμως ἀνταπέδωκας εἰς αὐτὸν τὰς χάριτας,
    ἀχαριστίας ἀνταποδοὺς αὐτῷ,
        κακὰ ἀντὶ καλῶνᵏ   66

        καὶ θλῦψιν ἀντὶ χαρᾶς
        καὶ θάνατον ἀντὶ ζωῆς·
(91) ὑπὲρ οὗ καὶ ἀποθανεῖν σε ἔδει.

91 Εἶτα ἐὰν μὲν ἔθνους ἁρπαγῇ βασιλεὺς ὑπὸ ἐχθρῶν,
    δι' αὐτὸν πόλεμος συνίσταται,   66
    δι' αὐτὸν τεῖχος ῥήγνυται,
    δι' αὐτὸν πόλις ἀναρπάζεται,
    δι' αὐτὸν λύτρα πέμπεται,
    δι' αὐτὸν πρέσβεις ἀποστέλλονται
        ἢ ἵνα ζῶν ἀναλημφθῇ   670
        ἢ ἵνα νεκρὸς ταφῇ.

92 σὺ δὲ τὴν ἐναντίαν κατὰ τοῦ κυρίου σου ἤνεγκας ψῆφον·
    ὃν γὰρ τὰ ἔθνη προσεκύνουν
      καὶ ἀκρόβυστοι ἐθαύμαζον
      καὶ ἀλλόφυλοι ἐδόξαζον,¹   675
    ἐφ' ᾧ καὶ Πιλᾶτος ἐνίψατο τὰς χεῖρας,ᵐ
    σὺ τοῦτον ἀπέκτεινας ἐν τῇ μεγάλῃ ἑορτῇ.

93 Τοιγαροῦν πικρά σοι ἡ τῶν ἀζύμων ἑορτὴ καθώς σοι γέγραπται·
    Ἔδεσθε ἄζυμα μετὰ πικρίδων.ⁿ
    πικροί σοι ἧλοι οὓς ὤξυνας,   680
    πικρά σοι γλῶσσα ἣν παρώξυνας,
    πικροί σοι ψευδομάρτυρες οὓς ἔστησας,ᵒ
    πικροί σοι βρόχοι οὓς ἡτοίμασας,

657 αἱ Testuz: ᾳ[A: a B   658–9 τὰς χάριτας αχαριτιας A(-ιστίας
Bonner): τὰς χαρειστειας B(sic): gratias ingratas C: ingratitudinem G   660 καλῶν
B: ἀγαθῶν A   661 χαρᾶς BC: χάριτος A: vs. om. G   664 ἐὰν μὲν
ε[[χ]]θνους B: μὲ[ν ἔ]θνος A: fit enim (γάρ) si nationis C   665 πόλεμος
A: ὁ π. B   665–6 συνίσταται–τεῖχος AB: om. C   670 ἤ–671 ἵνα: ἤ
εινα ζῶν ἀναπεμφθῇ μεινα A: ἵνα ληψθῇ ἵνα εἰς ζωὴν αναπεμθη B: ut recipiatur
vivens seu (ἤ) C, unde txt. Chadwick   672 τὴν ἐναντίαν A: ἐναντίον B
673 προσεκύνουν B(C): προσκυνεῖ A   674–5 vss. ABC: inv. G   676 ἐνί-
ψατο B: επενειψατο A(ἀπενίψ- Bonner)   678 τοιγαροῦν B: τυνυν A(τοί-)
680–92 κύριον cont. S¹   680 ὤξυνας B: εξυνας A   Post 681 ponit 685 S¹
683 txt. BC: om. AS¹: amara est tibi spongia plena aceto et felle G

90 No value can be set on his benefits to you,
        and you set no value on them when you gave him his thanks,
            repaying him with ungrateful acts,
                evil for good   660
                and affliction for joy
                and death for life;
1)   in recompense for that you had to die.

91 Furthermore, if a nation's king is seized by enemies,
            for him a war is waged,   665
            for him a wall is breached,
            for him a city is sacked,
            for him ransoms are sent,
            for him ambassadors are dispatched,
                either so that he may be received back alive,   670
                or so that he may be buried if dead.
92 But you cast the opposite vote against your Lord.
        For him whom the gentiles worshipped
            and uncircumcised men admired
            and foreigners glorified,   675
        over whom even Pilate *washed his hands*,
    you killed him at the great feast.

93 Bitter therefore for you is the feast of unleavened bread, as it is
                                        written for you:
        You shall eat unleavened bread with bitter flavours.[53]
        Bitter for you are the nails you sharpened,   680
        bitter for you the tongue you incited,
        bitter for you the false witnesses you instructed,
        bitter for you the ropes you got ready,

    k Ps. 38 (37 LXX): 21.   l Cf. Matt. 8: 5–13 par.; John 12: 20–1.
    m Matt. 27: 24.   n Exod. 12: 8.   o Cf. Matt. 26: 59–60.

---

53 According to Mishnah *Pesahim* x. 5 R. Gamaliel required that the Passover Haggadah should include reference to the Passover (i.e. the lamb), the
unleavened bread, and the bitter herbs served with the meal. Some such
tradition may survive in Melito. See S. G. Hall, *JTS* n.s. 22 (1971) 38–40,
following F. L. Cross.

πικραί σοι μάστιγες ἃς ἔπλεξας,
πικρός σοι Ἰούδας ὃν ἐμισθοδότησας,^P   685
πικρός σοι Ἡρώδης ᾧ ἐξηκολούθησας,
πικρός σοι Καιάφας ᾧ ἐπείσθης,^q
πικρά σοι χολὴ ἣν ἐσκεύασας,
πικρόν σοι ὄξος ὃ ἐγεώργησας,
πικρά σοι ἄκανθα ἣν ἤνθισας,   690
πικραί σοι χεῖρες ἃς ᾕμαξας·
ἀπέκτεινάς σου τὸν κύριον ἐν μέσῳ Ἰερουσαλήμ.

94 Ἀκούσατε πᾶσαι αἱ πατριαὶ τῶν ἐθνῶν^r καὶ ἴδετε·
καινὸς φόνος γέγονεν ἐν μέσῳ Ἰερουσαλήμ,
ἐν πόλει νομικῇ,   695
ἐν πόλει ἑβραϊκῇ,
ἐν πόλει προφητικῇ,
ἐν πόλει δικαίᾳ νομιζομένῃ.
καὶ τίς πεφόνευται; τίς δὲ ὁ φονεύς;
εἰπεῖν αἰδοῦμαι καὶ λέγειν ἀναγκάζομαι.   700
εἰ μὲν γὰρ νύκτωρ γεγόνει ὁ φόνος,
ἢ ἐπ' ἐρημίας ἦν ἐσφαγμένος,
σιγᾶν εὔχρηστον ἦν.
νῦν δὲ ἐπὶ μέσης πλατείας καὶ ἐν μέσῳ πόλεως
μέσης ἡμέρας πάντων ὁρώντων   705
γέγονεν δικαίου ἄδικος φόνος.
95 καὶ οὕτως ὕψωται ἐπὶ ξύλου ὑψηλοῦ·
καὶ τίτλος πρόσκειται τὸν πεφονευμένον σημαίνων.
τίς οὗτος; τὸ εἰπεῖν βαρὺ καὶ τὸ μὴ εἰπεῖν φοβερώτερον.

684 vs. ABCG: om. S¹   686–7 vss. ABCG: om. S¹   689 vs. ABCS¹:
om. G   690 ἤνθισας Testuz: ηνθησ[ας A: ημβησας B: plicasti C: fecisti
coronam G: vs. om. S¹   693–729 cont. S²   693 πᾶσαι ABG¹S²: om. C
αἱ A: om. B   ἐθνῶ B(-ῶν)CS²: ἀν]θρώπων AG¹   καὶ ειδετε ABG¹(S²):
om. C   694 Ἰ[ερουσ.–700 αἱ]δοῦμαι deest A   697 vs. BCG¹: om. S²
702 ἐσφαγμένος B: ἀπεσφ- A   704 ἐ|[πὶ μέση]ς πλατιας A(Bonner recte):
εμ μέσης πλατείας B: in mediis plateis C(inter plateas GS²) unde ἐν μέσαις πλατείαις
forsitan legendum   καὶ ἐν μέσῳ πόλεως scripsi cf. BG: καὶ πόλεως A: καὶ
πόλεως ἐν μέσῳ πόλεως B: civitatis CS²: in medio civitatis G   705 μέσης
[ἡμέρας] A(Hall)CG: om. BS²   706 δικαίου B(CGS²): . . .]ως A
707–26 cont. S¹   707 οὕτως A: οὕτω B: om. C: illum G: hic S¹: sic S²
υψωτε B(-ται)(CG): ὑψοῦ[ται A(S¹S²)   ὑψηλου AGS²: om. BCS¹   709 τὸ¹–
φοβερώτερον BC: τὸ μὴ εἰπεῖν φωβεροτερον A: μὴ ante εἰπεῖν¹ pon. GS¹S²

bitter for you the scourges you plaited,
bitter for you Judas whom you hired,   685
bitter for you Herod whom you followed,[54]
bitter for you Caiaphas whom you trusted,
bitter for you the gall you prepared,
bitter for you the vinegar you produced,
bitter for you the thorns you culled,   690
bitter for you the hands you bloodied;
you killed your Lord in the middle of Jerusalem.[55]

94 Listen, all *you families of the nations*, and see!
An unprecedented murder has occurred in the middle of Jeru-
    salem,
    in the city of the law,   695
    in the city of the Hebrews,
    in the city of the prophets,
    in the city accounted just.
And who has been murdered? Who is the murderer?
I am ashamed to say and I am obliged to tell.   700
For if the murder had occurred at night,
    or if he had been slain in a desert place,
        one might have had recourse to silence.
But now, in the middle of the street and in the middle of the city,
    at the middle of the day[56] for all to see,   705
        has occurred a just man's unjust murder.
95 Just so he has been lifted up on a tall tree,
    and a notice has been attached to show who has been murdered.[57]
Who is this? To say is hard, and not to say is too terrible.

p Cf. Matt. 26: 15 par.   q Cf. Matt. 26: 65–6 par.; John 11: 49–53.
r Ps. 96 (95 LXX): 7.

---

[54] Following *Evangelium Petri* i. 1–2 in making Herod a principal agent on behalf of the Jews in condemning Jesus; contrast Luke 23: 7–12, 15.

[55] The repeated assertion in §§ 93–4 that Christ died in the middle of Jerusalem may be connected with the fact that the traditional site of the crucifixion was enclosed within Herod Agrippa's wall of A.D. 41–4, and with Melito's claim to have visited Palestine (Fr. 3). See A. E. Harvey, 'Melito and Jerusalem', *JTS* N.S. 17 (1966) 401–4.

[56] Apparently contradicting 'in the evening' of § 71 (499). But both are compatible with a condemnation about noon as in John 19: 14. The source may be ἦν δὲ μεσημβρία in *Evangelium Petri* v. 15.

[57] In view of 96 (716) the reference is to *Evangelium Petri* iv. 11, where the superscription reads 'This is the king of Israel', rather than to the canonical gospels where it reads (with variations) 'The king of the Jews' (Mark 15: 26 par.).

πλὴν ἀκούσατε τρέμοντες δι' ὃν ἐτρόμαξεν ἡ γῆ.   710

96 ὁ κρεμάσας τὴν γῆν κρέμαται·
ὁ πήξας τοὺς οὐρανοὺς πέπηκται·
ὁ στηρίξας τὰ πάντα ἐπὶ ξύλου ἐστήρικται·
ὁ δεσπότης ὕβρισται·
ὁ θεὸς πεφόνευται·   715
ὁ βασιλεὺς τοῦ Ἰσραὴλ ἀνῄρηται ὑπὸ δεξιᾶς Ἰσραηλίτιδος.

97 ὦ φόνου καινοῦ, ὦ ἀδικίας καινῆς·
ὁ δεσπότης παρεσχημάτισται γυμνῷ τῷ σώματι,
καὶ οὐδὲ περιβολῆς ἠξίωται ἵνα μὴ θεαθῇ.
διὰ τοῦτο οἱ φωστῆρες ἀπεστράφησαν   720
καὶ ἡ ἡμέρα συνεσκότασεν,ˢ
ὅπως κρύψῃ τὸν ἐπὶ ξύλου γεγυμνωμένον,
οὐ τὸ τοῦ κυρίου σῶμα σκοτίζων
ἀλλὰ τοὺς τῶν ἀνθρώπων ὀφθαλμούς.

98 καὶ γὰρ τοῦ λαοῦ μὴ τρέμοντος ἐτρόμαξεν ἡ γῆ·ᵗ   725
τοῦ λαοῦ μὴ φοβηθέντος ἐφοβήθησαν οἱ οὐρανοί·ᵘ
τοῦ λαοῦ μὴ περιεσχισμένου περιεσχίσατο ὁ ἄγγελος·ᵛ
τοῦ λαοῦ μὴ κωκύσαντος ἐβρόντησεν ἐξ οὐρανοῦ κύριος
καὶ ὕψιστος ἔδωκεν φωνήν.ʷ

99 Διὰ τοῦτο, ὦ Ἰσραήλ,   730
ἐπὶ τοῦ κυρίου οὐκ ἐτ[ρόμαξ]ας,
⟨impugnatus ab hostibus contremuisti;⟩

710 ἀκούσατε τρέμοντες BCGS¹: -σαντες -ετε A   ἐτρόμαξεν (οὐρανὸς καὶ add.) A: ετραμησε B: tremuit C(G)S¹S²   712 τοὺς BC: om. A   713 τὰ πάντα ABCS²: terram S¹   714 ὕβριστε A(-ται)(CGS²): παρυβριστε B: nudo corpore add. S¹   715 πεφόνευται AB(inv. πεφ. et 714 ὕβρισταιC)S¹S²: πέπονθεν Anastasius Sinaiticus   716 τοῦ B: om. A   Ἰσραηλίτιδος Bonner cum S¹S²: ισλ'ραηλιτιδος A: ιηλ B(C)   717 φόνου . . . ἀδικίας ABS²: inv. S¹: invidia . . . visio G: ὦ ἀδ. κ. om. C   καινῆς Bonner cum (G)S¹S²: κενης AB   719 ἠξίωται A: ηξιώθη B   ἵνα μὴ θ. ABCS¹: om. GS²   722 κρύψῃ AB: celarent CG: velarent S¹S²   τὸν ABC: deum add. S¹: corpus add. S²   723 οὐ τὸ Bonner cum CGS¹S²: ουτως A: ᵒᵘτο B(sic)   σκοτίζων B: -ον A: tenebrantes C(GS¹S²)   724 τῶν ACS¹S²: τούτων B(G)   725 ἐτρ[ο]μαξεν A: ἔτρεμεν B   727 -ίσατο ὁ ἄγγελος ACG: -ίσθησαν ἄγγελοι B: velum add. C(καταπετασμα graece): velum templi add. G: περιεσχ.–728 κωκύσαντος om. S²   728 κωκύσαντος BCG: κολυσ- A   729 καὶ B: ὁ add. A cum LXX   Post 729 desinit S²   730–47 cont. L   730 ὦ B(CG)L: om. A   731 AGL: om. B   732 L: om. ABCG

Yet listen, trembling at him for whom the earth quaked.   710

96   He who hung the earth is hanging;
    he who fixed the heavens has been fixed;
    he who fastened the universe has been fastened to a tree;
    the Sovereign has been insulted;
    the God has been murdered;[58]   715
    the King of Israel has been put to death by an Israelite right
                                 hand.

97 O unprecedented murder! Unprecedented crime!
    The Sovereign has been made unrecognizable by his naked body,
      and is not even allowed a garment to keep him from view.
    That is why the luminaries turned away,   720
      and the day was darkened,
  so that he might hide the one stripped bare upon the tree,
    darkening not the body of the Lord
      but the eyes of men.

98 For when the people did not tremble, the earth quaked;   725
    when the people were not terrified, the heavens were terrified;
    when the people did not tear their clothes, the angel tore his;[59]
    when the people did not lament, *the Lord thundered out of heaven*
      and the Highest gave voice.

99 Therefore, O Israel,   730
    you did not quake in the presence of the Lord,
      so you quaked at the assault of foes;

---

    s Cf. Mark 15: 33 par.; *Evangelium Petri* v. 15.   t Cf. Matt. 27: 51;
Evangelium Petri vi. 21.   u Cf. *Evangelium Petri* vi. 21.   v Cf. Mark 15:
38 par.; *Evangelium Petri* v. 20.   w Ps. 18 (17 LXX): 14; cf. Mark 15: 34
par., 37 par.; *Evangelium Petri* v. 19.

---

    58 For Melito's theopaschite statements see Introduction, p. xliii.
    59 For full account of early Christian interpretations of the tearing of the
temple veil see Bonner 41–5. To his references add New Fr. II. 11.

ἐπὶ τοῦ κυρίου οὐκ ἐφοβήθης,

⟨. . . . . . .⟩

ἐπὶ τοῦ κυρίου οὐκ ἐκώκυσας,   73

ἐπὶ τῶν πρωτοτόκων σου ἐκώκυσας·

κρεμαμένου τοῦ κυρίου οὐ περιεσχίσω,

ἐπὶ τῶν πεφονευμένων περιεσχίσω·

ἐγκατέλιπες τὸν κύριον,

[οὐχ] εὑρέθης ὑπ' αὐτοῦ·   74

οὐκ ἐ[δέξω τὸν κύριον],

οὐκ ἠλεήθης ὑπ' αὐτοῦ·

ἠδάφισας τὸν κύριον,

ἠδαφίσθης χαμαί.

(100) καὶ σὺ μὲν κεῖσαι νεκρός,   745

ἐκεῖνος δὲ ἀνέστη ἐκ νεκρῶν

καὶ ἀνέβη εἰς τὰ ὑψηλὰ τῶν οὐρανῶν.

100 Κύριος ἐνδυσάμενος τὸν ἄνθρωπον

καὶ παθὼν διὰ τὸν πάσχοντα

καὶ δεθεὶς διὰ τὸν κρατούμενον   750

καὶ κριθεὶς διὰ τὸν κατάδικον

καὶ ταφεὶς διὰ τὸν τεθαμμένον

101 ἀνέστη ἐκ νεκρῶν καὶ ταύτην ἐβόησεν τὴν φωνήν·

Τίς ὁ κρινόμενος πρὸς ἐμέ; ἀντιστήτω μοι.ˣ

ἐγὼ τὸν κατάδικον ἀπέλυσα·   755

ἐγὼ τὸν νεκρὸν ἐζωογόνησα·

ἐγὼ τὸν τεθαμμένον ἀνίστημι·

(102) τίς ὁ ἀντιλέγων μοι;

102 ἐγώ, φησὶν ὁ Χριστός,

733 A(B post 735)Gᵃ⁽ᵗ⁾L: om. C   734 vs. deperditum iudico
736 ABC(L): om. G   σου BC: om. A(super mortuos filios habet L)
737 ABCGᵃ: om. GᵗL   738 BC(Gᵃ)(L cf. 736): om. AGᵗ   πεφον. B:
filios add. C(L): pueros add. G   740 AGᵗL: om. BCGᵃ   αὐτοῦ AL:
domino Gᵗ   741 οὐκ ἐ[. . . A: non accepisti dominum Gᵗ: vs. om. BCGᵃL
742 ABCG: om. L   742 αὐ[τοῦ–746 ἐκεῖνος] paene deest A
743–7 cont. S¹   746–7 ἐκ-οὐρανῶν BCLS¹: ἐκ ν[εκρῶν καὶ ἀνέβη εἰς τὸν]
ουρανων vel simile breviore lacuna A: e mortuis et exaltatus ad caelum G
749–52 cont. S¹   749 παθὼν AB(G)S¹: mortuus est C   754 ἐμέ A: με B
756 ἐζωογόνησα (A prima manus)B: ἐζωοποίησα A corrector   758 ὁ B:
om. A   759 χ̅ς̅ A(Χριστός)C: χριστος χ̅ς̅ B

you were not terrified in the presence of the Lord,

⟨. . . . . .⟩

you did not lament over the Lord,   735

   so you lamented over your firstborn;

you did not tear your clothes when the Lord was hung,

   so you tore them over those who were slain;

you forsook the Lord,

   you were not found by him;   740

you did not accept the Lord,

   you were not pitied by him;

you dashed down the Lord,

   you were dashed to the ground.

00) And you lie dead,   745

   but he has risen from the dead

    and gone up to the heights of heaven.

100 The Lord, when he had clothed himself with man

   and suffered because of him that was suffering

   and been bound because of him that was held fast   750

   and been judged because of him that was condemned

   and been buried because of him that was buried,

101 arose from the dead and uttered this cry:

  '*Who takes issue with me?—let him stand against me.*

   I released the condemned;   755

   I brought the dead to life;

   I raise up the buried.

02)   Who is there that contradicts me?

102 I am the one', says the Christ,

^x Isa. 50: 8.

ἐγὼ ὁ καταλύσας τὸν θάνατον   760
καὶ θριαμβεύσας τὸν ἐχθρὸν[y]
καὶ καταπατήσας τὸν ᾅδην
καὶ δήσας τὸν ἰσχυρὸν[z]
καὶ ἀφαρπάσας τὸν ἄνθρωπον εἰς τὰ ὑψηλὰ τῶν οὐρανῶν·
ἐγώ, φησιν ὁ Χριστός.   765

103 τοίνυν δεῦτε πᾶσαι αἱ πατριαὶ τῶν ἀνθρώπων
αἱ ἐν ἁμαρτίαις πεφυραμέναι
καὶ λάβετε ἄφεσιν ἁμαρτημάτων.[a]
ἐγὼ γάρ εἰμι ὑμῶν ἡ ἄφεσις,
ἐγὼ τὸ πάσχα τῆς σωτηρίας,   770
ἐγὼ ὁ ἀμνὸς ὁ ὑπὲρ ὑμῶν σφαγείς·
ἐγὼ τὸ λύτρον ὑμῶν,
ἐγὼ ἡ ζωὴ ὑμῶν,[b]
ἐγὼ τὸ φῶς ὑμῶν,[c]
ἐγὼ ἡ σωτηρία ὑμῶν,   775
ἐγὼ ἡ ἀνάστασις ὑμῶν,[d]
ἐγὼ ὁ βασιλεὺς ὑμῶν·
ἐγὼ ὑμᾶς ἀναστήσω διὰ τῆς ἐμῆς δεξιᾶς·
ἐγὼ ὑμᾶς ἀνάγω εἰς τὰ ὑψηλὰ τῶν οὐρανῶν·
ἐκεῖ ὑμῖν δείξω τὸν ἀπ᾽ αἰώνων πατέρα.   780

104 Οὗτός ἐστιν ὁ ποιήσας τὸν οὐρανὸν καὶ τὴν γῆν
καὶ πλάσας ἐν ἀρχῇ τὸν ἄνθρωπον,
ὁ διὰ νόμου καὶ προφητῶν κηρυσσόμενος,
ὁ ἐπὶ παρθένῳ σαρκωθείς,

---

764 ἀφαρπάσας BC: καθαρμασας A   ὑψηλὰ B: ὕψη A   765 ὁ B: om.
A   766–78 cont. L   766 αἱ B: om. A   767 αἱ ἐν AC: λιν B
768 ἁμαρτημάτων B: ἁμαρτιῶν A   770 σωτηρίας B(A): *vestrae* add. C(G)
771 ὑμῶν σφαγις B: νεφαγεις A   772 λ[ύτρον A(Bonner, perpaucis in
lacuna restituendis): λουτρὸν BC: *liberatio* G: *redemptio* L   773 BCGL: om.
A   Post 773 pon. 776 BC   774 ABCG: om. L   775 ἡ σωτηρία
BCL: ὁ σω[τὴρ A: *liberator creaturarum* G   776 ἡ ἀν. ὑμῶν B: ὕμιν ἡ ἀν. A
777 ἐγὼ ὁ β. ὑμῶν B: [. . . . . . .] ὁ β. A   778–80 txt. C: ordinem 779,
780, 778 A: 779 (ἐγὼ ὑμᾶς ἀναστήσω add., cf. 778), 780, 778 B: 779, 780G:
778 L   779 τὰ ὑψηλὰ B: τ[ὰ ὕψη] A   780 ἐκεῖ BCG: ἐγὼ A
781 cont. L   781–9 cont. S¹ tunc desinit   781 ἐστιν ὁ ποιήσας
BCGLS¹: brevius A, ut ἐπ[οίησεν]   783 νόμου AC(G)S¹: νόμων B
784 ἐπὶ B(C): ε[A: e G: *in* S¹

'I am the one that destroyed death[60]   760
    and *triumphed over* the enemy
    and trod down Hades
    and *bound the strong one*
    and carried off man to the heights of heaven;
I am the one', says the Christ.   765

03 'Come then, all you families of men who are
        compounded with sins,
    and *get forgiveness of sins.*[61]
For I am your forgiveness,
    I am the Pascha of salvation,   770
    I am the lamb slain for you;
    I am your ransom,
    I am your *life,*
    I am your *light,*
    I am your salvation,   775
    I am your *resurrection,*
    I am your king.
I will raise you up by my right hand;
I am leading you up to the heights of heaven;
    there I will show you the Father from ages past.'   780

04 It is he that made heaven and earth
    and fashioned man in the beginning,
    who is proclaimed through the law and prophets,
    who was enfleshed upon a virgin,

ʸ Cf. Col. 2: 15.   ᶻ Matt. 12: 29 par.   ᵃ Acts 10: 43; 26: 18.
ᵇ Cf. John 11: 25; 14: 6.   ᶜ Cf. John 8: 12.   ᵈ Cf. John 11: 25.

---

[60] This hymnic passage resembles Hippolytus, *Apostolic Tradition* 4. 8 as well as various texts related to Melito such as Ps.-Epiphanius, *De resurrectione* 8 (Nautin p. 157); Fr. 13; New Fr. II. 14. There may be a common liturgical root (J. Kroll, *Gott und Hölle* (Leipzig, 1932) 1–125). The absence of extended mythology of the descent into Hades confirms the early date of *Peri pascha* (A. Grillmeier, *Zeitschrift für katholische Theologie* 71 (1949) 8–12).

[61] 103 is an invitation to baptism. But it should not be inferred with Perler (p. 204) that a baptismal rite follows the homily (R. Cantalamessa, *L'omelia 'In S. Pascha' dello pseudo-Ippolito di Roma* (Milan, 1967) 282–7).

ὁ ἐπὶ ξύλῳ κρεμασθείς,   785
ὁ εἰς γῆν ταφείς,
ὁ ἐκ νεκρῶν ἀνασταθεὶς
   καὶ ἀνελθὼν εἰς τὰ ὑψηλὰ τῶν οὐρανῶν,
ὁ καθήμενος ἐν δεξιᾷ τοῦ πατρός,
ὁ ἔχων ἐξουσίαν πάντα σώζειν,   790
δι' οὗ ἐποίησεν ὁ πατὴρ τὰ ἀπ' ἀρχῆς μέχρι αἰώνων.
105   οὗτός ἐστιν τὸ ᾱ καὶ τὸ ῶ·
οὗτός ἐστιν ἀρχὴ καὶ τέλος,ᵉ
   ἀρχὴ ἀνεκδιήγητος καὶ τέλος ἀκατάλημπτον·
οὗτός ἐστιν ὁ Χριστός·ᶠ   795
οὗτός ἐστιν ὁ βασιλεύς·
οὗτός ἐστιν Ἰησοῦς·
οὗτος ⟨ὁ⟩ στρατηγός·
οὗτος ὁ κύριος·
οὗτος ὁ ἀναστὰς ἐκ νεκρῶν·   800
οὗτος ὁ καθήμενος ἐν δεξιᾷ τοῦ πατρός·
   φορεῖ τὸν πατέρα καὶ ὑπὸ τοῦ πατρὸς φορεῖται·
   ᾧ ἡ δόξα καὶ τὸ κράτος εἰς τοὺς αἰῶνας. ἀμήν.

Μελίτωνος Περὶ πάσχα.

785–8 cont. L tunc desinit   785 ὁ A: om. B   787 ἀναστα]θεὶς A: ἀναστις B   788 εἰς] desinit A   790 πάντα σώζειν scripsi: πάντα κρινε σωζιν B: salvare C: discernendi vivos et mortuos G   Post 794 discrepat G   795 ἐστιν B: Iesus add. C cf. 797   797 B: vs. om. C   798 ὁ suppl. Testuz cum C: om. B   803 αἰῶνας B: aetates aetatum C   Post 804 ιρηνη τῷ γράψαντι καὶ τῷ ἀναγινώσκοντι καὶ τοῖς ἀγαπῶσι τὸν κν ἐν ἀφελότητι καρδίας add. B

who was hung upon a tree, 785
who was buried in the earth,
who was raised from the dead
   and went up to the heights of heave,
who sits at the Father's right hand,
who has power to save every man, 790
through whom the Father did his works from beginning to
                        eternity.

5 He is *the Alpha and the Omega*;
he is *beginning and end,*
   beginning inexpressible and end incomprehensible;
he is the Christ; 795
he is the king;
he is Jesus;
he is the captain;
he is the Lord;
he is the one who rose from the dead; 800
he is the one who sits at the Father's right hand;
   he carries the Father and is carried by the Father.
   To him be glory and power for ever. Amen.

Melito's *On Pascha*.

e Rev. 1: 8; 21: 6.   f John 7: 26, 41; Acts 9: 22.

Fragment 1*

4 Ἐν δὲ τῷ πρὸς τὸν αὐτοκράτορα βιβλίῳ τοιαῦτά τινα καθ᾽
ἡμῶν ἐπ᾽ αὐτοῦ γεγονέναι ἱστορεῖ·

5 Τὸ γὰρ οὐδεπώποτε γενόμενον, νῦν διώκεται τὸ τῶν θεοσεβῶν
γένος καινοῖς ἐλαυνόμενον δόγμασιν κατὰ τὴν Ἀσίαν. οἱ
γὰρ ἀναιδεῖς συκοφάνται καὶ τῶν ἀλλοτρίων ἐρασταὶ τὴν ἐκ   5
τῶν διαταγμάτων ἔχοντες ἀφορμήν, φανερῶς ληστεύουσι,
νύκτωρ καὶ μεθ᾽ ἡμέραν διαρπάζοντες τοὺς μηδὲν ἀδικοῦντας.

6 καὶ μεθ᾽ ἕτερά φησιν·
καὶ εἰ μὲν σοῦ κελεύσαντος τοῦτο πράττεται, ἔστω καλῶς
γινόμενον· δίκαιος γὰρ βασιλεὺς οὐκ ἂν ἀδίκως βουλεύσαιτο   10
πώποτε, καὶ ἡμεῖς ἡδέως φέρομεν τοῦ τοιούτου θανάτου τὸ
γέρας· ταύτην δέ σοι μόνην προσφέρομεν δέησιν ἵνα αὐτὸς
πρότερον ἐπιγνοὺς τοὺς τῆς τοιαύτης φιλονεικίας ἐργάτας,
δικαίως κρίνειας εἰ ἄξιοι θανάτου καὶ τιμωρίας ἢ σωτηρίας
καὶ ἡσυχίας εἰσίν. εἰ δὲ καὶ παρὰ σοῦ μὴ εἴη ἡ βουλὴ   15
αὕτη καὶ τὸ καινὸν τοῦτο διάταγμα, ὃ μηδὲ κατὰ βαρβάρων
πρέπει πολεμίων, πολὺ μᾶλλον δεόμεθά σου μὴ περιιδεῖν ἡμᾶς
ἐν τοιαύτῃ δημώδει λεηλασίᾳ.

7 τούτοις αὖθις ἐπιφέρει λέγων·
ἡ γὰρ καθ᾽ ἡμᾶς φιλοσοφία πρότερον μὲν ἐν βαρβάροις ἤκμασεν,   20
ἐπανθήσασα δὲ τοῖς σοῖς ἔθνεσιν κατὰ τὴν Αὐγούστου τοῦ
σοῦ προγόνου μεγάλην ἀρχήν, ἐγενήθη μάλιστα τῇ σῇ
βασιλείᾳ αἴσιον ἀγαθόν. ἔκτοτε γὰρ εἰς μέγα καὶ λαμπρὸν
τὸ Ῥωμαίων ηὐξήθη κράτος· οὗ σὺ διάδοχος εὐκταῖος
γέγονάς τε καὶ ἔσῃ μετὰ τοῦ παιδός, φυλάσσων τῆς βασιλείας   25
τὴν σύντροφον καὶ συναρξαμένην Αὐγούστῳ φιλοσοφίαν, ἣν
καὶ οἱ πρόγονοί σου πρὸς ταῖς ἄλλαις θρησκείαις ἐτίμησαν,

8 καὶ τοῦτο μέγιστον τεκμήριον τοῦ πρὸς ἀγαθοῦ τὸν καθ᾽ ἡμᾶς
λόγον συνακμάσαι τῇ καλῶς ἀρξαμένῃ βασιλείᾳ, ἐκ τοῦ

29 ἐκ τοῦ: τὸ legendum?

---

* For the text see pp. xxix, xlviii.

4 In his book to the Emperor[1] [Melito] relates that things of this
kind happened against us in his day:

5 Something that has never happened at all before, the race of the
godly is persecuted, being harassed by new decrees throughout
Asia.[2] For the shameless informers and lovers of other men's goods
are taking advantage of the ordinances to commit open robbery,
by night and day plundering those who do no wrong.

6 Later he says:
If it is at your command that this is done, let it count as rightly
happening! A just king would not ever purpose wrong, and we are
glad to win the prize of such a death. The only petition which we
make to you is this, that you first personally acquaint yourself with
those whose actions cause such strife, and fairly decide whether
they deserve death and punishment or safety and peace. But if in
fact you are not the source of this decision and this new ordinance,
which is not fit to be used even against barbarian enemies, then far
more we implore you not to leave us suffering such public pillage.

7 He adds further to this when he says:
Our philosophy first flourished among barbarians, but it blos-
somed out among your peoples during the great reign of your
ancestor Augustus, and became especially for your empire an
auspicious benefit. For from that time the power of Rome grew
to become great and splendid. To that power you have become
a successor desired in prayer, and will continue to be so, together
with your son, if you guard the philosophy of the empire which
was nursed with and began with Augustus, and which your
8 ancestors respected alongside the other cults. This also is the
surest proof that it was for good that our thinking flourished together with the empire which began so well—the fact that nothing

---

[1] The emperor is Marcus Aurelius. See Introduction, p. xii.

[2] The 'new decrees' which broke a long peace for Christians have been
variously interpreted, as by H. Grégoire, 'Nouvelles observations sur le nombre
des martyrs', *Bulletin de l'Académie royale* 38 (1952) 37–60 (decrees of the *Commune Asiae*); J. Zeiller, 'A propos d'un passage énigmatique de Méliton de
Sardes', *Revue des études augustiniennes* 2 (1956) 257–63 (imperial legislation
against disturbing peace by religious novelties). Note also the Senatusconsultum
of 176 or 177 permitting criminals to be used instead of gladiators; see J. H.
Oliver and R. E. A. Palmer, 'Minutes of an act of the Roman Senate', *Hesperia*
24 (1955) 320–49, criticized by T. D. Barnes in *JTS* N.S. 19 (1968) 517–19.

μηδὲν φαῦλον ἀπὸ τῆς Αὐγούστου ἀρχῆς ἀπαντῆσαι, ἀλλὰ   30
τοὐναντίον ἅπαντα λαμπρὰ καὶ ἔνδοξα κατὰ τὰς πάντων εὐχάς.

9 μόνοι πάντων, ἀναπεισθέντες ὑπό τινων βασκάνων ἀνθρώπων,
τὸν καθ᾽ ἡμᾶς ἐν διαβολῇ καταστῆσαι λόγον ἠθέλησαν Νέρων
καὶ Δομετιανός, ἀφ᾽ ὧν καὶ τὸ τῆς συκοφαντίας ἀλόγῳ
συνηθείᾳ περὶ τοὺς τοιούτους ῥυῆναι συμβέβηκεν ψεῦδος·   35

10 ἀλλὰ τὴν ἐκείνων ἄγνοιαν οἱ σοὶ εὐσεβεῖς πατέρες
ἐπηνωρθώσαντο, πολλάκις πολλοῖς ἐπιπλήξαντες ἐγγράφως,
ὅσοι περὶ τούτων νεωτερίσαι ἐτόλμησαν· ἐν οἷς ὁ μὲν
πάππος σου Ἀδριανὸς πολλοῖς μὲν καὶ ἄλλοις, καὶ Φουνδανῷ
δὲ τῷ ἀνθυπάτῳ, ἡγουμένῳ δὲ τῆς Ἀσίας, γράφων φαίνεται,   40
ὁ δὲ πατήρ σου, καὶ σοῦ τὰ σύμπαντα διοικοῦντος αὐτῷ,
ταῖς πόλεσι περὶ τοῦ μηδὲν νεωτερίζειν περὶ ἡμῶν ἔγραψεν,
ἐν οἷς καὶ πρὸς Λαρισαίους καὶ πρὸς Θεσσαλονικεῖς καὶ

11 Ἀθηναίους καὶ πρὸς πάντας Ἕλληνας. σὲ δὲ καὶ μᾶλλον
περὶ τούτων τὴν αὐτὴν ἐκείνοις ἔχοντα γνώμην καὶ πολύ γε   45
φιλανθρωποτέραν καὶ φιλοσοφωτέραν, πεπείσμεθα πάντα
πράσσειν ὅσα σου δεόμεθα.

Fragment 2*

Μελίτων Σαρδιανῶν ἐπίσκοπος μετὰ πολλὰ τῶν ἐπιδοθέντων
παρὰ τοῦ αὐτοῦ Ἰουστίνου φησίν·
Οὐκ ἐσμὲν λίθων οὐδεμίαν αἴσθησιν ἐχόντων θεραπευταί,
ἀλλὰ μόνου θεοῦ τοῦ πρὸ πάντων καὶ ἐπὶ πάντων καὶ τοῦ
Χριστοῦ αὐτοῦ ὄντος θεοῦ λόγου πρὸ αἰώνων ἐσμὲν
θρησκευταί,   5
καὶ τὰ ἑξῆς.

Fragment 3*

12 Ἐν δὲ ταῖς γραφείσαις αὐτῷ Ἐκλογαῖς ὁ αὐτὸς κατὰ τὸ
προοίμιον ἀρχόμενος τῶν ὁμολογουμένων τῆς παλαιᾶς

40 δὲ² om. pauci   41 σύμπαντα διοικ-: πάντα συνδιοικ- legendum
47 πράσσειν: πράξειν legendum?   3. 2 προοίμιον: αὐτῷ vel αὐτὸ add. alii

---

* For the text see pp. xxx, xlviii.

---

3 For the rescript see Justin, 1 Apology 68 and Eusebius, HE 4. 9.

4 It is possible that this passage either prompted the fabrication of the
Rescript to the Commune Asiae preserved in Eusebius, HE 4. 13 and in the manuscript of Justin's Apologies, or was itself prompted by a version of that rescript.

ignoble befell it from the rule of Augustus, but on the contrary
everything splendid and glorious in accordance with the prayer
9 of all. Alone among all, yielding to the persuasion of certain
malicious persons, Nero and Domitian were willing to subject our
thinking to slanderous attack; from that source, by unthinking
habit, the flood of false information against such people has come
10 about. But their ignorance was corrected by your religious fathers,
who many times rebuked in writing those many who dared to use
violence against these men. Among them, your grandfather
Hadrian clearly wrote to (besides many others) Fundanus the
proconsul, who was also governor of Asia;[3] and your father, while
you also were sharing the general administration with him, wrote
that no violence should be used in connection with us, notably
to the Larissans and to the Thessalonians and Athenians and to
11 all the Greeks.[4] And in your case, since you hold the same opinion
as they did concerning these men, and are in your humanity and
your philosophy far greater, we are even more convinced that you
will do all that we ask you.

Melito, bishop of Sardis, after many of the things which are also
produced by the same Justin,[5] says:
We are not devotees of stones which have no sensation, but we
are worshippers[6] of the only God who is before all and over all,
and of his Christ who is the Word of God before the ages,[7]
and so forth.

12 In the *Extracts* written by him, the same author in his preface
as he begins makes a catalogue of the acknowledged books of

The extant rescript is generally regarded as a Christian forgery, though it
could conceivably contain genuine elements. In the Justin manuscript it
purports to come from Antoninus Pius, and this fits Melito's description, but its
destination mentions only Asia, not Larissa, Athens, etc. In Eusebius it has the
name of Marcus Aurelius, despite the fact that Eusebius attributes it to Antoninus. If the rescript originally had Marcus Aurelius' name, it perhaps pur-
ported to be a favourable response to Melito. For documented discussion, see
notes of H. J. Lawlor and J. E. L. Oulton, *Eusebius bishop of Caesarea The ecclesiastical history and The martyrs of Palestine* ii (London, 1928, repr. 1954) 128-9;
G. Bardy, *Eusèbe de Césarée Histoire ecclésiastique* (SC 31, Paris, 1952) 177-8.

   [5] The compiler of the *Chronicon pascale* appears to have had a substantial and
perhaps complete copy of Melito's *Petition*, and found it in agreement with
Justin's *Apologies*.

   [6] As often among the Apologists, Melito seems to be rebutting a charge of
atheism; cf. Justin, *1 Apology* 6; Athenagoras, *Supplicatio* 4-10.

   [7] The terminology has biblical roots in Col. 1 : 17; Rom. 9 : 5; Ps. 2 : 2 (Acts
4 : 26); Rev. 19 : 13; 1 Cor. 2 : 7.

διαθήκης γραφῶν ποιεῖται κατάλογον· ὃν καὶ ἀναγκαῖον
καταλέξαι, γράφει δὲ οὕτως·

13 Μελίτων Ὀνησίμῳ τῷ ἀδελφῷ χαίρειν. ἐπειδὴ πολλάκις 5
ἠξίωσας, σπουδῇ τῇ πρὸς τὸν λόγον χρώμενος, γενέσθαι σοι
ἐκλογὰς ἔκ τε τοῦ νόμου καὶ τῶν προφητῶν περὶ τοῦ σωτῆρος
καὶ πάσης τῆς πίστεως ἡμῶν, ἔτι δὲ καὶ μαθεῖν τὴν τῶν
παλαιῶν βιβλίων ἐβουλήθης ἀκρίβειαν πόσα τὸν ἀριθμὸν καὶ
ὁποῖα τὴν τάξιν εἶεν, ἐσπούδασα τὸ τοιοῦτο πρᾶξαι, 10
ἐπιστάμενός σου τὸ σπουδαῖον περὶ τὴν πίστιν καὶ
φιλομαθὲς περὶ τὸν λόγον ὅτι τε μάλιστα πάντων πόθῳ τῷ πρὸς
τὸν θεὸν ταῦτα προκρίνεις, περὶ τῆς αἰωνίου σωτηρίας
14 ἀγωνιζόμενος. ἀνελθὼν οὖν εἰς τὴν ἀνατολὴν καὶ ἕως τοῦ
τόπου γενόμενος ἔνθα ἐκηρύχθη καὶ ἐπράχθη, καὶ ἀκριβῶς 15
μαθὼν τὰ τῆς παλαιᾶς διαθήκης βιβλία, ὑποτάξας ἔπεμψά σοι·
ὧν ἐστι τὰ ὀνόματα· Μωυσέως πέντε, Γένεσις Ἔξοδος
Ἀριθμοὶ Λευιτικὸν Δευτερονόμιον, Ἰησοῦς Ναυῆ, Κριταί, Ῥούθ,
Βασιλειῶν τέσσαρα, Παραλειπομένων δύο, Ψαλμῶν Δαυίδ,
Σολομῶνος Παροιμίαι ἡ καὶ Σοφία, Ἐκκλησιαστής, Ἇισμα 20
Ἀισμάτων, Ἰώβ, Προφητῶν Ἡσαΐου Ἰερεμίου τῶν δώδεκα
ἐν μονοβίβλῳ Δανιὴλ Ἰεζεκιὴλ Ἔσδρας· ἐξ ὧν καὶ τὰς
ἐκλογὰς ἐποιησάμην, εἰς ἓξ βιβλία διελών.

Fragment 4*

3 Ἐν μὲν οὖν τῷ Περὶ τοῦ πάσχα τὸν χρόνον καθ᾽ ὃν
συνέταττεν, ἀρχόμενος σημαίνει ἐν τούτοις·
Ἐπὶ Σερουιλλίου Παύλου ἀνθυπάτου τῆς Ἀσίας ᾧ Σάγαρις

10 εἶεν: εἰδέναι   12 μάλιστα delendum?   18 Ἀριθμοὶ Λευιτικὸν:
inv.   20 ἡ καὶ: καὶ vel καὶ ἡ   4. 3 Σερουιλλίου: Σεργίου

* For the text see pp. xxx, xlviii.

8 One cannot identify Onesimus with the bishop of Ephesus of that name
(Ignatius, *Ephesians* 1) because a more honorific designation than *brother* would
be expected (J. B. Lightfoot, *The Apostolic Fathers* II. ii (London², 1889) 32).
9 Cf. the title and opening of Fr. 15, where there is similar reference to law
and prophets, with Christ as subject and faith in the title.
10 If St. Paul's journeys are excluded, Melito was the first recorded Christian
pilgrim to Palestine. A. D. Nock (*JTS* N.S. 11 (1960) 63–4 n. 4) regards the
visit as a literary figment: 'It was hardly necessary to go to Palestine to get the

the Old Covenant, which we must also detail here. He writes
thus:

13 Melito to Onesimus[8] his brother, greeting. Inasmuch as you
have often made request, in the zeal which you show for the
word, to be made possessor of extracts from both the law and
the prophets concerning the Saviour and all our faith,[9] and
further have desired also to be precisely informed about the
ancient books, both as to their number and as to their arrangement,
I was zealous to do such a thing, recognizing your zeal for the
faith and studious application to the word, and that you prefer
these things more than any in your love to God, as you strive
14 for eternal salvation. So, going back to the east and reaching the
place where it was proclaimed and done,[10] I got precise information about the books of the Old Covenant,[11] of which I now send
you a list.[12] Their names are: Of Moses five, Genesis, Exodus,
Numbers, Leviticus, Deuteronomy; Jesus son of Nave;[13] Judges;
Ruth; of Kingdoms, four; of Omissions, two;[14] of Psalms, David;
of Solomon, Proverbs (called also Wisdom),[15] Ecclesiastes, Song of
Songs; Job; of the prophets, Isaiah, Jeremiah, The Twelve in one
book, Daniel, Ezekiel, Esdras.[16] From these I have also made the
extracts, dividing them into six books.

3 In his book *On the Pascha*[17] he indicates at the beginning the time
when he composed it in these words:
Under Servillius Paulus,[18] proconsul of Asia, at the time when

facts.' But this underestimates the likely difficulties, since local Asiatic Jews
would probably not be cooperative. The truth of Melito's claim is supported by
the character of his list of books, and by the evidence of *PP* 93–4; see p. 53
n. 55, and n. 12 below.

[11] This biblical expression (2 Cor. 3: 14) is here first used to refer to the
Bible itself, the Old Testament.

[12] Melito's list nearly agrees with the Hebrew canon, probably fixed by the
rabbis at Jamnia between A.D. 70 and 100, but omitting Esther. The order
accords, with some exceptions, with Greek patristic and synodical lists. See
tables in H. B. Swete, *An Introduction to the Old Testament in Greek* (Cambridge²,
1902) 200–14.

[13] i.e. Joshua.

[14] i.e. 1 and 2 Chronicles.

[15] Eusebius, *HE* 4. 22. 9, clearly attests the common use of the title Wisdom
for Proverbs in the earliest Christian period. Melito seems to know what we call
the Wisdom of Solomon (*PP* 18–30 and notes), but does not mention it here.

[16] i.e. Ezra–Nehemiah.

[17] On the relation of this fragment to *PP* see Introduction, pp. xix–xxi.

[18] Probably either L. Sergius Paulus or Q. Servilius Pudens; see Introduction,
pp. xxi–xxii.

καιρῷ ἐμαρτύρησεν, ἐγένετο ζήτησις πολλὴ ἐν Λαοδικείᾳ
περὶ τοῦ πάσχα, ἐμπεσόντος κατὰ καιρὸν ἐν ἐκείναις ταῖς
ἡμέραις, καὶ ἐγράφη ταῦτα. 5

4 τούτου δὲ τοῦ λόγου μέμνηται Κλήμης ὁ Ἀλεξανδρεὺς ἐν
ἰδίῳ περὶ τοῦ πάσχα λόγῳ, ὃν ὡς ἐξ αἰτίας τῆς τοῦ
Μελίτωνος γραφῆς φησιν ἑαυτὸν συντάξαι.

Fragment 5*

Μελίτων γοῦν ὁ ἐν τῇ Ἀσίᾳ φησὶν αὐτὸν εἶναι τύπον τοῦ
διαβόλου ἐπαναστάντος τῇ Χριστοῦ βασιλείᾳ, καὶ τούτου
μόνου μνησθεὶς οὐκ ἐπεξειργάσατο τὸν τόπον.

Fragment 6*

228D Ὁ θεῖος καὶ πάνσοφος ἐν διδασκάλοις Μελίτων, ἐν τῷ
περὶ σαρκώσεως Χριστοῦ λόγῳ τρίτῳ, λίαν ἐπιμέμφεται
ἐξηγητὴν τὸν βουλόμενον ἐκ τῶν μετὰ τὸ βάπτισμα ὑπὸ
Χριστοῦ πραχθέντων παραστῆσαι ἢ πιστώσασθαι τὸ ἀληθὲς
τῆς ψυχῆς ἢ τοῦ σώματος αὐτοῦ ἢ τῶν φυσικῶν καὶ 5
ἀναμαρτήτων αὐτοῦ πραγμάτων· λέγω δὴ πείνης, δίψης,
ὕπνου, δακρύου, πτύσματος, ἱδρῶτος, ἐκκρίσεως τῆς διὰ
ῥινός, καὶ ἐκκρίσεως καὶ ἀποβολῆς τῆς φθειρομένης καὶ
πεττομένης βρώσεως καὶ πόσεως φυσικῶς· οὐ μόνον δέ,
ἀλλὰ καὶ τῶν κατὰ ψυχὴν ὁμοίως ἀδιαβλήτων καὶ φυσικῶν 10
229A ἡμῖν ὄντων, τοῦτ’ ἔστι τῆς λύπης καὶ ἀγωνίας καὶ ἀθυμίας.
φησὶ γὰρ κατὰ Μαρκίωνος συντάττων ὁ θεόσοφος Μελίτων,
ἀπηρνεῖτο γὰρ καὶ ὁ Μαρκίων καθάπερ Σευῆρός τε καὶ
Γαϊανὸς τὴν ἔνσαρκον Χριστοῦ οἰκονομίαν, τὰς αὐτὰς
προτάσεις καὶ χρήσεις εὐαγγελικὰς ἅσπερ νῦν οὗτοι πρὸς 15
ἡμᾶς οἱ Μαρκίωνος τοῦ Ποντικοῦ μαθηταί· πρὸς ὃν λίαν
ἐχεφρόνως ὁ Μελίτων ἀπεκρίνατο φάσκων ὡς
Οὐδεμία ἀνάγκη τοῖς νοῦν ἔχουσιν ἐξ ὧν μετὰ τὸ βάπτισμα
ὁ Χριστὸς ἔπραξε παριστᾶν τὸ ἀληθὲς καὶ ἀφάνταστον τῆς
ψυχῆς αὐτοῦ καὶ τοῦ σώματος τῆς καθ’ ἡμᾶς ἀνθρωπίνης 20
φύσεως. τὰ γὰρ μετὰ τὸ βάπτισμά, φησιν, ὑπὸ Χριστοῦ
πραχθέντα, καὶ μάλιστα τὰ σημεῖα, τὴν αὐτοῦ κεκρυμμένην

---

* For the text see pp. xxx, xlviii.

Sagaris bore witness,[19] there was a great dispute at Laodicea[20] about the Pascha, which had coincided according to season in those days;[21] and these things were written.

4 Clement of Alexandria mentions this work in his own work *On the Pascha*, which he says he composed because of Melito's writing.[22]

Melito of Asia says that he[23] is a model of the devil who rebelled against the kingdom of Christ. Having simply mentioned this, he does not add any further detail on the passage.

The divine and all-wise among teachers Melito, in his third book about the incarnation of Christ,[24] seriously blames an exegete who wants, on the basis of what was done by Christ after the baptism, to set out or demonstrate the reality of his soul or body or of his natural and sinless functions, I mean of hunger, thirst, sleep, weeping, spittle, sweat, dripping from the nose, and emission and excretion of the corrupt and digested food and drink in a natural manner. Not only that, but also of those functions of the soul which are similarly blameless and natural, i.e. sorrow and conflict and depression. For writing against Marcion the divinely wise Melito says (for Marcion also, like Severus and Gaianus,[25] denied the fleshly economy of Christ, posing the same problems and gospel texts as these present disciples of Marcion of Pontus put to us), against him Melito very sagely replied:
There is no need to illustrate to the intelligent from what Christ did after the baptism the real and non-imaginary nature of his soul and body, of his human nature like ours. For (he says) what was done by Christ after the baptism, and especially the signs, showed

[19] Referring either to the actual time when Sagaris was martyred, or to his anniversary festival.

[20] Laodicea in Asia, addressed in Rev. 3: 14–22, was the place of Sagaris' burial (Eusebius, *HE* 5. 24. 5).

[21] The meaning is quite obscure.

[22] See also *HE* 6. 13. 9. Clement may be Eusebius' source for the 'quotation', and indeed for all his information about Melito's *On the Pascha*.

[23] Origen is discussing the identity of Absalom in the title to Psalm 3.

[24] From this it has been wrongly deduced that Melito composed a three-book work called *On the Incarnation of Christ*.

[25] Anastasius' real argument is with the theology associated with the sixth-century writers, Severus the great Monophysite of Antioch, and Gaianus the Aphthartodocetic patriarch.

ἐν σαρκὶ θεότητα ἐδήλουν καὶ ἐπιστοῦντο τῷ κόσμῳ. θεὸς
229B γὰρ ὢν ὁμοῦ τε καὶ ἄνθρωπος τέλειος ὁ αὐτὸς τὰς δύο αὐτοῦ
οὐσίας ἐπιστώσατο ἡμῖν· τὴν μὲν θεότητα αὐτοῦ διὰ τῶν   25
σημείων ἐν τῇ τριετίᾳ τῇ μετὰ τὸ βάπτισμα· τὴν δὲ
ἀνθρωπότητα αὐτοῦ ἐν τοῖς τριάκοντα χρόνοις τοῖς πρὸ τοῦ
βαπτίσματος, ἐν οἷς διὰ τὸ ἀτελὲς τὸ κατὰ σάρκα ἀπέκρυβε
τὰ σημεῖα τῆς αὐτοῦ θεότητος, καίπερ θεὸς ἀληθὴς
προαιώνιος ὑπάρχων.   30

Fragment 7*

Μελίτωνος ἐπισκόπου Σάρδεων ἐκ τοῦ λόγου τοῦ εἰς τὸ
πάθος·
Ὁ θεὸς πέπονθεν ὑπὸ δεξιᾶς Ἰσραηλίτιδος.

Fragment 8a*

Τὰ γὰρ Εἰρηναίου τε καὶ Μελίτωνος καὶ τῶν λοιπῶν τίς
ἀγνοεῖ βιβλία, θεὸν καὶ ἄνθρωπον καταγγέλλοντα τὸν Χριστόν;

Fragment 8b*

Μελίτωνος ἐπισκόπου Σάρδεων Περὶ λουτροῦ

1 Ποῖος δὲ χρυσὸς ἢ ἄργυρος ἢ χαλκὸς ἢ σίδηρος πυρωθεὶς
οὐ βαπτίζεται ὕδατι, ὁ μὲν αὐτῶν ἵνα φαιδρυνθῇ διὰ τῆς
χρόας, ὁ δὲ ἵνα τονωθῇ διὰ τῆς βαφῆς; ἡ δὲ σύμπασα γῆ
ὄμβροις καὶ ποταμοῖς λούεται, καὶ λουσαμένη καλῶς   5
γεωργεῖται. ὁμοίως καὶ ἡ Αἰγυπτιακὴ γῆ λουσαμένη ποταμῷ
πληθύνοντι αὔξει μὲν τὸ λήϊον, πληροῖ δὲ τὸν στάχυν,
ἑκατοντάχοα δὲ γεωργεῖ διὰ καλοῦ λουτροῦ. ἀλλὰ μὴν καὶ
αὐτὸς ὁ ἀὴρ λούεται ταῖς τῶν ψεκάδων καταπομπαῖς.
λούεται καὶ ἡ τῶν ὄμβρων μήτηρ πολυανθὴς ἶρις, ὁπόταν   10
κατὰ ῥευμάτων κυρτώσῃ ποταμούς, ὑδραγωγῷ πνεύματι
προσκαλουμένη.

8b. 2 χαλκὸς A: -οῦς V   11 κυρτώσῃ V: κυρωσει A: κυρτωθῇ Wilamowitz
12 προσκαλουμένη AV: προκ- Wilamowitz

* For the text see pp. xxxi–xxxii, xlviii–xlix.

and proved to the world his godhead hidden in flesh. For the same one being at once God and perfect Man, he proved his two essences to us: his godhead through the signs in the three years after the baptism, and his manhood in the thirty seasons before the baptism,[26] when because of his fleshly immaturity he hid the signs of his godhead, although he was true God pre-eternally existing.

Melito bishop of Sardis, from his work *On the passion*:[27]
God has suffered by an Israelite right hand.[28]

For who does not know the books of Irenaeus and Melito and the rest, which proclaim Christ as God and Man?

Melito bishop of Sardis, On baptism

1 What sort of[29] gold or silver or bronze or iron is not made red hot and dipped in water, in one case to be brightened by the colour, in another to be tempered by the dipping? The whole earth, too, bathes in rains and rivers, and after bathing yields well. So also the land of Egypt after bathing in a swollen river increases its corn, fills out its ear, and yields a hundredfold through the goodly bathing. Yes, and even the air itself is bathed by the descents of the rain-drops. The many-coloured rainbow, the mother of rains, also bathes, when she swells rivers down channels, summoning them with water-laden breath.

---

[26] This distinction, implying that each nature was exhibited exclusively in the period described, is difficult to parallel.

[27] This title was at first adopted for *PP* because of the citation following. See Introduction, p. xvii.

[28] *PP* 96 (716) has slightly different wording.

[29] Theophilus, *Ad Autolycum* I. 12, uses the same kind of question and some remarkably similar examples on the subject of chrism.

2 Εἰ δὲ βούλῃ τὰ οὐράνια θεάσασθαι βαπτιζόμενα, ἐπείχθητι
νῦν ἐπὶ τὸν ὠκεανόν, κἀκεῖ σοι δείξω θέαμα καινόν· πέλαγος
ἀναπεπταμένον καὶ θάλασσαν ἀόριστον καὶ ἀπείρητον βυθὸν   15
καὶ ἀμέτρητον ὠκεανὸν καὶ ὕδωρ καθαρόν, τὸ τοῦ ἡλίου
βαπτιστήριον καὶ τὸ τῶν ἀστρῶν λαμπ⟨ρυν⟩τήριον καὶ τὸ τῆς
σελήνης λουτρόν. τὸ δὲ πῶς λούονται μυστικῶς παρ᾽ ἐμοῦ
μάθε πιστῶς.

3 Ἥλιος μέν, διανύσας τὸν τῆς ἡμέρας δρόμον πυρίνοις   20
ἱππεύμασι, τῇ περιδινήσει τοῦ δρόμου πυροειδὴς γενόμενος
καὶ ὡς λαμπὰς ἐξαφθείς, διακαύσας δὲ τὴν μέσην τοῦ δρόμου
ζώνην, ὡς, ἂν πλήσιον ὀφθῇ, δέκα ἀκτινοβόλοις ἀστραπαῖς
καταφλέξαι τὴν γῆν δυσωπούμενος κάτεισιν εἰς τὸν ὠκεανόν.
καθάπερ σφαῖρα χαλκῆ, πυρὸς ἔνδοθεν γέμουσα, πολὺ φῶς   25
ἀναστράπτουσα, λούεται ἐν ὕδατι ψυχρῷ μέγα ἠχοῦσα,
λαμπρυνομένη δὲ †απαυγει†· τὸ δὲ πῦρ ἔνδοθεν οὐ σβέννυται,
ἀλλὰ πάλιν ἀναστράπτει ἀνακαυθέν· οὕτω δὴ καὶ ὁ ἥλιος,
πεπυρωμένος ὡς ἀστραπή, ὅλως οὐ τελευτῶν λούεται ἐν ὕδατι
ψυχρῷ, ἀκοίμητον ἔχων τὸ πῦρ· λουσάμενος δὲ βαπτίσματι   30
μυστικῷ σφόδρα εὐφραίνεται, τὸ ὕδωρ ἔχων τροφήν. εἷς δὲ
καὶ αὐτὸς ὤν, ὡς καινὸς τοῖς ἀνθρώποις ἀνατέλλει ἥλιος,
τετονωμένος ἐκ βυθοῦ, κεκαθαρμένος ἐκ λουτροῦ· τὸ δὲ
νυκτερινὸν ἐξελάσας σκότος λαμπρὰν ἐγέννησεν ἡμέραν.
Κατὰ δὲ τὸν τούτου δρόμον καὶ ἡ τῶν ἄστρων κίνησις καὶ ἡ   35
τῆς σελήνης φάσις ἐνεργεῖ. λούονται γὰρ εἰς τὸ τοῦ ἡλίου
βαπτιστήριον ὡς καλοὶ μαθηταί. οἱ γὰρ ἀστέρες μετὰ τῆς
σελήνης κατ᾽ ἴχνος τοῦ ἡλίου διώκουσιν, καθαρὰν ἕλκοντες
αὐγήν.

4 Εἰ δὲ ἥλιος σὺν ἄστροις καὶ σελήνη λούεται ἐν ὠκεανῷ,   40
διὰ τί καὶ ὁ Χριστὸς ἐν Ἰορδάνῃ οὐ λούεται; βασιλεὺς
οὐρανῶν καὶ κτίσεως ἡγεμών, ἥλιος ἀνατολῆς, ὃς καὶ τοῖς
ἐν ᾅδου ἐφάνη καὶ τοῖς ἐν κόσμῳ βροτοῖς, καὶ μόνος ἥλιος
οὗτος ἀνέτειλεν ἀπ᾽ οὐρανοῦ.

13 ἐπιχθητι A : ἐπαχθητι V   17 λαμπ⟨ρυν⟩τήριον Wilamowitz : λαμπτηριον
AV   20 διανύσας A : -οισας V : -οίξας Perler   21 περιδινήσει V : παραδ- A
22 διακαύσας V : διασώσας A   23 ὀφθῇ A : οφθηται V   δέκα AV : δοκεῖ
Wilamowitz   25 καθάπερ V : ἔνθαπερ A   27 απαυγει A : ἐπ᾽ αὐγῇ V :
ἀπ᾽ αὐγῆς Pitra coni. : ἀπαυγεῖ Wilamowitz : ἀπολείπει legendum?   29 οὐ

2 If you wish to observe the heavenly bodies being baptized, make haste now to the Ocean, and there I will show you a strange sight:[30] outspread sea, and boundless main, and infinite deep, and immeasurable Ocean, and pure water; the sun's swimming-pool,[31] and the stars' brightening-place, and the moon's bath. And how they symbolically bathe, learn faithfully from me.

3 When the sun has with fiery chariotry fulfilled the day's course, having in the whirling of his course become like fire and flared up like a torch, and when he has blazed through his course's meridian, (then) as though reluctant, if he should appear close by, to burn up the land with ten radiant lightning-shafts, he sinks into the Ocean. Just as a ball of bronze, full of fire within, flashing with much light, is bathed in cold water, making a loud noise, and in the polishing process stops glowing; yet the fire within is not quenched, but flares up again when roused: just so also the sun, inflamed like lightning, wholly undying bathes in cold water, but keeps his fire unsleeping; and when he has bathed in symbolic baptism, he exults greatly, taking the water as food. Though one and the same, he rises for men as a new sun, tempered from the deep, purified from the bath; he has driven off the nocturnal darkness, and has begotten bright day. Along his course, both the movement of the stars and the appearance of the moon operate. For they bathe in the sun's swimming-pool like good disciples; for the stars with the moon pursue the sun's track, soaking up pure brilliance.

4 Now if the sun, with stars and moon, bathes in Ocean, why may not Christ also bathe in Jordan?[32] King of heavens and creation's Captain, Sun of uprising who appeared both to the dead in Hades and to mortals in the world, he also alone arose a Sun out of heaven.

[30] A similar expression appears in *PP* 19; but even closer similarities appear in Theophilus, *Ad Autolycum* I. 13, where resurrection is argued from the monthly resurrection of the moon.

[31] One might translate 'baptistery', a meaning probably partly intended in line 37.

[32] Misgivings about the propriety of Christ's baptism are already indicated by Matt. 3: 14. Later it was rejected by Marcion, whose gospel began at Luke 4: 31, and by sects who identify Christ with the divine spirit or power who descended on Jesus at or after his baptism, such as the Ophites in Irenaeus, *Haer.* I. 30. 13–14.

AV: del. Wilamowitz   36 φάσις scripsi: φύσις A: φύσει V   38 ἕλκοντες
A: ἔχοντες V   43 ἐφάνη V: φαίνει A

Fragment 9*

Τοῦ μακαρίου Μελίτωνος Σάρδεων·
Ὡς γὰρ κριὸς ἐδέθη,
φησὶ περὶ τοῦ κυρίου ἡμῶν Ἰησοῦ Χριστοῦ,
καὶ ὡς ἀμνὸς ἐκάρη
καὶ ὡς πρόβατον εἰς σφαγὴν ἤχθη^a   5
καὶ ὡς ἀμνὸς ἐσταυρώθη·
καὶ ἐβάστασε τὸ ξύλον ἐπὶ τοῖς ὤμοις αὐτοῦ
ἀναγόμενος σφαγῆναι ὡς Ἰσαὰκ ὑπὸ τοῦ πατρὸς αὐτοῦ.^b
ἀλλὰ Χριστὸς ἔπαθεν, Ἰσαὰκ δὲ οὐκ ἔπαθεν·
τύπος γὰρ ἦν τοῦ μέλλοντος πάσχειν Χριστοῦ.   10
ἀλλὰ καὶ ὁ τύπος τοῦ Χριστοῦ γενόμενος
ἔκπληξιν καὶ φόβον παρεῖχεν τοῖς ἀνθρώποις.

ἦν γὰρ θεάσασθαι μυστήριον καινόν,
υἱὸν ἀγόμενον ὑπὸ τοῦ πατρὸς ἐπ᾽ ὄρος εἰς σφαγήν,
ὃν συμποδίσας ἔθηκεν ἐπὶ τὰ ξύλα τῆς καρπώσεως^c   15
ἑτοιμάζων μετὰ σπουδῆς τὰ πρὸς τὴν σφαγὴν αὐτοῦ.
ὁ δὲ Ἰσαὰκ σιγᾷ πεπεδημένος ὡς κριός,
οὐκ ἀνοίγων τὸ στόμα οὐδὲ φθεγγόμενος φωνῇ.^d
τὸ γὰρ ξίφος οὐ φοβηθεὶς
οὐδὲ τὸ πῦρ πτοηθεὶς   20
οὐδὲ τὸ παθεῖν λυπηθεὶς
ἐβάστασεν καρτερῶν τὸν τύπον τοῦ κυρίου.
ἦν οὖν ἐν μέσῳ προκείμενος Ἰσαὰκ πεποδισμένος ὡς κριός,
καὶ Ἀβραὰμ παρεστὼς καὶ κρατῶν γυμνὸν τὸ ξίφος,^e
οὐκ αἰδούμενος φονεῦσαι τὸν υἱὸν αὐτοῦ.   25

7 αὐτοῦ om. permulti   10 Χριστοῦ om. pauci   13–25 om. plerique

---

* For the text of Frs. 9–12 see pp. xxxii–xxxiv, xlix.

---

³³ In *PP* 64 and Frs. 10. 2 and 11. 6 the same unusual wording εἰς σφαγήν appears; cf. also *PP* 4.

³⁴ Isaac carrying the firewood anticipated Christ bearing the cross. For the typology cf. Irenaeus, *Haer.* 4. 5. 4, and more especially Tertullian, *Adv. Marcionem* 3. 18. 2; *Adv. Judaeos* 10. 6. Melito is the earliest known example of this exegesis.

³⁵ God the Father is typologically represented by Abraham, reflecting New Testament ideas (John 3 : 16; Acts 2 : 23; and especially Rom. 8 : 23, see C. K. Barrett, *A Commentary on the Epistle to the Romans* (London, 1957) 172).

Of blessed Melito of Sardis:
For as a ram he was bound
(he says concerning our Lord Jesus Christ),
   and *as a lamb* he was shorn,
   and as a sheep he was led to slaughter,[33]
   and as a lamb he was crucified;
and he carried the wood on his shoulders[34]
   as he was led up to be slain like Isaac by his Father.[35]
But Christ suffered, whereas Isaac did not suffer;
   for he was a model of the Christ who was going to suffer.
But by being merely the model of Christ
   he caused astonishment and fear among men.[36]
For it was a strange mystery to behold,[37]
   a son led by his father to a mountain for slaughter,
   whose feet he bound and whom he put on the wood of the
                                     offering,
   preparing with zeal the things for his slaughter.
But Isaac was silent, bound like a ram,
   not opening his mouth nor uttering a sound.[38]
For not frightened by the sword
   nor alarmed at the fire
   nor sorrowful at the suffering,
he carried with fortitude the model of the Lord.[39]
Thus Isaac was offered in the midst[40] foot-bound like a ram,
   and Abraham stood by and held the sword unsheathed,
      not ashamed to put to death his son.

---

[a] Isa. 53: 7.   [b] Cf. Gen. 22: 6; John 19: 17.   [c] Cf. Gen. 22: 9.
[d] Isa. 53: 7.   [e] Gen. 22: 10.

---

[36] The astonishing nature of the deed is not biblical, but found already in Philo, *De Abrahamo* 193. It is emphasized as pointing to the even more amazing sacrifice of Christ (D. Lerch, *Isaaks Opferung christlich gedeutet* (Tübingen, 1950) 30–2).

[37] Similarly *PP* 19, 29, etc.

[38] The absence of any words of Isaac in Gen. 22: 8–13 leads to the assertion that he was silent, like Christ at his trial and the lamb of Isa. 53: 7. Jewish exegesis emphasized Isaac's assent (G. Vermes, *Scripture and tradition in Judaism* (Studia postbiblica 4, Leiden, 1961) 193–204), and Melito sees the same idea in his silent assent. Cf. D. Lerch, loc. cit.

[39] Not just carrying the wood, but enduring all that pointed typologically to Christ (D. Lerch, op. cit. 32).

[40] Apparently suggesting a public act, contrary to the Genesis text but in keeping with lines 11–12 above. The same phrase occurs of Christ's death in the middle of Jerusalem in *PP* 94, and cf. the emphatic reference to Jerusalem in Fr. 11. 5.

Fragment 10

Μελίτωνος Σάρδεων·

Ὑπὲρ Ἰσαὰκ τοῦ δικαίου ἐφάνη κριὸς εἰς σφαγήν,
ἵνα δεσμῶν Ἰσαὰκ λυθῇ.[a]
ἐκεῖνος σφαγεὶς ἐλυτρώσατο τὸν Ἰσαάκ·
οὕτως καὶ ὁ κύριος σφαγεὶς ἔσωσεν ἡμᾶς   5
καὶ δεθεὶς ἔλυσε
καὶ τυθεὶς ἐλυτρώσατο.

4 σφαγεὶς : σφαγῆς pauci

Fragment 11

Καὶ μετ᾽ ὀλίγα·

Ἦν γὰρ ὁ κύριος ἀμνὸς ὡς ⟨ὁ⟩ κριός,
ὃν εἶδεν Ἀβραὰμ κατεχόμενον ἐν φυτῷ Σαβέκ.[a]
ἀλλὰ τὸ φυτὸν ἀπέφαινε τὸν σταυρόν,
καὶ ὁ τόπος ἐκεῖνος τὴν Ἰερουσαλήμ,
καὶ ὁ ἀμνὸς τὸν κύριον ἐμπεποδισμένον εἰς σφαγήν.   5

2 ἀμνὸς : ὁ ἀ. edd.   ὁ ante κριός suppl. Pitra

Fragment 12

Τοῦ αὐτοῦ·

Τὸ Κατεχόμενος τῶν κεράτων[a] ὁ Σύρος καὶ ὁ Ἑβραῖος
Κρεμάμενός φησιν, ὡς σαφέστερον τυποῦν τὸν σταυρόν.
ἀλλὰ καὶ τὸ Κριὸς[a] τοῦτο ἀκριβοῖ· οὐ γὰρ εἶπεν Ἀμνός,
νέος ὡς ὁ Ἰσαάκ, ἀλλὰ Κριός, ὡς ὁ κύριος, τέλειος.   5
ὥσπερ δὲ φυτὸν Σαβέκ,[a] τοῦτ᾽ ἔστιν ἀφέσεως, ἐκάλεσε τὸν
ἅγιον σταυρόν, οὕτω καὶ Ἰεζεκιὴλ ἐν τῷ τέλει ὕδωρ ἀφέσεως[b]

---

[41] The deliverance of Isaac by the slaughter of the ram foreshadows the deliverance of mankind by the death of Christ (D. Lerch, op. cit. 33–4). This develops a hint in Fr. 9 (lines 2 and 17) that Christ is represented by the ram as well as by Isaac; but F. Nikolasch goes too far in suggesting that this double representation corresponds to the two natures of Christ (*Das Lamm als Christussymbol in den Schriften der Väter* (Vienna, 1963) 27). Note similarities to *PP* 100–2; Fr. 13. 36–9.

Of Melito of Sardis:
On behalf of Isaac the righteous one, a ram appeared for slaughter,
  so that Isaac might be released from bonds.
That ram, slain, ransomed Isaac;
so also the Lord, slain, saved us,
  and bound, released us,
  and sacrificed, ransomed us.[41]

And a little further on:
For the Lord was a lamb like the *ram*
  which *Abraham saw caught in a Sabek-tree.*
But the tree displayed the cross,[42]
  and that place, Jerusalem,[43]
  and the lamb, the Lord fettered for slaughter.

Of the same:
Caught by the horns the Syriac and Hebrew express as *hanged*, which
prefigures in the plainest way the cross.[44] But the word *ram* also
makes this explicit: it did not say *a lamb*, young like Isaac, but
a ram, full-grown like the Lord.[45] And just as it called the holy
cross *a tree of Sabek*, that is *of forgiveness*,[46] so Ezekiel near the end

^a Cf. Gen. 22: 13.   ^b Ezek. 47: 3.

---

[42] The Greek fathers generally interpret the φυτὸν Σαβέκ as a tree which
signifies the cross; see F. Nikolasch, op. cit. 25–40.

[43] Isaac was offered on Mount Moriah (Gen. 22: 2), which tradition identified with the site of the Jerusalem temple (2 Chron. 3: 1); some Jews saw the
offering of Isaac as a prototype of the temple sacrifices (G. Vermes, *Scripture and
tradition in Judaism* (Leiden, 1961) 208–11). Melito may have done the same,
though D. Lerch deduces the contrary (*Isaaks Opferung christlich gedeutet* (Tübingen, 1950) 35).

[44] *Caught* (κατεχόμενος) in fact renders the Hebrew correctly, and *hanged*,
though easier to interpret typologically of Christ, is wrong. The writer must
have in mind some reading of the Syriac or Aramaic (called *Hebrew*) versions;
but both the Peshitta and the Targum of Ps.-Jonathan agree with the Greek.

[45] The exegesis of *ram* as *full-grown* is unusual; parallels adduced by F.
Nikolasch (op. cit. 58–60) are inexact.

[46] The two words φυτὸν σαβέκ represent the single Hebrew word *ṣbak*, which
means *bush* or *thicket*. The writer here mistakenly traces σαβέκ to the Aramaic
and Syriac *shbaq*, a verb meaning *release* or *forgive*.

ἐκάλεσε τὸ ἐκτυποῦν τὸ ἅγιον βάπτισμα. δύο γὰρ συνέστη τὰ ἄφεσιν ἁμαρτημάτων παρεχόμενα, πάθος διὰ Χριστὸν καὶ βάπτισμα. 10

9 παρεχόμενα : χαριζόμενα

called what expressed the holy baptism *the water of forgiveness*. For two things constitute provision for the forgiveness of sins: suffering for Christ, and baptism.[47]

[47] For early examples of the view that martyrdom could give or repeat the benefits of baptism, see *Martyrdom of S. Perpetua* 18. 3; 21. 2–3; Tertullian, *Apology* 50; Origen, *Exhortation to martyrdom* 30. E. Lohse, *Märtyrer und Gottesknecht* (Göttingen, 1955) has a valuable *Exkurs* (pp. 211–13), in which he emphasizes that this fragment, if by Melito, would be the earliest example.

Fragment 13*

Melito, Bishop of Sardis, from his treatise On Soul and Body:[48]
For this reason the Father sent his incorporeal Son from heaven,[49]
so that, enfleshed in the virgin's womb and born as man,
he might bring man to life and gather his parts,
which death had scattered when he divided man. 　　　　5
And further on:
The earth quaked and its foundations shook,[50]
the sun fled and the elements turned away,
and the day was changed;
for they could not bear ⟨to see⟩[51] their Lord hanging on a tree. 　10
And creation, shuddered, stupefied, and said,
'What can this strange mystery be?
The judge is judged, and is silent;
the invisible is seen, and is not ashamed;
the incomprehensible is seized, and is not vexed; 　　　　15
the immeasurable is measured, and does not resist;
the impassible suffers, and does not retaliate;
the immortal dies, and takes it patiently;
the heavenly one is buried, and submits.
What is this strange mystery?' 　　　　　　　　　20
Creation was stupefied.
But when our Lord arose from the dead,
having trodden down death
and bound the strong one
and released man, 　　　　　　　　　　　　　25

* For the text see p. xlix.

---

[48] On this title and the contents see Introduction, pp. xxxiv–xxxvii.
[49] For lines 2–5 see New Fr. II. 4 (32–8) and notes.
[50] For lines 7–40 see New Fr. II. 11–14 and notes. The Greek is reconstructed by Richard 316–17: Ἐτρόμησεν ἡ γῆ . . . ἔφυγεν ὁ ἥλιος ⟨καὶ⟩ τὰ στοιχεῖα ἀπεστράφη, καὶ ἡ ἡμέρα ἠλλοιώθη. (10) οὐ γὰρ ἐβάσταζον ὁρῶντες τὸν ἑαυτῶν δεσπότην κρεμάμενον ἐπὶ ξύλου. ἐξεπλάγη ἡ κτίσις ξενιζομένη καὶ λέγουσα· Τί ἄρα εἴη τοῦτο τὸ καινὸν μυστήριον; ὁ κριτὴς κρίνεται καὶ σιωπᾷ· ὁ ἀόρατος ὁρᾶται καὶ οὐκ ἐπαισχύνεται. (15) ὁ ἀκράτητος κρατεῖται καὶ οὐκ ἀγανακτεῖ. ὁ ἀμέτρητος μετρεῖται καὶ οὐκ ἀντιτάσσεται· ὁ ἀπαθὴς πάσχει καὶ οὐκ ἀνταποδίδωσιν· ὁ ἀθάνατος θνήσκει καὶ καρτερεῖ· ὁ ἐν οὐρανοῖς θάπτεται καὶ ὑπομένει. (20) τί τοῦτο τὸ καινὸν μυστήριον; . . . ἀλλ' ὁ κύριος ἀνέστη ἐκ νεκρῶν, καταπατήσας τὸν θάνατον καὶ δήσας τὸν ἰσχυρὸν (25) καὶ λύσας τὸν ἄνθρωπον . . .
[51] Words restored from Greek and parallel texts.

then all creation understood that it was for man's sake[52]
that the judge was judged
   and the invisible was seen
   ⟨and the incomprehensible was seized,⟩[53]
   and the immeasurable was measured,   30
   and the impassible suffered,
   and the immortal died,
   and the heavenly one was buried.
For our Lord, having become man,
   was judged in order to bestow kindness,   35
   was bound in order to release,
   was seized in order to set free,
   suffered in order to have compassion,
   died in order to make alive,
   was buried in order to raise up.   40

Fragment 14*

The same, from the treatise On the Cross:[54]
For this cause he came to us;
for this cause, though incorporeal,[55]
   he wove himself a body of our texture.[56]
He was seen as a lamb, but remained a shepherd;   5
he was reputed a servant, but did not refuse the rank of Son;
carried in the womb by Mary, and clothed with his Father;[57]
treading the earth, and filling heaven;
appearing as a boy, and not falsifying the eternity of his nature;[58]
wearing a body, and not restricting the simplicity of his divine
                               nature; 10
seen as poor, and not depriving himself of his wealth;
wanting food, inasmuch as he was man,
   and not ceasing to nourish the world, inasmuch as he was God;

* For the text see pp. xxvii, xlix.

---

[52] These words, vital for the purpose of Fr. 13, are not in New Fr. II. 13. But
they are probably original, being attested by the *Additamentum* (Nautin 59. 34)
and the Coptic homily (fo. 160b col. 1; Budge p. 272).

[53] Line supplied by editors, but apparently wanting in parallel texts also.

[54] No work of Melito by this name is otherwise known, but the title at the
head of New Fragments should be compared.

[55] Compare Fr. 13. 2.

[56] Fr. 14 repeatedly uses the imagery of clothing in relation to the incarnation, a device also repeated in *PP* 47, 66, 100.

[57] Cf. *PP* 105 (803).

[58] References to Christ's eternal, divine, or unchangeable nature are elements
in the fragment unlikely to come from Melito.

putting on the likeness of a servant,
    and not changing his likeness to the Father.   15
He was all things with his nature immutable.
He stood before Pilate, and sat with the Father;
He was fastened to the tree, and held the universe.

Fragment 15*

Melito the bishop, On Faith.[59, 60]
From the law and the prophets we have collected the things
which are proclaimed about our Lord Jesus Christ, so that we
may demonstrate to your affection that he is perfect mind, the
Word of God who was *begotten before the morning star*.[a61] He is 5
the Creator [with the Father], the shaper of 'man[62] who was *all
things in all*:[b63]
[who was] among patriarchs a patriarch,
[who was] in the law a law,
    among the priests a chief of priests,   10
    among the kings the captain,
    among the prophets a prophet,
    among the angels an angel,[64]
in the utterance a Word,
    among spirits a Spirit,[65]   15
in the Father a Son,[66]

* For the text see pp. xxxvii–xxxviii, xlix–l.

---

[a] Ps. 110 (109 LXX): 3.   [b] 1 Cor. 15: 28.

[59] On the title see Introduction, p. xvi.
[60] Most sources attribute a form of this text to Irenaeus. Words and phrases
peculiar to the 'Irenaeus' form are printed in diamond brackets. Words
peculiar to the Melito text-form, if unlikely to be original, are printed in
square brackets. Instead of lines 2–4 the 'Irenaeus' form reads: ⟨The law, the
prophets, and the gospels proclaimed that Christ was born from a virgin, and
suffered on a tree, and was seen from the dead, and ascended into heaven, and
was glorified by the Father; and he is perfect mind . . .⟩. The Greek appears in a
catena published by M. Richard; see *Le Muséon* 86 (1973) 265: Ὁ νόμος καὶ
οἱ προφῆται καὶ τὰ εὐαγγέλια ἐκήρυξαν τὸν Χριστὸν γεννηθέντα ἐκ παρθένου καὶ
παθητὸν ἐπὶ ξύλου καὶ ὁρατὸν ἐκ νεκρῶν καὶ εἰς οὐρανοὺς ἀνερχόμενον καὶ ὑπὸ τοῦ
πατρὸς δοξαζόμενον καὶ βασιλέα εἰς τοὺς αἰῶνας. The last phrase corresponds to
line 18 or 70 of the Fragment.
[61] Cf. *PP* 82 (594).   [62] Cf. *PP* 82 (607).   [63] Cf. *PP* 9 (54).
[64] 'Irenaeus' has here been followed where the Melito text-form has *chief of
angels*.
[65] Instead of lines 14–15 'Irenaeus' has *among men a Man*, which Nautin regards
as a theological 'improvement'; Richard 332–3 judges all three lines original.
[66] With lines 16–17 cf. *PP* 105 (803); Fr. 14. 6–7; Fr. 16b.

in God a God,
King for ever and ever.
It is he that steered Noah,[67, 68]
who led Abraham,   20
who was with Isaac bound,
who was with Jacob exiled,
who was with Joseph sold,
who was with Moses a captain,
⟨who gave the people the law,⟩   25
who with Joshua son of Nun divided the inheritance,
who in David and in the prophets predicted his sufferings,
who was enfleshed in a virgin,[69]
who was born in Bethlehem,
who in the manger was swathed with bandages,   30
who was recognized by shepherds,
who was praised by angels,
who was worshipped by magi,
who was preached beforehand by John,
⟨and was baptized in Jordan,⟩   35
⟨who was tempted in the desert,⟩
⟨who was found to be the Lord,⟩
who gathered the apostles,
who preached the kingdom,
who cured the lame,[70]   40
⟨who cleansed the lepers,⟩

[67] For lines 19–27 there are close parallels in *PP* 59, 69; New Fr. II. 3; cf.
also *PP* 61–5, 83–5.

[68] For a Greek reconstruction of lines 19–69, see Richard 324–7: . . . ὁ τὸν
Νῶε κυβερνήσας, (20) ὁ τὸν Ἀβραὰμ ὁδηγήσας, ὁ τῷ Ἰσαὰκ συνδεθείς, ὁ τῷ
Ἰακὼβ συγξενιτεύσας, ὁ τῷ Ἰωσὴφ συμπαθείς, ὁ τῷ Μωυσεῖ συστρατηγήσας, (25) ὁ
(τὸν λαὸν) νομοθετήσας, (. . .) αὐτὸν κληροδοτήσας, ὁ ἐν παρθένῳ σαρκωθείς, ὁ ἐν
Βηθλεὲμ γεννηθείς, (30) ὁ ἐν φατνῇ σπαργανωθείς, ὁ ὑπὸ ποιμένων γνωρισθείς, ὁ ὑπ᾽
ἀγγέλων ὑμνηθείς, ὁ ὑπὸ μάγων προσκυνηθείς, ὁ ὑπὸ Ἰωάννου προκηρυχθείς, (35) ὁ
ἐν Ἰορδάνῃ βαπτισθείς, ὁ ἐν ἐρήμῳ πειρασθείς, ὁ κύριος εὑρεθείς, ὁ τοὺς ἀποστόλους
συναθροίσας, ὁ βασιλείαν οὐρανῶν ἀναδείξας, (40) ὁ τοὺς χωλοὺς θεραπεύσας, ὁ
τοὺς λεπροὺς καθαρίσας, ὁ τοὺς τυφλοὺς φωταγωγήσας, ὁ τοὺς νεκροὺς ἀναστήσας,
ὁ ἐν τῷ ναῷ ὀφθείς, (45) ὁ ὑπὸ τοῦ λαοῦ ἀπιστηθείς, ὁ ὑπὸ Ἰουδαίων παραδοθείς, ὁ
ὑπὸ ἀρχιερέων συλληφθείς, ὁ ὑπὸ Ἡρώδου προαχθείς, ὁ ὑπὸ Πιλάτου ἀνακριθείς,
(50) ὁ ἐν σαρκὶ προσηλωθείς, ὁ ἐπὶ ξύλου κρεμασθείς, καὶ ἐκ νεκρῶν ἀναστάς, (55) ὁ
εἰς τοὺς οὐρανοὺς ἀναλημφθείς, ὁ ἐν δεξιᾷ τοῦ πατρὸς καθήμενος. . . . ἡ ἀνάστασις
τῶν τεθανατωμένων, ἡ σωτηρία τῶν ἀπολλυμένων, (62) ὁ ὁδηγὸς τῶν πεπλανημένων, ἡ καταφυγὴ τῶν ἀπεγνωσμένων, ὁ ποιμὴν τῶν σωζομένων, (65) ὁ νυμφίος
τῆς ἐκκλησίας, ὁ ἡνίοχος τῶν χερουβίμ, ὁ ἀρχιστράτηγος τῶν ἀγγέλων, θεὸς ἐκ
θεοῦ, υἱὸς τοῦ πατρός.

[69] Cf. *PP* 70 (489); 104 (784); Fr. 16b. 4.

[70] For lines 40–3 see *PP* 72 (508–11).

who gave light to the blind,
who raised the dead,
who appeared in the temple,
who was not believed by the people,[71]   45
who was betrayed by Judas,
who was arrested by the priests,
⟨who was led before Herod,⟩
who was judged by Pilate,
who in the flesh was nailed up,   50
who was hung on a tree,[72]
who was buried in earth,
who arose from the dead,
who appeared to the apostles,
who was taken up to the heavens,   55
who sits at the Father's right,
and by him is glorified.
He is the repose[73] of the dead,[74]
the finder of the lost,
the light of those who are in darkness,   60
the redeemer of the captives,
the guide of the wanderers,
the refuge of the forlorn,
⟨the shepherd of those who are saved,⟩
the bridegroom of the Church,[75]   65
the charioteer of the cherubim,
the chief of the army of angels,
God from God,
Son from the Father,
Jesus Christ, King for ever. Amen.   70

Fragment 16b*

Μελίτωνος ἐπισκόπου Σάρδεων ἐν τῷ ⟨περὶ⟩ τῆς κυριακῆς λόγῳ·
Τίς γὰρ ἔγνω νοῦν κυρίου ἢ τίς σύμβουλος αὐτοῦ ἐγένετο;[a]

* For the text see pp. xxxviii, l.

---

[71] With lines 45–50 cf. PP 92–3.
[72] For lines 51–2 see PP 70 (490–1), 104 (785–6).
[73] i.e. ἀνάπαυσις, cf. Matt. 11 : 29. The Greek has *resurrection*; cf. New Fr. II.
19 (189).
[74] For this and most remaining lines see New Fr. II. 19, where other parallel
texts are cited.
[75] For the thought cf. Fr. 17. 5.

ἢ ὁ λόγος ὁ ἐν παρθένῳ σαρκωθεὶς
καὶ εἰς γῆν τεθεὶς
καὶ ἐκ νεκρῶν ἀναστάς,   5
ὁ εἰς οὐρανοὺς ὑψωθεὶς
καὶ ἐν πατρὶ δοξασθείς.

Of Melito Bishop of Sardis, in his work On the Lord's day:[76]
For who knows the mind of the Lord, or who was his counsellor?[a]—
except the Word, who was enfleshed in a virgin[77]
and was put in earth
and arose from the dead,   5
who was lifted up to heaven
and was glorified in the Father.

Fragment 17*

Ὑμνήσατε τὸν πατέρα οἱ ἅγιοι·
ᾄσατε τῇ μητρὶ παρθένοι.
Ὑμνοῦμεν, ὑπερυψοῦμεν ἅγιοι.
Ὑψώθητε νύμφαι καὶ νυμφίοι,
ὅτι ηὕρατε τὸν νυμφίον ὑμῶν Χριστόν.   5
εἰς οἶνον πίετε, νύμφαι καὶ νυμφίοι, . . .

---

6 οἶνον: αἶνον Perler

Hymn the Father, you holy ones;[78]
sing to your Mother, virgins.
We hymn, we exalt (them) exceedingly, we holy ones.
You have been exalted to be brides and bridegrooms,   5
for you have found your bridegroom, Christ.
Drink for wine, brides and bridegrooms, . . .

* For the text see pp. xxxviii–xxxix, l.

---

a Isa. 40: 13; Rom. 11: 34.

---

76 The title appears in Eusebius' list; see Introduction p. xiii. The whole
fragment so resembles Hesychius of Jerusalem, *Homily on Pascha* I. 5. 17–20 (SC
187 p. 66) that some literary connection is certain.
77 Lines 3–7 resemble elements in *PP* 74, 104; Fr. 15.
78 The fragment is apparently a ritual dialogue after some kind of initiation
ceremony. See Introduction, p. xxxviii.

New Fragments I–III*

I   Word of Athanasius[1] the bishop on the truth of the holy
    cross and upon which (?) Christ suffered.
    Hear words of truth[2]
    and parables of doctrines
    and utterances of prophets   5
    and words of peace
    and thoughts of the Father
    and the preparation of the Lamb
    and the building of churches
    and the appearing of the cross.[3]   10
    It is better for you if you hear
    and obey these words on hearing;
    but better for us,[4] at God the Father's command and by the
                              appearing of Christ,
    to say and teach also the slavery of this our body.
    And utter voices . . .   15

II. 1 . . . from the beginning the Word of the Father, loving mankind,
    descended because of man and lived with them,
    and separated the bad from the just,
    and revealed the just as a heavenly people.
  2 With some he was killed,[5]   5
    with some he was an exile,
    with some he was put to flight,
    with some he was sawn apart,
    with some he was in a ship,
    with some he was flogged,   10
    with some he was tempted,
    with some he was sold,
    with some he was in hunger and thirst.

---

  * For texts see pp. xxxix, l.

  [1] *Athanasius* vE: *holy Athanasius* L.

  [2] A homily with this *incipit* is attributed to Alexander of Alexandria in the lemma to a Syriac fragment (see Van Esbroeck 92–3). But the fragment which it introduces is from *Peri Pascha* (S²) and not from this homily.

  [3] The repeated emphasis on church-building and on the cross in these fragments refers to the festival of 13–15 September, when the Elevation of the Cross (associated with the foundation of various churches) was celebrated at Jerusalem, which is also repeatedly mentioned. These elements may have been added at a late date to the original homily, since the festival commemorates the events of A.D. 629; though some are perhaps original, and attracted the attention of those seeking ancient homilies for a collection concerned with the festival (Van Esbroeck 94–5).   [4] I have altered *vos* of L into *us*.

  [5] With the typology of II. 2–3 cf. *PP* 59; 69; Fr. 15. 18–27.

3 And so from the beginning the Word suffered with all the just,
   and will be with (them) for ever.   15
   With Abel he was killed,
   with Noah he was in the water-flood,
   with Abraham [he was] on pilgrimage,
   with [Isaac he was offered],
   with [Jac]ob he was an exile,   20
   with Joseph he was sold,
   and with Moses he was in flight,
   and with Jesus son of Nave he was at war;
   with David he was in flight,
   with Isaiah he was sawn apart,   25
   and in his own body he lived among these.
4 He put on a body from a virgin because of men,
   he who is Word with you;
   and God is Word,
   and Word is Man,   30
   and Man is with God.
   For God visited his own creation,[6]
   which he had made in his image and likeness.
   He sent out his own Son from heaven to earth incorporeal,
   and he took a body from a virgin.   35
   He was born a man,
   and he raised up lost man
   and gathered his scattered members.[7]
   And why does Christ die?[8]
5 Was there no need for the judgement of death?[9]   40
   Or why [does he take flesh?]
   Was he not [clothed in glo]ry?
   Or [why] did he become man?
   Was he not God?
   Or why did he descend to earth?   45
   Was he not King in heaven?
6 Why did it concern God,
   descent to earth,

---

[6] Lines 32–8 occur in the witnesses to Alexander, *De anima* (PG 18. 595A–B; *Additamentum*, Nautin 58. 1–5; etc.) and, abbreviated, at the beginning of Fr. 13.

[7] Cf. *PP* 55–6.

[8] Lines 39–56 agree closely with Alexander, *De anima* (PG 18. 595B–6D). Lines 39–67 agree with *Additamentum* (Nautin 58. 5–59. 15) and the paraphrase of 'Athanasius' fos. 153b–154b (Budge pp. 266–7).

[9] Better with the other witnesses to read: 'Did he deserve the punishment of death?'

and conception in the body from a virgin,
and wrapping in bandages, 50
and laying in a manger,
and sucking milk in a mother's bosom,
and baptism in Jordan by John,
and mockery on the wood of the cross,[10]
and burial in earth, 55
and resurrection from the dead on the third day,
and the building of the churches?

7 What was the concern for man?
But so that these lost men might be saved,
thou hast given thyself for redemption,[11] 60
soul for soul
⟨and body for body,⟩[12]
and blood for blood,
man for man,
and death for death. 65
[The death which man owed[13]
Christ paid by his] de[ath.]

8 See Israel's repayment![14, 15]
They slew the helper of Jews;[16]
they repaid bad for good 70
and misery for joy
and death for life;
him who raised their dead
and healed the lame
and cleansed the lepers 75

[10] The *Additamentum* text of lines 52–4 is preferable: 'taking milk at the breast, being baptized in Jordan, being mocked by the people, being fixed on the tree'.

[11] For the Greek of 60–5 see Ps.-Epiphanius, *De resurrectione* 1 (Nautin 155. 6–7): δοὺς λύτρον ψυχὴν ἀντὶ ψυχῆς καὶ σῶμα ἀντὶ σώματος, ὅλον ἄνθρωπον ἀντὶ ἀνθρώπου (65) καὶ θάνατον ὑπέρ θανάτου.

[12] Line wanting in Georgian, supplied from *Additamentum* and Greek.

[13] For the Greek of lines 66–7 see Ps.-Epiphanius, *De resurrectione* 1 (Nautin 155. 4–5): ὅνπερ ὤφειλεν θάνατον ὁ ἄνθρωπος, τοῦτον ἔλυσεν ὁ Χριστὸς ἀποθανών.

[14] For the Greek of lines 68–77 see Richard 323 = Ps.-Epiphanius, *De resurrectione* 3 (Nautin 155. 11–16): ὁ ἀσεβὴς λαὸς τῶν Ἰουδαίων ἀπέκτειναν τὸν ἑαυτῶν εὐεργέτην, (70) ἀποδόντες αὐτῷ πονηρὰ ἀντὶ ἀγαθῶν καὶ θλίψιν ἀντὶ χαρᾶς καὶ θάνατον ἀντὶ ζωῆς. τὸν γὰρ ἐγείροντα τοὺς νεκροὺς αὐτῶν καὶ θεραπεύοντα τοὺς χωλοὺς (76) καὶ φωταγωγοῦντα τοὺς τυφλούς, τοῦτον ἀπέκτειναν κρεμάσαντες ἐπὶ ξύλου.

[15] With lines 68–85 cf. witnesses to Alexander, *De anima* (PG 18. 597B–8D; 'Athanasius' fos. 155b–156b (Budge 268–9)); *PP* 90; 72.

[16] The other witnesses read: 'their own benefactor'.

and restored light to their blind[17]
him they slew by hanging on a tree.
9 O strange and unspeakable mystery![18, 19]
They hung on a tree him who founded the earth,
they fixed with nails on a cross ⟨him who fixed the world,⟩   80
and they prepared burial for him who measured the heavens,
and they bound him who frees from sin,
and they gave him vinegar to drink who gives drinks of justice,
and fed with gall him who saves and feeds with salvation;
[they disfigured hands and feet of him who] heals [their] hands
                                                    and feet.[20] 85
10 O strange and unspeakable mystery,[21, 22]
that the judge was judged,
and he who loosed the bound was bound,
and he who created the world was fixed with nails,[23]
and he by whom heaven and earth are measured was measured,[24] 90
and he who gives creatures life ⟨died⟩,
and he who raises the dead was buried.

---

[17] caecis L: eorum add. vE.

[18] For the Greek of 78–85 see Ps.-Epiphanius De resurrectione 4 (Nautin 155. 16–22): ἴδετε οἱ ἄνθρωποι, ἴδετε πᾶσαι αἱ πατριαὶ τὰ καινὰ τολμήματα· ἐκρέμασαν τὸν κρεμάσαντα τὴν γῆν, (80) καὶ προσέπηξαν ξύλῳ τὸν πήξαντα τὸν κόσμον, καὶ ἐμέτρησαν τὸν μετρήσαντα τοὺς οὐρανούς, καὶ ἔδησαν τὸν λύσαντα τοὺς ἁμαρτωλούς, καὶ ἐπότισαν ὄξος τὸν ποτίσαντα δικαιοσύνην, καὶ ἐψώμισαν χολὴν τὸν ψωμίσαντα ζωήν, (85) καὶ ἠφάνισαν χεῖρας καὶ πόδας τοῦ θεραπεύσαντος αὐτῶν χεῖρας καὶ πόδας.

[19] The Greek, supported by Alexander (PG 18. 598B) and 'Athanasius' (fo. 156a col. 1), has: 'See, you men, see, all you families, the unprecedented audacities!'

[20] The Greek, supported by Alexander (PG 18. 598D) and 'Athanasius' (fo. 156b col. 2) adds: 'and they forced him to shut his eyes who had made them see again, and they buried him who had raised their dead' (Nautin 155. 22–3: καὶ ἠνάγκασαν καμμύσαι τὸν ποιήσαντα αὐτοὺς ἀναβλέψαι, καὶ ἔθαψαν τὸν ἐγείραντα τοὺς νεκροὺς αὐτῶν).

[21] For the Greek of 86–92 see Ps.-Epiphanius, De resurrectione 5 (Nautin 155. 24–157. 4): ὦ μυστηρίου καινοῦ καὶ θαύματος παραδόξου· ἐκρίθη ὁ κριτής, καὶ ἐδήθη ὁ λύων τοὺς πεπεδημένους, καὶ προσεπάγη ὁ πήξας τὴν γῆν, καὶ ἐκρεμάσθη ὁ κρεμάσας τὸν κόσμον, (90) καὶ ἐμετρήθη ὁ μετρήσας τοὺς οὐρανούς, καὶ ἐψωμίσθη χολὴν ὁ ψωμίσας ζωήν, καὶ ἀπέθανεν ὁ ζωογονῶν τὰ πάντα, καὶ ἐτάφη ὁ ἀνιστῶν τοὺς νεκρούς.

[22] Lines 86–153 appear, with some omissions, in the Additamentum (Nautin 59. 16–43), and much expanded in 'Athanasius' fos. 156b–161a (Budge 269–73). With II. 10 generally cf. PP 96.

[23] The Greek, supported by 'Athanasius' fo. 157a col. 1, adds: 'and he that hung the world was hung.'

[24] The Greek, supported by the Additamentum (Nautin 59. 18–19) adds: 'and he who fed with life was fed with gall.'

11　Then the powers of heaven were astonished,[25, 26]
　　and angels shuddered,
　　and the armies of heaven were afraid,　　　　　　　　　95
　　and the mountains were shaken,[27]
　　and the hills jumped;
　　the sea became calm,
　　and the deeps trembled,
　　and God's whole creation was afraid;　　　　　　　　　100
　　stars withheld their light,
　　the sun was darkened,[28]
　　and angels horrified quit the temple,
　　and seraphim cried out with their noise,
　　[the ve]il was torn,　　　　　　　　　　　　　　　105
　　and shadows filled all the earth.
12　When the Saviour shut his eyes upon the cross,
　　light shone in hell;
　　because the Lord descended to destroy hell,
　　not in body but in soul;　　　　　　　　　　　　110
　　because the Lord descended and ravished all hell with his soul,
　　but with his body the earth.
　　When they hung on the tree the Lord with his body,[29]
　　then tombs opened,
　　and hell was destroyed,　　　　　　　　　　　　115
　　and he released many souls,
　　and dead men arose;
　　and creation could not bear it,[30, 31]

---

[25] For the Greek of lines 93–4 see Ps.-Epiphanius *De resurrectione* 7 (Nautin 157. 10–11): τότε οἱ ἄγγελοι ἐξενίσθησαν καὶ αἱ δυνάμεις τῶν οὐρανῶν ἐξεπλάγησαν. Richard 312 deduces a different wording from Ps.-Chrysostom, *In ascensionem hom.* iii (*PG* 52. 797).

[26] The portents of II. 11 appear in much briefer form in Melito Fr. 13. 7–10, and more fully in other witnesses (see n. 22 above). To these should be added for lines 93–117 Alexander, *De anima* (*PG* 18. 599B–602A). Cf. also *PP* 97–8.

[27] For the Greek of lines 96–106 see Richard 313 (based on Ps.-Chrysostom, *In ascensionem hom.* iii, in *PG* 52. 797): ἐτρόμησε γὰρ ἡ γῆ, ἐκινήθη ἡ θάλασσα, ἐκλυδωνίσθη ἡ ἄβυσσος, (100) πᾶσα ἡ κτίσις ἐταράχθη. ἐφοβήθησαν φωστῆρες οὐρανῶν, ἔφυγεν ὁ ἥλιος καὶ ἡ σελήνη, ἀστέρες ἐξέλιπον, ἡμέρα οὐχ ὑπέμεινεν, ἄγγελος ἐξήλατο τεταραγμένος τοῦ ναοῦ, (105) περιεσχισμένου τοῦ καταπετάσματος τοῦ οἴκου. σκότος ἐπλήρωσε τὴν γῆν.

[28] The Greek, supported by other witnesses, adds: 'stars failed, day could not endure it.'

[29] For the Greek of lines 113–17 see Ps.-Epiphanius, *De resurrectione* 6 (Nautin 157. 5–6): τοῦ γὰρ κυρίου κρεμαμένου ἐπὶ τοῦ ξύλου ἐρράγησαν οἱ τάφοι, (115) καὶ ὁ ᾅδης ἠνεῴχθη, καὶ ἀνέστησαν νεκροί, καὶ ἐξήλλοντο ψυχαί.

[30] For the Greek of lines 118–28 see Richard 316. Lines 118–19 are recon-

because they saw their own Lord hung on the cross.
13 The whole creation shuddered, and they said,   120
'What is this new creation?'[32]
The judge is judged and is silent;
the invisible is seen on the cross and is not ashamed;
the infinite is con[tained and does not complain],[33]
[the im]passible suffers and does not [seek vengeance],   125
the immortal dies and [says nothing],
the King of heaven is buried and endures it.
What is this strange mystery?'
For all creation was astonished and trembled.
But the Lord arose from the dead,[34]   130
and then creation knew that the judge had been judged,
and the invisible had been seen,[35]
and the impassible had suffered,
the immortal had died,
and the heavenly one had been buried in the earth.   135
14 And the Lord was born a man[36]
and was judged in order to pity man,
he was bound in order to loose,
he was flogged in order to pardon,
he suffered passion for you by the cross to free you from passions, 140
he died by the cross to make you alive by the cross,
he was buried to raise you.
Because the Lord suffered in the likeness of men[37]
by that likeness [the passions of mankind were destroyed];

structed from Ps.-Chrysostom, *In ascensionem hom.* iii (*PG* 52. 797), the remainder
direct from Ps.-Epiphanius, *De resurrectione* 7 (Nautin 157. 12–17): οὐ γὰρ
ἐβάσταζον ὁρῶντες τὸν ἑαυτῶν δεσπότην κρεμάμενον ἐπὶ ξύλου. (120) ἐξεπλάγη ἡ
κτίσις ξενιζομένη καὶ λέγουσα· Τί ἄρα εἴη τοῦτο τὸ καινὸν μυστήριον; ὁ κριτὴς
κρίνεται καὶ σιωπᾷ· ὁ ἀόρατος ὁρᾶται καὶ οὐκ ἐπαισχύνεται. ὁ ἀκράτητος κρατεῖται
καὶ οὐκ ἀγανακτεῖ. ὁ ἀμέτρητος μετρεῖται καὶ οὐκ ἀντιτάσσεται. (125) ὁ ἀπαθὴς
πάσχει καὶ οὐκ ἀνταποδίδωσιν· ὁ ἀθάνατος θνῄσκει καὶ καρτερεῖ· ὁ ἐν οὐρανοῖς
θάπτεται καὶ ὑπομένει. τί τοῦτο τὸ καινὸν μυστήριον;

31 Lines 118–42 are attested, with divergences, by Fr. 13 as well as by other
witnesses already noted.

32 *creation* vE : *mysterium* L.

33 The Greek and other sources add : 'the immeasurable is measured and
does not resist.'

34 For this line cf. Ps.-Epiphanius, *De resurrectione* 8 (Nautin 157. 18): ἀλλ' ὁ
βουλήσει παθὼν κύριος ἀνέστη ἐκ τῶν νεκρῶν.

35 Fr. 13 and 'Athanasius' (fo. 160b col. 1) here add : (*and*) *the immeasurable
had been measured*. But the two *Additamentum* texts agree with the Georgian here,
and the omission may be deliberate.

36 With this and following lines compare *PP* 100.

37 With this and following lines compare *PP* 66.

he slew [death] with death.

15 He perceived the taste of death and pitied those
who were below in the condemnation[38] of death.
He was buried and he raised the dead,
just as [our Saviour] gave life to [the prisoners]
and led them to light.   150
But death he destroyed and slew;[39]
therefore the Lord descended from heaven[40] to earth,
to put death to death and to break his head like a murderer's.

16 What is this strange mystery?[41, 42]
Or for what did you descend from heaven,   155
but for men?
For in all the world your good image was dispersed.
Yet, had you but given the word,
all bodies would have stood before you.
But you came to earth   160
and sought the lost who are your creatures,
and restored again Adam and a royal treasure.

17 And [every race of men] has received life from Christ.[43]
One was judged and many were saved.[44]
One was buried and many arose.   165
The Lord died for all and rose for all,
and he put on humanity,
[ascended] to the heights, to heaven,
and offered the Father a gift,
not gold nor silver nor precious pearls,   170
but man, whom he made in his image
and perfected in his likeness.

---

[38] *condemnation* vE : *umbra* L.

[39] *and slew* om. L : add. vE.

[40] *from heaven* om. L : add. vE.

[41] For the Greek of lines 154–6 see Ps.-Epiphanius, *De resurrectione* 7 (Nautin 157. 17): τί τοῦτο τὸ καινὸν μυστήριον; ἢ πάντως διὰ τὸν ἄνθρωπον;

[42] Lines 154–181 agree approximately with the last part of Alexander, *De anima* (PG 601c–4B) and with the last part of 'Athanasius' (fos. 161a col. 2–162a col. 2; Budge 273–4).

[43] For the Greek of lines 163–75 see Ps.-Epiphanius, *De resurrectione* 11–13 (Nautin 159. 9–16): πᾶσαι δὲ αἱ πατριαὶ τῶν ἐθνῶν ἐσώθησαν ἐν τῷ Χριστῷ. εἷς γὰρ ἐκρίθη καὶ μυριάδες ἐσώθησαν. (165) ὁ γὰρ κύριος ἀπέθανεν ὑπὲρ πάντων. οὗτος δὲ ὁμοίως ἐνδυσάμενος ὅλον τὸν ἄνθρωπον ἀνῆλθεν εἰς τὰ ὕψη τῶν οὐρανῶν, ἀναφέρων δῶρον τῷ πατρὶ (170) οὐ χρυσόν, οὐκ ἄργυρον, οὔτε λίθον τίμιον, ἀλλ' ἄνθρωπον ὃν ἔπλασεν κατ' εἰκόνα καὶ ὁμοίωσιν αὐτοῦ. τοῦτον ὁ πατὴρ ὑψώσας ἐν δεξιᾷ αὐτοῦ ἐπὶ θρόνου (175) ὑψηλοῦ κεκάθικεν.

[44] Lines 164–5 appear in the *Additamentum* (Nautin 60. 44–5) as well as in other witnesses.

18 But him the Father exalted,
   and has made him sit at the right of his throne
   in high places and abundance;   175
   and him he made judge of the people
   and leader of angels
   and prince of cherubim
   architect of Jerusalem[45]
   and son of a virgin   180
   and king for ever,
   this one whom we see wholly as man with him.[46]
   He is older than the morning star;
   he is brighter than the rising sun,
   more brilliant than the lightning-flash,   185
   higher than the heavens,
   creator of creatures.
19 He is mediator of God and man;[47]
   he is the reviver of the dead,[48]
   and saviour of the lost,   190
   and guide of the deceived,
   comforter of the oppressed,
   and saviour of the created,
   and shepherd of the sheep,
   and giver of rest to the weary,   195
   and salvation of the people,
   and boast of the apostles,
   and crown of witnesses,
   and bishop of martyrs;
   charioteer of the cherubim,[49]   200
   and Lord of angels,[50]

[45] Not necessarily a late touch, since it might refer to the heavenly Jerusalem, and appears in the 'Athanasius' homily unrelated to the festival of the cross (fo. 162a col. 2; Budge 274).

[46] This line apparently means that the preceding epithets apply to the humanity of the Lord; what follows describes his divine nature (Van Esbroeck ad loc.).

[47] Lines 188–203 appear in abbreviated form in the *Additamentum* (Nautin 60. 2–5); cf. also Fr. 15. 58–70.

[48] Lines 189–91 appear in Greek in a fragment first published by A. Ehrhard, *Überlieferung und Bestand der hagiographischen und homiletischen Literatur der griechischen Kirche* ii (*TU* 51, Leipzig, 1938) 256 n. 3, and reproduced in Nautin 72 and Richard 323. The order of lines is there reversed: ὁδηγὸς τῶν πεπλανημένων, ποιμὴν τῶν σωζομένων, ζωὴ τῶν τεθανατωμένων.

[49] The *Prayer* cited by Richard 320 incorporates the Greek: ὁ ἡνίοχος τῶν χερουβίμ.

[50] The continuation of the fragment cited for lines 189–91 may supply the original of lines 201–2: στρατηγὸς τῶν ἀγγέλων, βασιλεὺς τῶν αἰώνων.

and king of Israel,
and reviver of the fallen,
and builder of Jerusalem.

20 It is he that spread out the heavens,[51, 52]   205
and founded the earth,
and contained the deeps,
and made all things,
and adorned the world.
For he is the Word of his Father,   210
and the Spirit of his power,
and the perfector of peace who came from heaven,
the giver of Holy Spirit of the prophets.
Christ conceived a body from a human being;
he was wrapped in bandages;   215
he was laid in a manger;
he cleansed men.

21 He did all this for men of obedience.
Because men are disobedient to the law,
and whereas they have no faith in the living cross   220
nor in the Word who was crucified upon it
inasmuch as he was despised,[53]
and whereas they impiously mock, (saying,)
'He died as a malefactor
and is buried as one dead',   225
they mourn him as one dead;
but he rose from the dead inasmuch as he is God.[54]

22 And because he was God and is God,[55]
little in body and great in soul,
despised on earth and glorified in the heavens,   230
scorned by men and magnified by the Father,
this is the Man who was sent by the Father to the world because
he is God,
both Man upon earth and God in heaven,
and he is God over all creation.

23 It is he that led you [to the Father . . .];   235
he makes you believe in him [and] loves you.
Now he is the true Christ,
and his is the glory for ever.

[51] A Greek reconstruction of 205–7 may be made from the *Prayer* (lines 9–11)
reproduced by Richard 318 (cf. 330): ὁ τὸν οὐρανὸν ἐκτείνας . . . ὁ τὴν γῆν
τεθεμελιώσας . . . ὁ τὰς ἀβύσσους κατακλείσας.

[52] Lines 205–9 resemble lines 598–602 in *PP* 82–3.

[53] *was despised* vE: *patiebatur* L.

[54] Similarly *PP* 8.

[55] With lines 228–34 cf. the balanced expressions of Fr. 14.

24 But we see this image of disobedience:[56]
   (those) who multiplied upon earth with men from city to city,   240
   and crowded from region to region, heartless, with all who are
                                                              theirs;
   who in one way misappropriate words, and in another more fully
                                                   name the truth;
   who are bold and speak—impious men—
   in order to make (people) believe in truth (mixed) with falsehood,
   and unity of churches with heresy and disobedience and violence, 245
   and holiness with fornication,
   and uprightness with impiety,
   and virginity with hate;
   and thus they are disobedient to Christ,[57]
   and spurn the Father,   250
   and teach the disorder of men.

25 And after . . .

i. 1 . . . of prophecy.
   Prophets [also suff]er,
   the just are killed with the sword,
   witnesses are tortured,
   martyrs are racked.   5

2 Now, beloved, once more God then said,
   'O Eve, enough for you was your husband whom I gave you.'[58]
   Did he not give you a serpent?
   For this reason they brought accusations,
   so that she might be delivered from pains.[59]   10

3 And God said to the serpent,
   '*You shall go on chest and stomach.*'[60]
   He cursed the chest,
   because in it heart and heart's rage there[61] arise.
   '*You shall go on stomach*',   15
   because it deceived for food.
   (It shall have) soil to eat all the days of its life[60]
   because Adam was from the soil of the earth.[62]

---

[56] The attack on heretical churches in this section, though possible in Melito's day, is more likely to belong to a later period. The shift in emphasis at this point may also indicate a point where the compiler left his ancient source.

[57] *to Christ* vE: *coram Christo* L.

[58] Perhaps derived from Gen. 3: 16.

[59] These three obscure lines are probably corrupt. The accusations are perhaps the recriminations of Gen. 3: 12–3.

[60] Cf. Gen. 3: 14.

[61] *there* add. vE: om. L.   [62] Cf. Gen. 2: 7.

4 Receive the definition of the same three:
    because the same three made sin,   20
    because from a tree the transgression of commandments [. . .
    . . .] on the cross the king fixed the curse with nails.
    Just as from a tree came sin, so also from a tree came salvation.
5 By the cross death is destroyed,
    and by the cross salvation shines;   25
    by the cross the gates of hell are burst,
    and by the cross the gates of paradise are opened.
    The cross has become the way of saints and martyrs;
    the cross has become the chain of the apostles
    and the shield of faith of prophets.   30
    The cross is the guide of the fallen;
    the cross is the comfort of the possessed,
    and an immovable wall to believers.
    The cross is the strength of the weak,
    and the lifting up of the lowly.   35
    The cross is the guide of the faithful robber;[63]
    the cross is the destroyer of hell.
6 For all this we offer glory [to the Father
    . . . of all now and always . . .] for ever. Amen.

[63] Cf. Luke 23: 40-3.

INDEX OF PASSAGES

FROM SCRIPTURE AND *EVANGELIUM PETRI*

NOTE: The passages cited are the citations, allusions, and more important parallels referred to in the notes to the text of Melito. References are to the lines (verses) of this edition where the relevant annotations occur. Unless otherwise stated, the line numbers refer to *PP*.